STRESEMANN AND THE POLITICS OF
THE WEIMAR REPUBLIC

STRESEMANN

AND THE POLITICS

OF THE WEIMAR REPUBLIC

BY HENRY ASHBY TURNER, JR.

PRINCETON, NEW JERSEY

PRINCETON UNIVERSITY PRESS

1963

Publication of this book
has been aided by the Ford Foundation program
to support publication, through university presses,
of works in the humanities and social sciences,
and by a grant from the Fluid Research Fund
of Yale University

✤

Printed in the United States of America by
Princeton University Press, Princeton, New Jersey

PREFACE

THE OPENING of Stresemann's papers to research in 1953 has produced a flood of scholarly literature dealing with his career. For the most part, these recent studies have centered on his controversial six-year term of office as Germany's Foreign Minister. As a result, his role in domestic politics has been relegated to the background. This is unfortunate, for Stresemann was not only the foremost Foreign Minister of the Weimar Republic but also the founder and leader of an important political party, Chancellor during a crucial period of the republican era, and the most influential member of the cabinet during the Republic's years of stabilization. By focusing on the domestic side of his career, this book attempts to contribute both to the literature on Stresemann and to the political record of Germany's first Republic.

❖

The research for this study, in Washington and in Germany, was made possible by grants from the Social Science Research Council and the Penfield Traveling Scholarship Fund. I am also indebted for assistance and cooperation to: the staff of the Foreign Affairs Branch of the National Archives; Dr. Wolfgang Mommsen and Dr. Hans Booms of the Bundesarchiv, Koblenz; Herr Jürgen Huch, formerly of the Bundesarchiv; the staff of the Politisches Archiv of the Auswärtiges Amt, Bonn; Dr. Gerhard Zwoch of the Bundeshaus-Bibliothek, Bonn; Dr. Thilo Vogelsang of the Institut für Zeitgeschichte, Munich; the staff of the Hauptarchiv, Berlin; Henry Bernhard; Rudolph Bernhard; Louis P. Lochner; Dr. Otto Most; Hans von Raumer; Dr. Harald Schinkel; Dr. Erich Heinz Schlottner; and Dr. Wolfgang Stresemann.

I am grateful to Professor Cyril E. Black for his suggestions and encouragement during the early phase of this work and to Professor Hans W. Gatzke, whose careful reading of the manuscript eliminated a number of mistakes. Finally, I should like to express my gratitude to Professor Gordon A. Craig for his critical guidance and advice throughout the preparation of this study.

CONTENTS

STRESEMANN AND THE POLITICS OF
THE WEIMAR REPUBLIC

I. THE REVOLUTION AND THE FAILURE OF LIBERAL UNITY, 1918

SHORTLY before nine o'clock on a chill and cloud-laden autumn morning in 1918, Gustav Stresemann, member of the German Reichstag and chairman of the National Liberal Party's delegation, left his apartment in the fashionable suburb of Charlottenburg, just to the west of Berlin. Crossing the brown and somber expanse of the Tiergarten, he went to the Reichstag building, where he was scheduled to meet with the leaders of the other delegations. When he arrived at his destination, however, he found instead of the normal round of parliamentary activity a revolution.

The date was November 9. Two days earlier, the Social Democrats had bowed to the pressure of more radical groups and issued an ultimatum demanding the immediate abdication of the Emperor. When their demand had not been met by the evening of the 8th, they seized the initiative, withdrawing their ministers from the cabinet and proclaiming a general strike. Upon learning of these developments at the Reichstag, Stresemann went to his office on the second floor of the building, where he watched for a time as crowds of demonstrators streamed into the center of the city. Later in the morning, after the Social Democrats had failed to arrive at the meeting of delegation leaders, he went to the Reich Chancellery, several blocks away in the Wilhelmstrasse, with a number of deputies from the other non-socialist parties. There he and his companions were told that the Chancellor, Prince Max of Baden, was conferring with the Social Democratic leaders and could not receive them. After waiting in an antechamber for some time, they were finally handed a proclamation which announced that the Emperor had abdicated and that the chancellorship had been turned over to the Social Democrat Friedrich Ebert.

Shocked by this news, Stresemann returned to the Reichstag.

3

There he presided over the last meeting of the National Liberal delegation, which passed a resolution calling for the preservation of the monarchy under one of the Emperor's descendants even as the cheering throng outside the building was greeting the proclamation of the German Republic by Philipp Scheidemann of the Social Democratic Party. These rapid-fire developments, which in a matter of only a few hours had delivered the deathblow to the Hohenzollern Empire, left Stresemann stunned and shaken. Instead of leaving the Reichstag with the other deputies, he lingered on alone in the National Liberal caucus room, apparently at a loss as to what to do. Finally, late in the bleak, gray afternoon, the armed workers whom the revolutionary government had sent to occupy the building unceremoniously ordered him out.[1]

As for many other Germans, November 9, 1918, was for Stresemann a day on which "everything that had seemed permanent collapsed."[2] Throughout his life he had been an enthusiastic and loyal supporter of the old regime and when it fell he was on the threshold of what promised to be a long and distinguished career as one of the Empire's leading political figures. Born forty years earlier, the son of a modestly prosperous small-scale beer purveyor in a working-class district on the east side of Berlin, he had risen to national prominence with a rapidity that was little short of meteoric by the standards of Wilhelmine Germany. After three and a half years at the universities of Berlin and Leipzig, he completed his doctorate in 1900 with a dissertation on the Berlin beer industry. Having decided upon a career in business, he then accepted an administrative position in the struggling industrial association movement in Saxony. Within five years he made an outstanding success of this

[1] Based on his article, "Zum Jahrestag der Revolution" (dated 5.11. 1919), in his *Von der Revolution bis zum Frieden von Versailles* (Berlin, 1919), pp. 186ff. Also, Hjalmar Schacht, *76 Jahre Meines Lebens* (Bad Wörishofen, 1953), pp. 191f.

[2] His article, "Die Neuen Parteien" (dated 26.11.1918), in his *Von der Revolution*, p. 47.

4

venture and greatly expanded the scope of his activities by taking an active part in the national organization of light industry, the *Bund der Industriellen*. But in spite of the prospects of a highly lucrative business career, his interests were already turning to politics. In 1903 he joined the National Liberal Party and during the next few years became increasingly involved in its affairs. His successes in business quickly won him recognition in the party, which was strongly oriented toward industry, and in 1907, at the age of only twenty-eight, he was elected to the imperial Reichstag. Thereafter, with the exception of a two-year hiatus occasioned by a defeat in the elections of 1912, he served in that body until the revolution ended its existence in 1918.[3]

In appearance, Stresemann could not be described as an imposing figure. In most respects he conformed physically to the popular stereotype of the phlegmatic German *Bürger*, complete with short, corpulent body, thick neck, round, balding head, and nondescript mustache. His personality, however, almost invariably left those who encountered him with the impression of an alert and energetic man of exceptional intelligence. An example of this is provided by Lord Edgar D'Abernon, British Ambassador in Berlin from 1920 to 1926, who was moved to compare him with a prominent Englishman four years his senior: "A first impression of Stresemann was that he might have been Winston Churchill's brother. The same silhouette—almost identical colouring. And in temperament and mental characteristics a close analogy. . . . Both brilliant, daring and bold. In both, more than a dash of recklessness. . . . Minor differences of

---

[3] There is as yet no adequate study of his early years. The information used above was drawn from the following: Walter Görlitz, *Gustav Stresemann* (Heidelberg, 1947); Rudolf Olden, *Stresemann* (Berlin, 1929); Rochus Freiherr von Rheinbaben, *Stresemann* (Dresden, 1928); Annelise Thimme, "Gustav Stresemann, Legende und Wirklichkeit," *Historische Zeitschrift*, CLXXXI (1956), 287ff.; Annelise Thimme, *Gustav Stresemann* (Hanover and Frankfurt/Main, 1957); Donald Warren, Jr., "Gustav Stresemann as Organizer of German Business Interests, 1901-1914" (Columbia dissertation, 1959).

course there were. Winston's voice is soft and lisping. . . . Stresemann's tones were resonant and clear. . . . And his mind was no less clear than his voice. No half tones; no blurred outlines."[4]

To this, D'Abernon might have added that Stresemann, like his English contemporary, also possessed a spontaneous eloquence which won him early recognition as one of Germany's foremost political speakers. Moreover, although he could never rival Churchill's mastery of language, he too commanded a clear prose style and dabbled extensively in journalism. His frequent articles on current affairs in various newspapers and periodicals did much to establish his reputation during the early years of his career. By 1917 he had placed his journalistic activities on a permanent basis by acquiring control of a national weekly magazine, *Deutsche Stimmen*, to which he regularly contributed editorials.

Politics offered Stresemann a means of satisfying both a restless craving for activity and a compelling ambition for advancement and recognition. Throughout his career he threw himself into his work unreservedly and one associate, Chancellor Hans Luther, was later to describe his approach to politics as that of "a possessed person."[5] Entering the Reichstag as its youngest member, he quickly attracted attention through his ability to master complex legislative questions rapidly and present his views to the chamber forcefully and effectively. He also soon excelled at the ceaseless give-and-take of parliamentary bargaining. A congenial table companion, and something of a gourmand, he was a tireless participant in the constant round of luncheons, dinners, and *Bierabende* that marked the political social life of the Berlin of his day and so came to know the special legislative interests and concerns of a large circle of his fel-

---

[4] Viscount Edgar D'Abernon, *An Ambassador of Peace* (3 vols., London, 1929-30), III, 10.

[5] Hans Luther, "Erinnerungen an Gustav Stresemann," *Schweizer Monatshefte*, XXXIV (1954), 426.

low deputies. When important measures came to the vote, he often made good use of this information in marshaling the support of waverers and potential opponents. The experience in bargaining which he gained in the Reichstag served him well in his subsequent career as Foreign Minister. However, it also stamped him indelibly as a middle-class, professional politician with the result that he was always to be somewhat out of place in the elegant world of international diplomacy into which his career eventually thrust him.

The abilities and accomplishments of the young Stresemann did not escape the attention of Ernst Bassermann, the veteran leader of the National Liberal Party. Soon after he entered the Reichstag, Bassermann adopted him as a protégé, introducing him into the inner circles of the party and giving him assignments that advanced his career. After Stresemann's setback at the polls in 1912, the party leader interceded to prevent the defeat from abruptly ending his career and helped him to regain his place in the Reichstag through a by-election in 1914. In view of his close ties to Bassermann, it came as no surprise when, after the latter's death in 1917, he was elected to succeed him as chairman of the National Liberal Reichstag delegation, thus moving into the foremost ranks of imperial politics.

The National Liberal Party within which Stresemann rose to prominence was still an important factor in German politics, but its strength had declined sharply since the early decades of the Empire, when it had been the country's largest party. Weakened by secessions and by the inroads of the burgeoning Social Democratic Party, it was left with only 45 of the 397 seats in the Reichstag after the last imperial elections, which were held in 1912. In addition, it was torn by internal dissension, with strong right and left wings battling each other for control. The dominant conservative right wing differed from the reactionary German Conservative Party only by virtue of the fact that most of its adherents lacked the aristocratic titles of the Conservatives and drew their backing from business circles rather than from large-scale agriculture. The left wing, on the other hand, stood close to the groups of leftist liberals which united in 1910 to form the Progressive People's Party. On social and economic issues Stresemann generally sided with this left wing. In his youth he had been strongly attracted to Friedrich Naumann's National Socialism and the ideas of social reform and class conciliation set forth by Naumann continued to influence his ideas long after he had broken with that movement. When he entered the National Liberal organization, he therefore aligned himself with the left-wing Young Liberal group, which favored close collaboration with the leftist liberal parties and an increased emphasis on social legislation designed to reduce the class antagonism that had come to mark German political and social life.

While he agreed with the Young Liberals on most social and economic issues, Stresemann differed sharply with them on the question of constitutional reform until late in his career in the National Liberal Party. During the pre-war period, he repeatedly joined with the right wing and the bulk of the party in opposing their demands for full parliamentary government in the Empire and equal suffrage in Prussia, where a discriminatory three-class electoral law was still in effect. In line with the older traditions of the party, he was not enthusiastic about thoroughgoing popular government and approved of the checks imposed upon the will of the populace by the imperial and Prussian systems. During the war, however, his thinking on the subject underwent a fundamental change. At the outset he had expected that Germany's basically authoritarian regime would be an important asset under wartime conditions, feeling that the complicated and often cumbrous parliamentary machinery of the Western democracies would be a source of weakness in times that called for rapid decisions and actions. But contrary to his expectations, the governments of England and France not only survived the strains of wartime but proved in many respects more efficient and flexible than the imperial system. In addition, the weak and vacil-

8

lating policies of Wilhelm II revealed to him the dangers involved in the existing system's concentration of sweeping powers in the hands of the Emperor.[6]

His patience with the old constitution came to an end in November 1916, when Karl Helfferich, the State Secretary for Internal Affairs, admitted to a committee of the Reichstag that the British parliamentary system had done a superior job of mobilizing civilian labor and that the imperial government was far behind with its own schedule.[7] From that time on, Stresemann favored the introduction of parliamentary government. At first, he felt the change would have to be postponed until the end of the war. But by early 1917 he had become convinced that only immediate concessions in the constitutional question could prevent the increasing dissatisfaction of the public from undermining the war effort and strengthening the radical groups that were seeking the overthrow of the entire governmental structure. He therefore threw his support behind the reform movement, arguing that if reforms were enacted promptly they could be held to a minimum but that delay would increase the danger of a more radical change.[8] His own preference was a form of parliamentary government which, like the British and French systems, would require the cabinet to have the confidence of a majority of the Reichstag, but which would differ from those systems by allowing the Emperor to appoint persons from outside the Reichstag as cabinet members. Such an arrangement, he hoped, would preserve the imperial tradition of non-party ex-

[6] See his Reichstag speeches: 26.10.1916, *Verhandlungen des Reichstags*, cccviii, 1820ff.; 29.3.1917, *ibid.*, cccix, 2855; 22.10.1918, *ibid.*, cccxiv, 6174 and 6177.

[7] His article, "Waffenstillstand und Wilsonprogramm" (dated 31.10. 1918), in his *Von der Revolution*, pp. 30f.

[8] Speech to a meeting of National Liberals, 28.2.1917, in his *Macht und Freiheit* (Halle, 1918), pp. 29ff. Also Reichstag speech of 29.3.1917, *Verhandlungen*, cccix, 2852ff. The change in his position was not influenced by the Russian Revolution since the earlier of these speeches predates the outbreak of the first serious demonstrations in Russia.

pert ministers (*Fachminister*), which he regarded as one of the most admirable aspects of the old regime.[9]

Even the prospect of this large a change left him somewhat apprehensive and he made no secret of his regret that the Empire had no hereditary upper chamber similar to the British House of Lords. There was already an upper house, the Bundesrat, but its members were named by the governments of the federal states. He realized that since those governments were almost certain to be democratized in the wake of a reform in the Empire, the Bundesrat would not provide a conservative check on the popular will in the future.[10] With regard to the Prussian reform, he at first favored only a system of plural voting, which would still preserve some of the advantages of the propertied classes. But when it had became obvious by the summer of 1917 that the public would be satisfied with nothing less than equal suffrage, he abandoned this halfway solution.[11]

After altering his own position, Stresemann managed to win the support of the National Liberal Reichstag delegation for constitutional reform. Joining with the leaders of the Progressive and Social Democratic parties, he urged the imperial government to permit the constitutional alterations necessary for the introduction of the parliamentary system at the national level. At first these efforts met with no response, for the Emperor and his advisers would hear nothing of such changes. But in October 1918, after the military leaders had finally admitted that the war could not be won, the Empire's ruling circles reluctantly agreed to a reform in the hope that it would stave off trouble at home and insure more lenient treatment from the Western democracies. The resultant changes, which were completed late that month, coincided closely with Stresemann's views—establishing a constitu-

[9] His article, "Gedanken zur Krisis" (dated July 1917), in his *Macht und Freiheit*, p. 73.

[10] His article, "Die Herbstkrisis" (dated fall of 1917), in his *Macht und Freiheit*, p. 150.

[11] *Ibid.* Also, his article, "Gedanken zur Krisis" (dated July 1917), in his *Macht und Freiheit*, p. 73.

tional monarchy but leaving the Emperor with considerable freedom in the selection of his ministers.

Although he would have liked Wilhelm II to step down in favor of a younger member of the Hohenzollern line, Stresemann concluded that the October reform had stabilized the domestic situation.[12] Consequently, he greatly underestimated the seriousness of the uprisings of early November. As late as the 8th, he believed that further trouble could be averted by pushing through a reform in Prussia similar to that in the Empire. He spent that evening trying unsuccessfully to bring the chairman of the National Liberal Prussian delegation, Robert Friedberg, to support such a step.[13] He was therefore wholly unprepared for the momentous events of the following day.

The revolution left Stresemann deeply embittered. During the latter stages of the war, he had been increasingly critical of the policies of Wilhelm II, but his loyalty to the Hohenzollerns apparently made it impossible for him to see that the Emperor's refusal to abdicate voluntarily had brought on the revolution. He placed the responsibility primarily on Prince Max, who he felt had betrayed his sovereign by giving in to the Social Democrats without lifting a finger in defense of the monarchy. With regard to the motives of the Social Democrats and the Progressives (who had quickly endorsed the revolution), he saw only a cowardly attempt to purchase better peace terms from the Western democracies by turning Germany into a republic.[14] Moreover, he believed that the consequences of the revolution might turn out to be far different than its instigators expected. The destruction of the constitutional monarchy established in October was in his opinion a dangerous break with the country's

[12] His article, "Um Kaiser und Reich" (dated 6.11.1918), in his *Von der Revolution*, pp. 37ff.

[13] His article, "Zum Jahrestag der Revolution" (dated 5.11.1919), in his *Von der Revolution*, p. 185.

[14] Speech to Party Congress, 13.4.1919, in his *Reden und Schriften* (2 vols., Dresden, 1926), I, 266. Also, speech to DVP group, 22.2.1919, in his *Von der Revolution*, pp. 117f.

organic political development that could easily result in events similar to those that had swept Russia into communism a year earlier. In addition, he feared that the elimination of the imperial title, which was the original bond between the federal states, would loosen the unity established in 1871 and leave Germany divided and helpless before its former enemies.[15]

The harsh armistice terms which the Allies forced upon the representatives of the new German Republic on November 11 further intensified his bitterness toward the revolution and those who had carried it out. From the outset, he had been an enthusiastic supporter of the war effort and until the summer of 1918, when it became clear that Germany could not win a smashing victory, he had been one of the most ardent exponents of annexationist war aims. Moreover, he had supported the policies of the country's military leaders so uncritically, especially on the issue of unlimited submarine warfare, that he had won the sobriquet of "Ludendorff's young man."[16] This subservience to the military clique had been conspicuously evident at the time of the July crisis of 1917, when he had played an important role in effecting the ouster of Chancellor Bethmann-Hollweg, who had offended the Army by refusing to endorse its annexationist war aims.[17] Even after the military leaders had admitted their inability to carry the war further and had forced the civilian authorities to seek an immediate armistice in October 1918, Stresemann managed to preserve his faith in the invincibility of the German Army and the infallibility of its leaders. He therefore accepted without question the military's unfounded contention that only the revolution had weakened the country and pre-

[15] His article, "Der Umsturz" (dated 12.11.1918), in his *Reden und Schriften*, I, 211ff. Also, "Aufgaben der Nationalversammlung" (dated 3.2.1919), in his *Von der Revolution*, pp. 99ff.

[16] See Hans W. Gatzke, *Germany's Drive to the West* (Baltimore, 1950), *passim*. Also, A. Thimme, *Gustav Stresemann*, pp. 20ff. The quotation is from Philipp Scheidemann, *Memoiren eines Sozialdemokraten* (2 vols., Dresden, 1928), II, 36.

[17] Marvin L. Edwards, *Stresemann and the Greater Germany, 1914-1918* (New York, 1963), 99ff, p. 139ff.

vented it from rejecting the armistice and continuing the war until better terms could be obtained. Several months later he summed up his view: "Not the 2nd of October, when Germany's decision to request an armistice was made, but the 9th of November was the death day of Germany's greatness in the world."[18] As a result of his acceptance of the incipient stab-in-the-back legend, the revolution was always associated for him with humiliating defeat and collapse. Although he was later to become one of the leading figures of the Republic, he was never reconciled to the events which brought it into being. Whenever he referred to the revolution in later years, it was always as a black chapter in German history.

In spite of his dissatisfaction with the new state of affairs, Stresemann did not consider withdrawing from politics. Instead, he began preparations for the future as soon as it became known that the revolutionary socialist government would not exclude other parties from the elections to the National Assembly, which was to draw up the new constitution. On November 15 and 16 he took part in a series of discussions between the leaders of the National Liberal and Progressive parties aimed at increasing cooperation between the two wings of German liberalism. Since the schism of 1866-1867, they had differed principally in their attitudes toward the imperial system. The National Liberal Party, dominated largely by its conservative right wing, accepted the quasi-parliamentary system set up by Bismarck as well as most of the policies of the imperial governments. On the other hand, the left liberals, who after many years of division were united in the Progressive Party in 1910, demanded the introduction of full parliamentary government and took issue

[18] Germany, Auswärtiges Amt, Politisches Archiv, *Nachlass des Reichsaussenministers Dr. Gustav Stresemann*, microfilm, National Archives of the United States, reel 3079, serial 6918, frame 173177 (hereafter cited as *Nachlass*, 3079/6918/173177), manuscript of his article, "Zum Geleit," for *Niedersächsisches Wochenblatt*, 25.3.1919. See also his article, "Der Umsturz" (dated 12.11.1918), in his *Reden und Schriften*, I, 205f. Also, speech in Osnabrück, 19.12.1918, *ibid.*, 217f.

with many of the imperial regime's policies. This division persisted even in the face of the Social Democratic onslaught, which by 1912 had left the Progressives with only 42 Reichstag seats to the National Liberals' 45. At first, the war threatened to widen the gap between the two, but in its final stages they moved closer together when the National Liberals dropped their annexationist demands and joined the Progressives in calling for full parliamentary government. With the adoption of the October reform, the old system became a thing of the past and most of the former obstacles to a liberal reconciliation seemed outdated. As a result, even before the revolution there was strong sentiment in both parties for close cooperation and the National Liberals were scheduled to discuss the possibility of a merger at a meeting of their Central Committee on November 17. After the revolution, these cautious preparations were jettisoned and the leaders of the two parties opened discussions without waiting for the approval of their respective organizations.[19]

Although he joined his colleagues in the talks with the Progressives, Stresemann was not a member of the National Liberal group, led by banker-politician Jacob Riesser, which favored a merger of the two liberal parties. He objected strongly to the prospect of collaboration with the left wing of the Progressive Party, which he felt was too willing to make concessions to the Social Democrats.[20] In his opinion, this left-wing group had broken with the traditions of German liberalism and taken up the cause of extreme democratization, which to him meant the subordination of the government to the will of the people through plebiscites and referendums, coupled with a policy of social leveling. He accepted the idea of popular participation in government, but to his mind the principles of liberalism required

[19] Nationalliberale Partei, Reichsgeschäftsstelle, *Rundschreiben. Die Einigungsverhandlungen mit der Fortschrittlichen Volkspartei.—Gründung der Deutschen Volkspartei.* (One-page leaflet distributed with the magazine, *Deutsche Stimmen*, 24.11.1918.)

[20] *Nachlass*, 3068/6889/133498ff., letter to *Kölnische Zeitung*, 16.10. 1918 (publication refused).

that the representatives of the people should be completely free to exercise their own judgments and should not be subjected to the shifting pressures of mass opinion. Convinced of the necessity for high incentives and rewards, he also rejected any notion of social leveling and wanted to preserve the National Liberal Party as a middle-class bulwark against such a trend.[21] Accordingly, he went into the talks with the Progressives hoping that they would produce only an election alliance that would leave the National Liberal organization intact and uncommitted regarding the future.[22]

Once the discussions with the Progressives began, it became clear that most of the National Liberal leaders favored a full merger. Among those so inclined was Robert Friedberg, the elderly chairman of the National Liberal delegation in the Prussian House of Delegates, who had been elected as the party's highest officer, chairman of the Central Committee, at the time of Bassermann's death in 1917. Friedberg was a member of the right wing of the party and had previously displayed no enthusiasm for a merger with the Progressives. But in November 1918, his opposition was apparently overcome by a flood of letters and telegrams which revealed that the party's provincial organizations were overwhelmingly in favor of a united liberal party that could provide a counterpoise to the socialists.[23] The Progressive representatives at the talks, led by Friedrich Naumann and Hermann Pachnicke, were also favorably disposed to the idea of a merger and, after extensive discussion, it was agreed on November 16 to combine the two parties before the elections to the National Assembly. At the same time, it was decided not to announce this step publicly until details of organization, representation, and policy had been settled by subsequent

[21] His article, "Liberalismus oder Demokratie" (dated 10.12.1918), in his *Von der Revolution*, pp. 53ff. Also, *Nachlass*, 3068/6889/133645, letter to F. Schneider, 4.11.1918.

[22] *Nachlass*, 3069/6896/134553f., letter to Stubmann, 15.11.1918.

[23] *Deutsche Volkspartei Papers*, Bundesarchiv, Koblenz, Vols. 93a and 94.

meetings. It was established, however, that all members of the new party would have to recognize the Republic as the *de facto* legal government and agree to work within its framework. Otherwise, past differences were to be put aside and no doctrinal orthodoxy was to be demanded.[24]

Stresemann decided to join the other National Liberals in accepting the merger even though he remained convinced that it was a mistake. In a letter written several days later, he explained to an old party colleague that this decision had involved an "enormous sacrifice," but that he had felt compelled to "stay on board" to see to it that "if the black-white-red banner comes down at least the black-red-gold will go up, so that we will not have to go along with the disgrace of having the red or reddish banner of an international democracy waving on board the old National Liberal fleet." Additional remarks in the same letter reveal, however, that a concern for political self-preservation also played a role in his decision. These remarks indicate that he had realized that most of the National Liberal rank and file were in favor of a merger and had reconciled himself to the fact that opposition on his part would, in all probability, lead only to his exclusion from liberal politics.[25] Confronted with the alternatives of accepting a merger which included a group he disliked or bowing out of politics altogether, he had chosen the former course.

Even after accepting the new arrangement, he continued to hope that at least the entry of the left-wing Progressives into the united party could be blocked. It was with this possibility in mind that he watched with interest an event which coincided with the agreement to merge the two liberal parties: the founding of the German Democratic Party (*Deutsche Demokratische Partei* or DDP). The founders of this new organization, led by

[24] Nationalliberale Partei, *Rundschreiben.* Also, *Nachlass*, 3171/7353/166100f., entry in Stresemann's daily calendar. Also, *Nachlass*, 3110/7013/143871ff., exchange of letters with Otto Fischbeck (former Progressive leader), 1922.

[25] *Nachlass*, 3069/6896/134572ff., letter to Hugo, 18.11.1918.

16

the sociologist Alfred Weber and the editor of the influential newspaper *Berliner Tageblatt*, Theodor Wolff, were academicians, journalists, and members of other professions. Most of them had previously played no direct role in politics and consequently, the Democratic Party was not related to any of the older parties. Its program revealed, however, that on questions of economic and social policy it had adopted a position very similar to that of the left-wing Progressives. In addition, its leaders, most of whom had long been sharply critical of the imperial government, and especially of its wartime policies, had enthusiastically endorsed the Republic.[26] Naturally, such a party did not appeal to Stresemann. Nevertheless, he was interested in it, for he knew it would affect the projected liberal union and hoped it would serve his ends by drawing the left-wing Progressives out of the projected united liberal party, thereby removing his principal objection to it.[27]

The effect of the appearance of the Democratic Party was quite different from what he had expected. The Progressives quickly demanded that it be included in the united liberal party, and to his consternation, Friedberg and most of the other National Liberals agreed to attempt such an amalgamation. Although he was opposed to any cooperation with the Democrats, Stresemann again elected to accept the possibility of a merger he did not like rather than risk exclusion from a new united liberal party. He therefore joined Friedberg at the head of the National Liberal deputation which attended a meeting with the Progressives and the Democrats at the residence of the Reichstag President on November 18.[28]

[26] See Otto Nuschke, "Wie die Demokratische Partei Wurde," in *Zehn Jahre Deutsche Republik*, ed. Anton Erkelenz (Berlin, 1928), pp. 24ff. Also, Hjalmar Schacht, *76 Jahre*, pp. 189ff. Also, Theodor Wolff, *Der Marsch Durch Zwei Jahrzehnte* (Amsterdam, 1937), pp. 203ff.

[27] *Nachlass*, 3069/6896/134573, letter to Hugo, 18.11.1918.

[28] Nationalliberale Partei, *Rundschreiben*. Also, Deutsche Volkspartei, *Die Entstehung der Deutschen Volkspartei* (written by Stresemann) (Berlin, 1920), pp. 5ff.

17

When the three-cornered meeting opened under the chairmanship of Otto Fischbeck of the Progressive Party, the group of intellectuals who had launched the DDP lost no time in making it clear that they were not interested in a merger. Their spokesman, Alfred Weber, explained that they were determined to keep their party free of all ties to the past and so would consider no fusions with existing organizations. At the same time, he announced that the Progressives and most National Liberals would be welcomed into the new Democratic Party. But in remarks pointedly directed at Stresemann and some of the other National Liberals present, he left no doubt that the Democratic leaders regarded persons who had been associated with aggressive or annexationist war policies as "compromised" and hence unacceptable.[29] During this speech, Stresemann sat by impassively, taking desultory notes, which he concluded with the scrawled phrase, "guarantees against compromised persons," with "compromised" strongly underlined.[30] At the end of Weber's remarks, Friedberg wanted to deliver a rebuttal, but Stresemann convinced him that the Democrats' attitude made any reply superfluous. Finally, the two took advantage of a recess to withdraw the National Liberal deputation from the meeting, leaving the Progressives and Democrats to continue without them.[31]

At first, the outcome of the meeting of November 18 seemed highly satisfactory from Stresemann's standpoint. He was no more anxious to work with the Democrats than they were to work with him. Their open refusal of a merger therefore spared him the unpleasant necessity of having to decide whether to accept such an arrangement or face the possibility of political isolation. In addition, he apparently concluded that the Demo-

[29] Theodor Wolff, *Der Marsch*, pp. 208f. Wolff, who wrote his account many years later and apparently without notes, is wrong on many details, for instance his assertion that Stresemann and the other National Liberals were not invited to the meeting.
[30] *Ibid.* Also, *Nachlass*, 3069/6896/134581f., Stresemann's notes.
[31] Deutsche Volkspartei (Stresemann), *Entstehung*, p. 7.

crats' militant stance would have just the effect he desired and would attract the left-wing Progressives to them, thus leaving only the right wing to combine with the National Liberals. In this, he was wrong. By withdrawing from the meeting of the 18th without taking up the Democrats' challenge, he had given them an important advantage in their attempt to win the support of the Progressives and they made good use of it. Instead of splitting the Progressives, as he had hoped, they succeeded in winning over the entire party. On November 19 the Progressive leaders abandoned the merger with the National Liberals and turned their organization over to the Democratic Party. On the following day the new party scored still another success when it announced the entrance of four members of the National Liberal Reichstag delegation, Gustav Ickler, Johannes Junck, Friedrich List, and Baron Hartmann von Richthofen.[32]

Depressed by the desertion of his former colleagues, Stresemann reluctantly concluded that the National Liberal Party, with its strong ties to the imperial regime, had become a political liability under the new conditions. On November 22, in an attempt to keep the Democratic tide from assuming flood proportions, he joined with Friedberg and several other National Liberal spokesmen in hastily proclaiming a German People's Party (*Deutsche Volkspartei* or DVP). He and the other founders of this new organization then urged all National Liberals to transfer their support to it.[33] The new party's policies were outlined only in a very vague fashion, but the statement proclaiming its formation endorsed a "democratic" form of government. Thus, with regard to the critical question of the Republic, its position was equivocal, for a constitutional monarchy with a cabinet fully responsible to the Reichstag could meet this qualification just as well as a republican government.

[32] Nationalliberale Partei, *Rundschreiben.*
[33] *Nachlass*, 3171/7353/166101, his daily calendar for 20.11.1918. Also, Deutsche Volkspartei (Stresemann), *Entstehung*, pp. 10f. Also, *Deutscher Geschichtskalender*, L, 351ff.

19

Though the entry of two former Progressive Reichstag deputies, Julius Kopsch and Otto Wiemer, soon made it possible to
advertise the new DVP as a union of National Liberals and
Progressives, Stresemann and Friedberg had little success in
their attempts to establish it as a full-fledged party.[34] Contrary
to their hopes, no large-scale influx of Progressives developed.
Even more importantly, most of the National Liberal provincial
organizations ignored the instructions of the national headquarters to transfer their allegiance to the DVP. Many pointedly refused to do so and, keeping their identity as branches of the old
party, called upon its leaders to make another attempt at a
united liberal party.[35] Others, such as those in Leipzig and
Magdeburg, went even further and simply turned their organizations over to the DDP.[36] Stresemann, Friedberg, and the other
National Liberals who had joined them in founding the DVP
were thus left in the anomalous position of heading two political
parties, one existing in name only and the other on the verge
of dissolution.

By the end of November, Friedberg, who was inclined to place
practical considerations above old animosities and questions of
ideology, had decided that the DVP could not survive as an independent entity. Consequently, he began to sound out the
Democrats on the possibility of a merger.[37] He was in a good
position for such an undertaking since he was not among the
outspoken annexationists against whom Weber had inveighed
on November 18, having spent his career in Prussian politics,
which were concerned primarily with domestic affairs. In confidential talks with the Democrats he found that they were willing
to modify their earlier position and accept all with the exception
of the extreme right-wing National Liberals. The one obstacle

---

[34] *Schulthess' Europäischer Geschichtskalender*, LIX, Part 1, 514.
[35] *Deutsche Volkspartei Papers*, Vols. 93a and 94.
[36] *Berliner Tageblatt*, 18. and 22.11.1918 (Nos. 590 and 597).
[37] Stresemann, "Beiträge zur Nationalliberalen Parteigeschichte,"
Deutsche Stimmen, 27.6.1920. Also, *Nachlass*, 3079/6917/137027ff.,
letter to Günther, 3.2.1919.

was Stresemann. The Democratic leadership recognized that he wielded sufficient influence to jeopardize the success of a merger if he were completely excluded. On the other hand, they had still not forgiven him his annexationist past. They therefore indicated their willingness to accept him into a united party and grant him a candidacy to the Assembly. But as a condition for this they demanded his exclusion from all the governing bodies of the new organization, which would in effect bar him, from the start, from any position of influence or prominence.[38]

To Stresemann's indignation, Friedberg and most of the other National Liberal-DVP leaders concluded they had no choice except to agree to the Democrats' demand. He himself complained angrily that he was being "sacrificed" to "make way for those representatives of the left wing who are not burdened by the fact that they believed in a German victory."[39] But since he was unable to offer any alternative solution to the plight of the National Liberal-DVP group and was again unwilling to face the prospect of complete exclusion from a new liberal party, he ended by acquiescing to the Democrats' demand. As a face-saving concession, he was allowed to present his exclusion from the proposed party's governing bodies as his own decision. When the talks concerning the final terms of the merger began on December 1, he accordingly submitted to the two National Liberal negotiators, Friedberg and Eugen Leidig, a terse, one-sentence statement: "Dr. Stresemann firmly declines to enter any committee of the German Democratic Party."[40]

Despite his submission, the merger negotiations did not go smoothly. As soon as the discussion of concrete matters got under way it became evident that the Democratic leaders were

[38] Nuschke, "Wie die Demokratische Partei Wurde," p. 29. Also, *Nachlass*, 3079/6917/137056, letter to Holtermann, 5.2.1919. Also, *Nachlass*, 3069/6896/134620, letter to Loewy, 1.12.1918.
[39] *Nachlass*, 3068/6889/133633, letter to Vogel, 3.12.1918.
[40] *Deutsche Volkspartei Papers*, Vol. 94, press release entitled "Dr. Stresemanns Erwiderung," dated 18.1.1919. The Democrats acknowledged his statement in the *Berliner Tageblatt*, 5.12.1918 (No. 621), p. 4.

determined to exploit the disadvantageous position of the National Liberal-DVP group and attempt to absorb it as a helpless minority rather than accept it as a full partner. Friedberg had been instructed by the National Liberal leaders to hold out for a representation of ten in the executive committee of the new party and also to secure the postponement of the adoption of a program until the National Liberals could have a voice in determining its content. These were not exorbitant demands, but the Democrats were determined to press home their advantage and rejected them. They were willing to part with only four places in the committee and demanded that the original program of the Democratic Party be adopted without change. With only the crumbling National Liberal organization and the stillborn DVP behind him, Friedberg was in a weak bargaining position and apparently came to the conclusion that unity must be had, even at the Democrats' price. Knowing that such a move would encounter stiff opposition from the National Liberals, he accepted the Democratic terms on December 3 without consulting Stresemann or most of the other leaders of the party—including Leidig, his co-negotiator. Then he promptly announced to the press that a merger had been completed and that he was entering the executive committee of the DDP along with three other National Liberals, Wilhelm Blankenburg, Gerhart Bollert, and Frau Clara Mende.[41]

When he heard of the terms Friedberg had accepted, Stresemann angrily rejected the newly completed merger. This action was not, as Friedberg maintained during the ensuing campaign, the result of any disappointment at failing to obtain a leading position in the new party. From the beginning he had been reconciled to the fact that the most he could expect would be a nomination to the National Assembly and this still remained open to him. His reaction was in part based on his indignation

---

[41] Eugen Leidig, "Parteigeschichtliches zur Gründung der Deutschen Volkspartei," *Deutsche Stimmen*, 23.2.1919. Also, Deutsche Volkspartei (Stresemann), *Entstehung*, pp. 13f.

at Friedberg's surrender of the National Liberals' conditions without even consulting him. But still more important was his conviction that a merger on the terms which the Democrats had imposed was really a "capitulation."[42] He had been ready to enter a united party, even on terms disadvantageous to himself, if the National Liberals were given a representation roughly in proportion to their popular backing. Under such circumstances there was always hope that he could eventually overcome the initial handicap that was to be imposed upon him. But with Democratic leaders in complete domination of the new party, he concluded that his own position and that of the other National Liberals would be intolerable. Contrary to the Democrats' later accusations, his refusal to accept the merger was in no sense based upon any expectation of increased power or influence. In fact, at the time, his decision seemed almost certain to end, or at least interrupt, his political career. He himself fully expected that Friedberg would have no difficulty in exploiting the apparently hopeless plight of the National Liberals to bring the whole party into the DDP. He therefore resigned himself to the prospect of withdrawing from politics altogether.[43]

Several days after Friedberg's completion of the merger with the Democrats, Stresemann's fortunes suddenly improved. At that time it became evident that Friedberg's action had offended other National Liberals as well. Particularly significant was the fact that the important National Liberal organizations in Bremen, Hamburg, Hanover, Pomerania, and Westphalia had announced their refusal to join the Democratic Party and urged Stresemann to keep the DVP alive.[44] He also gained assurances of support for such a venture from Heinrich Rippler, editor of the Berlin newspaper *Tägliche Rundschau*, which had formerly been

[42] *Nachlass*, 3171/7353/166104, entry in his daily calendar.
[43] Heinrich Rippler, "Wie die DVP entstand," in *Erneuerung* (publication of the DVP), 13.5.1933.
[44] *Frankfurter Zeitung*, 8.12.1918 (No. 340). Also, *Deutscher Geschichtskalender*, L, 354. Also, *Deutsche Volkspartei Papers*, Vol. 94.

aligned with the National Liberals.[45] In addition, he received overtures from the new right-wing German National People's Party (*Deutschnationale Volkspartei* or DNVP), which was made up of German Conservatives, Free Conservatives, and Christian Socialists.[46]

Encouraged by these unexpected developments, Stresemann decided to fight for his political life. Unwilling to join the reactionary German Conservatives in the new DNVP, he set out to convert the DVP into a national political organization by capturing the machinery of the moribund National Liberal Party. Although many of its provincial organizations had already deserted to the Democrats, the old party had remained in existence, primarily because no meeting had been held to dissolve it. Friedberg, who was still national chairman despite the fact that he had already accepted an official post with the Democrats, had recognized the dangers inherent in this situation and had scheduled a meeting of the National Liberal Central Committee for the morning of December 15. At that time he hoped to secure the dissolution of the old organization and thus prevent it from falling into Stresemann's hands. Determined to thwart Friedberg and gain control of the party machinery, Stresemann set out to marshal support for the Committee meeting. In a bitter battle that ended in an acrimonious debate with Friedberg, he succeeded in winning over the important Berlin organization.[47] Then he dispatched letters and telegrams to those who had stood close to him in the old party, alerting them to the importance of the Committee meeting and inviting them to the formal founding of the DVP, which he scheduled for the afternoon of the 15th.[48] He thus undertook to capture the old organization and, at the same time, to ensure a respectable assemblage of im-

[45] Rippler, "Wie die DVP entstand."
[46] *Nachlass,* 3068/6892/134012f., letters to Kardorff (DNVP), 11. and 12.12.1918.
[47] Deutsche Volkspartei (Stresemann), *Entstehung,* p. 15.
[48] *Nachlass,* 3068/6892/134007ff., copies of the telegrams. Also, *ibid.,* 134022, letter to Baldrusch, 13.12.1918.

portant political figures at the meeting that would officially launch the DVP.

When the National Liberal Central Committee assembled on the morning of December 15, luck was on Stresemann's side. Only 61 of its 229 members had surmounted the difficulties of a paralyzed transportation system to reach Berlin and attend the meeting. Of those, 33 sided with him, voting to turn the old party's organization over to the DVP. Friedberg, who had the backing of 28 Committee members, protested with some justification that this was too small and fortuitous a majority to make such an important decision. Stresemann, however, exploited his momentary advantage to the full and secured the adoption of a formal resolution embodying his wishes.[49] Later that same afternoon, in line with his plans, a group of 94 persons, most of whom were members of the National Liberal organization in Berlin, met at the Savoy Hotel and proclaimed the founding of the DVP. As the new organization's uncontested leader, Stresemann was promptly elected its chairman by acclamation.[50]

❖

The events of December 15 saved Stresemann from an early political retirement and opened the way for his career in the Weimar Republic. But at the same time, those events also perpetuated the disunity of German liberalism which proved to be one of the great weaknesses of the Republic. The Democrats later blamed Stresemann for this disunity, but although he was not a partisan of liberal unity, he cannot justly be held responsible for its failure. Forced on several occasions to choose between withdrawing from liberal politics altogether or accepting mergers he regarded as undesirable, he had repeatedly reconciled himself to the latter course. Even at the time of the December

[49] *Schulthess' Europäischer Geschichtskalender,* LIX, Part 1, 571.
[50] "Gründung der Deutschen Volkspartei," by Clara Mende (a participant), *Deutsche Stimmen,* 20.12.1928.

merger negotiations with the DDP he had been willing to accept a united party on terms that would have relegated him to a secondary position for an indefinite period. The heavy responsibility for the failure of liberal unity falls, therefore, not on him but on the group of idealistic intellectuals who founded the DDP and controlled it during its first months. It was only their decision to seek to dominate the united party completely that finally brought him to reject the project. If they had not driven him to this step there could have been no second liberal party, for none of the remaining disaffected National Liberals possessed sufficient prestige to call such an organization into being on a national scale. As events were to show, the policy of the Democratic leadership was an extremely unfortunate one. It not only destroyed the ideal opportunity for union provided by the revolution but also created a residue of bitterness and resentment that was to plague all subsequent attempts to bring the two wings of German liberalism together. Ironically, more than one of the founding fathers of the DDP, most of whom quickly withdrew from active politics, later became reconciled with Stresemann and eventually came to regret the decision of December 1918.

II. FELLOW TRAVELER ON THE
RIGHT, 1919-1920

THE PARTY which Stresemann unveiled on the afternoon of December 15 was, despite its new name, simply a somewhat truncated reincarnation of the old National Liberal organization which had expired a few hours earlier. The two renegade Progressives who had entered the DVP when it had first been proclaimed in November, Kopsch and Wiemer, had long since returned to the Democratic Party. Consequently, the leaders of the new party consisted solely of those National Liberals who had refused to endorse Friedberg's acceptance of the Democrats' merger terms. It was thus in a sense a negative creation. Instead of being united by a common set of goals for the future, its leaders had been brought together primarily by their need for a vehicle of political survival.

Contrary to the generally accepted view, the DVP cannot be equated with the right wing of the National Liberal Party. The explanation for this lies in the fact that the domestic issues over which the two wings of the old party had differed were not decisive in the division of late 1918. They had been superseded by questions of the proper attitude toward the Republic and of the distribution of power within the new parties, as well as by the animosities of the war years. As a result, the National Liberals divided along lines different from those that had previously marked off their quarreling factions. It is true that the leaders of the extreme left wing switched their allegiance to the DDP. Along with them, however, went such prominent members of the right wing as Friedberg and Eugen Schiffer, who were not so burdened by annexationist speeches and who were willing, despite their earlier conservative outlook, to enter an outspokenly republican party dominated by Democrats and left-wing Progressives. Among those who remained with the DVP, on the other hand, were a large number who, like Stresemann, had been

27

associated with the left in the old party, including Rudolf Heinze, Professor Wilhelm Kahl, and Jacob Riesser. Moreover, the extreme right wing did not enter the DVP, for Stresemann pointedly insisted that its spokesmen be excluded.[1] As a result, the most apt description of the new party was Stresemann's own: the core of the National Liberal Party, shorn of its extreme wings.[2]

Unfortunately from Stresemann's viewpoint, the DVP's inheritance from the National Liberal Party had been shorn not only of its extreme wings but also of much of its party machinery. This was due mainly to the inroads the Democrats had made. In many towns and cities the defection of local groups had left the DVP with no representation in the campaign for the National Assembly elections, which had been set for January 19, 1919. Even more crippling was the total loss of the National Liberal organizations of eleven electoral districts to the Democrats. Lacking these key organizations, which were responsible for nominations, the DVP was forced to enter the campaign without candidates in almost a third of the country, including such areas of former National Liberal strength as Baden, Saxony, Silesia, and Thuringia. Also damaging to the party's election prospects was the loss to the DDP of the backing of many newspapers formerly aligned with the National Liberals.[3]

Stresemann was aware of all of the DVP's handicaps but he was able to do little about them before the elections. He could not even direct the party's national campaign since he had to devote most of his energy to securing his own election in the industrial region surrounding Osnabrück which he had represented since 1914. The unrest of the revolution had persisted there and he was faced with a difficult fight, having continually to contend with the hostility of the Socialists and the Communists. On one occasion, while speaking in the town of Nordhorn, he narrowly escaped assassination by persons he described

[1] *Nachlass*, 3068/6892/133974, letter to Neumann, 11.12.1918.
[2] *Ibid.*, 133995, letter to Duke of Schleswig-Holstein, 6.1.1919.
[3] DVP, *Bericht über den Ersten Parteitag* (Berlin, 1919).

as "rabble" and was driven, much to his humiliation, to take refuge in a cellar.[4] One serious problem with which he was forced to deal at once was that of the DVP's finances. The funds it had inherited from the National Liberal organization were quickly exhausted by the expenses of the campaign and the party went heavily into debt. Moreover, efforts at fund-raising were handicapped by the fact that the traditional National Liberal tie to the heavy industry of the Ruhr had been weakened when the right wing of the old party was not included in the DVP. This connection was not entirely broken, for Albert Vögler, an associate of multimillionaire industrialist Hugo Stinnes, accepted a DVP candidacy for the Assembly and was elected as the party's first treasurer. But in spite of Vögler's efforts on behalf of the DVP, the large subsidies formerly granted to the National Liberals were not forthcoming from the Ruhr. Stresemann therefore attempted to cover the campaign deficit by using his own contacts. Although his political career had long since taken precedence over his business affairs, he still had official posts in two of light industry's most important organizations, the Saxon *Verband Sächsischer Industrieller* and the national *Bund der Industriellen.* In addition, he served as a board member of a number of small industrial firms in Saxony and Berlin.[5] During December and January, he had appeals for funds sent to many of the companies with which he was acquainted, indicating that the DVP should be regarded as a continuation of the National Liberal Party and could be counted upon to defend the interests of industry.[6] It soon became clear, however, that these smaller light industries did not com-

---

[4] *Nachlass,* 3079/6917/136968f., letter to Uebel, 1.2.1919. Also, Olden, *Stresemann,* p. 131.

[5] For information on his business ties and his curious relations with Paul Litwin, General Director of the *Deutsche Evaporator A.G.,* see Hans W. Gatzke, "Stresemann und Litwin," *Vierteljahrshefte für Zeitgeschichte,* v (1957), 76ff.

[6] *Nachlass,* 3079/6917/136947ff., letter to Oechelhaeuser, 6.1.1919. Also, *Nachlass,* 3068/6891/133872ff., DVP national headquarters to Molchow, 23.2.1918.

mand the funds available to the industry of the Ruhr. The money that was obtained proved sufficient to preserve the party's credit, but at the end of the campaign it was left with a large deficit.[7]

The campaign which the DVP waged during the hectic weeks before the elections of January 19, 1919, was distinguished primarily by its caution and equivocation. Its platform consisted essentially of a rejection of any significant alteration of the prerevolutionary social and economic *status quo,* hedged about with a number of minor concessions to the revolutionary temper of the times. On the vital issue of economic policy, the platform rejected a socialization of the economy and called for the preservation of private enterprise. But at the same time, it announced that the party would not object to the nationalization of those areas of production that could be operated more economically by the state. Although most of the DVP's leaders were monarchists, no clear stand had been adopted with regard to the equally important question of the future form of the German state. On this point the platform contained only the same equivocal endorsement of a "democratic" government that had been announced in its first proclamation in November.[8] This enabled the party's spokesmen to avoid the issue altogether when confronting predominantly republican audiences. When dealing with monarchists, however, Stresemann made no secret of his personal preference for a constitutional monarchy of the sort that had been established in October 1918. To one member of the party he wrote: "I have emphasized in almost every one of my campaign meetings that I was a monarchist, am a monarchist, and shall remain a monarchist."[9]

From Stresemann's standpoint, the results of the elections to the National Assembly could hardly be termed a success. He secured election himself by a comfortable margin, but the DVP

[7] *Deutsche Volkspartei Papers,* Vol. 104a, minutes of Managing Committee, 1.5.1919.

[8] The platform is printed in Felix Salomon, *Die Deutschen Parteiprogramme,* Heft 3 (Berlin, 1920), pp. 86ff.

[9] *Nachlass,* 3068/6891/133896, letter to Behm, 6.1.1919.

did not fare at all well, obtaining only 22 of the 423 seats. Along with the Independent Socialists, who also won only 22 seats, it shared the distinction of sending the smallest delegation to the Assembly. Its two competitors for the votes of the Protestant middle classes, the Democrats and the Nationalists (DNVP), made much stronger showings, obtaining 75 and 44 seats respectively. The most successful parties were the Social Democrats (SPD), with 165 seats, and the Center, with 91.

In view of the handicaps it had faced, the DVP had done well to preserve at least its claim to the status of a national party, something many former National Liberals had believed would be impossible. Still, it was hardly encouraging to note that although the electorate had been more than doubled by admitting women and lowering the voting age from twenty-five to twenty-one, the DVP had failed to equal the total of votes amassed by the National Liberals in 1912. Of more than 30 million votes cast, it had obtained only 1,345,638. With regard to distribution, its support lay in the same industrial and commercial regions of northern Germany that had traditionally been the strongholds of the National Liberals.

Although the DVP had emerged from the January elections as one of the country's weakest parties, it offered Stresemann one great advantage—he was able to dominate it completely. In the National Liberal Party, following the death of Bassermann, Stresemann's power as chairman of the Reichstag delegation had been checked by that of Friedberg. The latter had succeeded Bassermann as the party's highest officer, chairman of the Central Committee (*Zentralvorstand*), and also as head of the important Managing Committee (*Geschäftsführender Ausschuss*), which handled short-term tactical decisions. In the DVP Stresemann was challenged by no such rival. Following the revolution, most of the prominent National Liberal leaders had decided either to join Friedberg in the Democratic Party or to withdraw from politics altogether. Therefore, the new party was staffed, for the most part, by obscure figures drawn from the lower echelons of

31

the old organization. Of the twenty-two members of the delegation to the Assembly, for instance, only three had served in an imperial Reichstag, and of these Stresemann was by far the most prominent. In the new party's organizational structure, which was patterned on that of the old, he was chairman of both the Central Committee and the Managing Committee. In these capacities he was able to control the national headquarters completely. This placed at his disposal the main source of information in the DVP and gave him a means of influencing opinion in its local organizations throughout the country. Also useful in reinforcing his control of the party was his weekly magazine, *Deutsche Stimmen*, which he turned into a semi-official organ of the DVP, although it was solely under his personal control.

Realizing that it would be difficult to hold all the major posts in the new party, he decided not to seek the chairmanship of the DVP Assembly delegation.[10] The result was the election of Rudolf Heinze, the last Minister-President of the Kingdom of Saxony and a member of the National Liberal Reichstag delegation from 1907 to 1911. This selection apparently caused him no concern at the time since Heinze was a stiff, pretentious bureaucrat who could hardly challenge him for the leadership of the party. Within a few months, however, he came to regret not having taken the post for himself. The explanation for this change was that on the fundamental question of the DVP's future Heinze had come to differ with him, feeling that the party was too weak to continue as an independent entity. The situation reached the crisis point in early June 1919, when Heinze urged the Assembly delegation to take steps toward the formation of a broad new organization which would embrace the DVP and the DNVP, as well as parts of the DDP and the Center.

From the beginning Stresemann was skeptical about such an undertaking. But in view of the favorable reception Heinze's proposal received from some of the DVP deputies, he was at least

---

[10] *Nachlass*, 3079/6917/137101, letter to Garnich, 27.2.1919.

willing to see what possibilities might arise.[11] Given this much encouragement, Heinze opened negotiations with the Nationalists on his own initiative. The leaders of the larger party were not interested in the sort of organization he hoped to create. They were, however, intrigued by the possibility of absorbing the DVP and, in an apparent attempt to win the support of the smaller party's rank and file for the idea, they announced to the press that overtures regarding a merger of the two parties had been received from the DVP.[12] This provided Stresemann and the others who were not in favor of Heinze's plan with an opportunity to demand that it be abandoned at once. Heinze protested that he had not contemplated a merger with the DNVP alone. But his attempts to defend himself met with little response, since it was quite clear that he had been badly outmaneuvered by the Nationalists. The majority of the delegation followed Stresemann's recommendation and denounced the whole project while reasserting their determination to keep the party independent.[13] The result was a sharp reduction of Heinze's stature in the party and in the delegation. He remained as chairman of the delegation, but there was no longer any doubt that Stresemann had the upper hand.

Stresemann's refusal to consider a merger with the Nationalists was in part based upon his aversion to the reactionary German Conservatives who were strongly represented in the new party. In addition, he was undoubtedly aware that the leaders of the stronger DNVP would be in a dominant position in a united party and that his own power would thus be greatly reduced. Also behind his rejection of a merger was the firm belief that if the DVP could preserve its independence it would in-

[11] *Nachlass*, 3079/6920/137549f., letter to Dette, 4.6.1919. Also, *Nachlass*, 3079/6919/137341ff., his draft of an article for *Deutsche Stimmen*, dated 12.6.1919.

[12] Lewis Hertzman, "The German National People's Party (DNVP), 1918-1924" (Harvard dissertation, 1955), pp. 100ff.

[13] *Nachlass*, 3079/6920/137590ff., minutes of Managing Committee, 29.6.1919.

evitably expand. The basis for this belief was his conviction that hundreds of thousands of middle-class voters would soon become disillusioned with the Democrats' close cooperation with the Social Democrats and would turn to the DVP. He therefore felt that the formation of a united party of the right through a merger of the DVP and the DNVP would serve only to strengthen the left by leaving no alternative for those Democrats who wished to change parties but who could not accept the groups which made up the DNVP.[14] After the collapse of Heinze's venture, Stresemann sought to encourage defection from the DDP by publicly emphasizing that the DVP was determined to retain its independence but stood ready to accept into its organization all those Democrats who rejected the policies of the DDP's left-wing leadership.[15] He did not have to wait long for results. By October 1919, a number of important Democratic local organizations had transferred their allegiance to the DVP. In the ten-month period since January, the party's total membership had risen from less than 100,000 to slightly over 250,000. Throughout the fall and winter this trend continued without interruption. By March 1920, the DVP was, with 395,000 members, larger than the prewar National Liberal Party, which had only 283,711 members in 1914-1915.[16] As a result of this rather spectacular vindication of his policies, Stresemann received most of the credit for the party's successes, which further enhanced his already unquestioned pre-eminence.

Stresemann's first chance to see the new parliamentary Republic in action came with the opening of the National Assembly

[14] His article, "Das Bittere Ende" (dated 22.6.1919), in his *Von der Revolution*, p. 176. Also, *Nachlass*, 3088/6921/137629ff., letter to Schmidgall, 24.3.1919.

[15] *Nachlass*, 3079/6919/137353, notes for speech at Osnabrück, 30.8.1919.

[16] *Deutsche Volkspartei Papers*, Vol. 104c, "Bericht über die Entwicklung der Organisation." On the NLP, see Thomas Nipperdey, *Die Organisation der deutschen Parteien vor 1918* (Düsseldorf, 1961), p. 100. The membership figures are not exactly comparable because of the increased political activity of women after 1918.

at Weimar in early February 1919. His initial reaction was far from favorable. He found the proceedings on the flower-bedecked stage of the National Theater slightly ludicrous in comparison to the stately sessions of the old imperial Reichstag. In addition, he was shocked by the partisan content of the speeches of the new ministers, which he contrasted unfavorably with the lofty tone that had characterized the pronouncements of imperial officials.[17] He also missed the old checks on the power of the legislature and deplored the resultant scramble for patronage among the republican parties that controlled the Assembly, fearing it would mean the end of the old professional bureaucracy.[18]

The first cabinet set up under the auspices of the Assembly was based upon the Weimar Coalition of Social Democrats, Democrats, and Centrists and was headed by the Social Democrat, Philipp Scheidemann. It was dedicated to a defense of the revolution and the Republic and commanded a firm majority of the votes in the Assembly. The DVP was thus left as part of an ineffectual opposition, along with the Independent Socialists and the Nationalists. Following the election of Ebert as provisional President of the Republic, one of the first important orders of business taken up by the Assembly involved the various proposals for the socialization of industry. Stresemann and his colleagues joined the Nationalists in roundly condemning all plans for the elimination of private ownership and management. They were unable, though, to prevent the passage on March 13 of a bill which empowered the government to seize, with compensation, any industries it considered "ripe" for socialization. Yet, aside from a few isolated instances, no immediate steps were taken to implement the new law, and even the Social Democrats openly admitted their reluctance to embark upon a thoroughgoing program of socialization until industry had recovered

[17] Speech to DVP meeting in Berlin, 22.2.1919, in his *Von der Revolution*, pp. 107f., p. 119.
[18] Speech to the Assembly, 4.3.1919, in *Verhandlungen der Verfassunggebenden Deutschen Nationalversammlung*, cccxxvi, 496f.

from the war and the revolution. Still, Stresemann and the rest of the DVP were convinced that the danger was great that the political revolution would spread to the economic realm.[19] Despite their fears, a socialization crisis never arose during the lifetime of the Assembly, for disagreements within the Weimar Coalition itself effectively blocked all attempts to set up a program for government seizure of industry.

During the first two months of the Assembly, it seemed certain that the DVP would take its place beside the DNVP as part of a monarchist opposition. Officially, its position on the form of government was still the equivocal one maintained during the campaign. But only a week after the elections, on January 27, Stresemann had publicly served notice that he intended to associate the party with the monarchist cause. At that time he joined with two other leaders of the DVP, Heinze and Ernst von Richter, in dispatching a telegraphic birthday greeting to the exiled Wilhelm II on behalf of the party. This telegram, which was immediately released to the press, brought strenuous protests from the republicans within the party since it had been sent without the knowledge of the Central Committee or the Assembly delegation and ended with the statement: ". . . millions of Germans, even under new circumstances and on a new foundation of political life, join us in acknowledging the monarchist principle and will oppose any unworthy renunciation of the high ideals of the German Empire and the Prussian Kingdom."[20]

In the face of this strong reaction, Stresemann retreated hastily. Resorting to dissimulation, he maintained in private that the text of the message had been garbled in the process of being telephoned to the telegraph office and should have read: ". . . millions of Germans, even while recognizing the new circumstances. . . ."[21] He also pointed out that the telegram was not

[19] Speech to the first Party Congress, 13.4.1919, in his *Reden und Schriften*, I, 270ff.

[20] *Nachlass*, 3079/6917/136976f.

[21] *Ibid.*, 136987f. and 137017ff., letters to Riesser, 1.2.1919, and Boehm, 3.2.1919. His original draft of the telegram is identical to the published version.

an official statement of party policy and insisted that there was still room within the DVP for both republicans and monarchists. He thus made it clear that he was unwilling to risk an exodus of the party's republican supporters by pressing the issue any further at that time. But since he had refused to dissociate the DVP from the telegram publicly, it appeared equally clear that he had only postponed his plan to take the party into the monarchist camp. For the time being he made no further public statements on the issue, but in private he made no secret of his own sentiments. In mid-February he wrote to the DVP organization in Frankfurt am Main: "I would refuse to remain for even twenty-four hours in a party which required me to commit myself as a republican. If this were demanded of me . . . I would prefer to leave public life altogether."[22]

In spite of these ringing words, Stresemann had within two months completely reversed his position and was preparing the DVP for an acceptance of the Republic. This abrupt reversal was not due to the sudden discovery of any previously overlooked virtues of republicanism. The explanation lay instead in the fact that during March the National Assembly of the rump Austrian state had voted for union with Germany. In Stresemann's opinion this projected *Anschluss* was one of the few consoling developments in the otherwise bleak period since the war and he saw it as the first step toward a restoration of Germany's position as a great power. He recognized, however, that the prospect of a restoration of the Protestant and Prussian Hohenzollerns would only increase the opposition to such a union within Catholic Austria. Faced with an apparent choice between the old imperial ruling house and an enlarged and strengthened Reich, he decided in favor of the latter. In April, therefore, he announced to the first Party Congress of the DVP: "We must be clear about one thing, that *Grossdeutschland* can only be constructed on a republican basis."[23] Once again, the adoption of an official policy

22 *Ibid.*, 137039, letter of 14.2.1919.
23 Speech of 13.4.1919, in his *Reden und Schriften*, I, 263.

on the form of government was deferred. But the absence of opposition to Stresemann's statement indicated that the party was ready to rally to the Republic.

When the Allied peace terms were received by the German government in early May, Stresemann was shocked and angered. He had been resigned to the possibility of a severe treaty but the terms presented by the Allies exceeded his worst expectations. In an article written a few days after the publication of the terms he announced: "We are perhaps lost if we do not sign this treaty, but we are certainly lost if we do sign it."[24] A month later his defiance had given way to sober acceptance of the necessity of signing the treaty, but he was confident that important concessions could be gained through negotiation.[25] This belief soon proved to be unfounded. The Allies refused to make any significant changes in their terms and demanded approval by 6 P.M., June 23. Bitterly disappointed, he decided that the DVP could not accept responsibility for such a peace.[26] A similar position was adopted by the Nationalists and also by the Democrats, who left the government in protest against the Allied terms. When the Assembly voted on the treaty on June 22, the DDP and the DNVP joined the DVP in opposing acceptance. The three parties remained a minority, however, and a hastily contrived cabinet of Social Democrats and Centrists, headed by Gustav Bauer of the SPD, was empowered to accept the treaty on the condition that the so-called points-of-honor, which included the war-guilt clause, were omitted.

In view of the DVP's opposition to conditional acceptance of the Versailles Treaty, it was ironic that this party was to provide the formula that led to unconditional approval. This peculiar reversal was a product of the sequence of events set off on June 23 by the Allies' unexpected rejection of conditional ac-

[24] His article, "Wilsons Frieden" (dated 14.5.1919), in his *Von der Revolution*, p. 171.

[25] *Nachlass*, 3079/6920/137510f., letter to Grashoff, 11.6.1919.

[26] His article, "Das Bittere Ende" (dated 22.6.1919), in his *Von der Revolution*, pp. 172ff.

ceptance. With only hours left before the deadline, the Center Party's delegation refused to accept the opprobrium attached to unconditional capitulation, thereby making it impossible to obtain a majority to ratify the treaty. Bauer at once offered to resign and turn the government over to the parties that had been opposed to even conditional acceptance so that they could reject the Allied terms. Despite their defiant attitude of the previous day, the DVP, represented by Stresemann and Heinze, and the DNVP were not at all enthusiastic about running the risk of an Allied invasion, which would apparently be the consequence of a failure to comply with the ultimatum. Accordingly, Stresemann and the leaders of the DNVP replied to Bauer's offer with highly noncommittal answers that clearly indicated their unwillingness to take over. In any case, the Democrats eliminated the possibility of a cabinet of the right by refusing to work with the DVP or the DNVP. In the face of this apparent stalemate, the danger became acute that the deadline would expire with Germany unable to give the Allies any answer—a situation which the Allies had let it be known they would regard as tantamount to rejection. Finally, Heinze provided a face-saving solution that was acceptable to all. He suggested that Bauer's SPD-Center cabinet avert an invasion by accepting the Allied terms unconditionally while, in return, the opposition parties would agree not to question the patriotism of those who supported this step. Shortly before the expiration of the ultimatum, this formula was adopted and the government submitted to the Allies.[27]

Stresemann's role in the compromise on the treaty is unclear. But in view of his dominant position in the DVP, it seems certain that Heinze's plan had at least been cleared with him before it was submitted, if indeed he was not its author. After the plan had been accepted he adhered to its terms. Even while sharply criticizing the attempts of Finance Minister Matthias Erzberger

[27] See the memoirs of two participants: Friedrich Payer, *Von Bethmann-Hollweg bis Ebert* (Frankfurt/Main, 1923), pp. 301ff., and Matthias Erzberger, *Erlebnisse im Weltkrieg* (Stuttgart, 1920), pp. 380ff.

to deal with the French and British behind the back of the regular German delegation at Versailles, Stresemann refrained from any direct attacks on the Social Democratic-Centrist cabinet which had reluctantly accepted the burden of signing the treaty.[28] This did not prevent him from placing the blame for Germany's humiliation on the new Republic, however. He realized that in June 1919, there was no alternative to acceptance of the treaty, but he was thoroughly convinced that the causes of this deplorable state of affairs could be traced directly to the republican revolution of November 1918. Once again, as after the armistice, the basis for his sincere though erroneous views was the stab-in-the-back legend. He remained convinced that the German Army would have been able to hold off the Allies until better terms had been obtained had not the revolution undermined it.[29]

The Versailles Treaty alienated Stresemann from the Republic in more ways than one, for it was also the decisive factor in his decision to lead the DVP in rejecting the Weimar constitution. In April he had been ready to drop his monarchism and reconcile himself to the Republic, but he had been willing to do this only for the sake of the expected *Anschluss* with Austria. With the adoption of the treaty, his brief flirtation with republicanism came to an abrupt end, since that document expressly ruled out an *Anschluss*. When the constitution came before the National Assembly during the summer of 1919, he threw his weight against the republican minority in the DVP, which was led by Julius Curtius of the Baden organization. This group contended that the best course for the DVP was to make its peace with the new state of affairs by accepting the republican constitution.[30]

[28] Speech of 18.10.1919, in DVP, *Bericht über den Zweiten Parteitag* (Berlin, 1920), p. 13. For an example of his attacks on Erzberger, see his article, "Das Bittere Ende" (dated 22.6.1919), in his *Von der Revolution*, pp. 174f.

[29] His article, "Zum Jahrestag der Revolution" (dated 5.11.1919), in his *Von der Revolution*, pp. 193f.

[30] *Nachlass*, 3088/6922/137842ff., Curtius' letter to Stresemann, 24.7.1919.

Since the great majority of the party's leaders upheld Stresemann's position, the Assembly delegation voted against the constitution when it was adopted in August. Stresemann had thus firmly aligned himself and his party with the lost cause of monarchism and had placed a barrier between himself and the Republic which was to complicate his subsequent career greatly. Ironically, his monarchism was the inadvertent work of the Allies. If they had not blocked the *Anschluss* in 1919 he would have taken his place in the new state as a republican, albeit a reluctant one.

Although Stresemann termed the constitution "an ephemeral piece of work," he found relatively little to object to aside from its creation of a republican form of government.[31] Basically, it established a parliamentary system, which he had favored since 1916. Also, the final draft did much to dispel one of his major concerns by providing for a popularly elected and potentially strong President. It thus created a counterweight to the parliament, of which he was still somewhat distrustful, especially in view of the numerical strength of the Social Democrats.[32] His own preference would have been to have still another counterweight in the form of a conservative upper house similar to the British House of Lords. He was thus dissatisfied with the second chamber created by the constitution, the Reichsrat, which was made up of representatives of the republican governments of the federal states, or *Länder*.[33] However he failed to specify how a conservative chamber of the sort he had in mind could have been created in the new democratic Germany. Another aspect of the constitution that displeased him was its failure to rule out the use of ministerial and high administrative posts as political pawns and patronage positions. In his opinion, this would

[31] Speech of 18.10.1919, in DVP, *Zweiten Parteitag*, p. 15.
[32] Speech of 22.2.1919, in his *Von der Revolution*, p. 112.
[33] See his article, "Vor wichtigen Entscheidungen," *Vossische Zeitung*, 28.8.1921 (No. 404).

41

bring the introduction of an American-style spoils system and spell the end of the highly trained professional bureaucracy which he regarded as one of Germany's assets.[34]

After the adoption of the constitution, he openly committed himself and the DVP to an eventual restoration of the Hohenzollerns. His monarchism was, however, never of the militant, divine-right variety found among some of the reactionary German Conservatives in the DNVP.[35] There was a strong emotional element involved, for throughout his life he had been a loyal subject of the Hohenzollerns and looked back on the imperial era as a "time of loftiest elation and joy."[36] In this respect, he was like many of his compatriots, contrasting the prosperous and powerful Empire with the weak and insecure Republic without recognizing that the plight of the latter was a product in large measure of the failings of the former. Yet, although his emotional tie to the Empire was strong, his monarchism was essentially utilitarian in nature. After considering the various alternatives, he had reached the conclusion that a constitutional monarchy would provide the best foundation for sound and stable government in Germany. Still very much concerned about the possibility that the unity of the Reich might be weakened or even destroyed, he was convinced that its best guarantee was the original bond, the imperial crown. It would, he felt, offer a better focus of unity than a president, who would be installed by the votes of only a part of the people.[37] Moreover, he was skeptical about the republican ideal of a citizen ruler, feeling that an hereditary chief of state was less susceptible to some of the pressures that beset governments: "The great danger of republics lies in the fact that they are more accessible to moneyed interests than monarchies. A monarch stands through tradition much too high ever to be impressed by a millionaire; a president

---

[34] Speech to the Assembly, 8.10.1919, in *Verhandlungen*, cccxxx, 2915f.
[35] Speech of 3.12.1920, in *Deutsche Stimmen*, 14.12.1920.
[36] *Nachlass*, 3068/6891/133897, letter to Behm, 6.1.1919.
[37] Speech of 18.10.1919, in DVP, *Zweiten Parteitag*, p. 15.

is in a very different position with regard to such pressures."[38] In any case, as his behavior at the time of the *Anschluss* episode had demonstrated, the question of a restoration was never the paramount one for him. As he explained to one party colleague, his rule of thumb was "first comes the Reich and then comes the monarchy."[39]

In view of the unsettled conditions of 1919, he therefore decided to de-emphasize the whole issue. If it were revived too soon after the revolution, he reasoned, it would probably increase the already severe internal divisions and possibly lead to a civil war that would produce total collapse and leave the country defenseless against its enemies and against communism.[40] In presenting his own position and that of the party to the public he was careful to indicate that he envisioned a restoration only at some future time when the country had thoroughly recovered from the war and the majority of the people had decided they wanted a return to constitutional monarchy. Moreover, in a speech to the National Assembly on October 8, he made a promise he was soon to violate, pledging that the DVP would cooperate loyally within the framework of the Weimar constitution, seeking to alter it only by legal means and rejecting attempts to overthrow the Republic by means of a Putsch.[41]

With the Republic apparently installed for an indefinite period, Stresemann concluded that the most important task ahead was to end the leftist domination of the government as soon as possible. As a first step in this direction he began laying plans in late August to nominate Field Marshal Paul von Hindenburg for the presidency of the Republic. In his opinion, only Hindenburg, with his seemingly unlimited popularity, could prevent the Social Democrats from using their mass support to secure perpetual control of the presidency. He believed that the Field

[38] *Nachlass*, 3079/6918/137189, speech of 6.4.1919.
[39] *Nachlass*, 3068/6891/133896, letter to Behm, 6.1.1919.
[40] *Ibid.*, 133897.
[41] *Verhandlungen* (Assembly), cccxxx, 2915.

Marshal would require the backing of most of the country's non-socialist voters to defeat a Social Democratic nominee. For this reason he was hopeful that Hindenburg could be named as a non-partisan candidate rather than being identified with any one party.[42] Therefore, when the Nationalists also decided to support Hindenburg, he joined forces with their leader, Oskar Hergt, in making preparations for the nomination. The Field Marshal proved receptive to their overtures but refused to commit himself until the situation became clearer.[43] This, however, did not happen. The constitution had left the scheduling of presidential elections to be settled by ordinary legislation and so the matter rested with the republican parties which controlled the Assembly. Since they were content to retain Ebert as President on a provisional basis, the question of the first regular presidential election was postponed indefinitely.

After his plan to reduce the power of the left through the presidency had been forestalled, Stresemann reached a decision that was to have important consequences for his subsequent career. He decided that the DVP must attempt to gain a place in the government as soon as possible and that in order to do this it would be necessary to agree to cooperate in a coalition with the Social Democrats. In January 1920, he revealed the reasons for this decision in a letter to Albrecht von Graefe, a Nationalist leader who had publicly called upon the DVP to join with the DNVP in forming a "National Bloc" to oppose the leftist parties:

"It seems to me that the immediate task at hand in our political development is to eliminate the Social Democrats' present overwhelming influence and to reduce it to more modest proportions. A government without the Social Democrats during the next two to three years seems to me quite impossible since

---

[42] *Nachlass, 3088/6922/137915 and 137950f., letters to Brües, 13.* and 25.9.1919. Also, *Nachlass,* 3088/6922/137870, minutes of Managing Committee, 24.8.1919.

[43] *Deutsche Volkspartei Papers,* Vol. 104a, minutes of Managing Committee, 16.10.1919.

otherwise we shall stagger along from general strike to general strike. . . .

"There is a very real danger that the two People's Parties [the DVP and the DNVP] will withdraw into the sulking-corner for many years if they do not at once receive a voice in government proportionate to their numerical strength. Our voters would not understand such an attitude and, further, the danger is great that the bureaucracy will be progressively alienated from us or replaced by persons from hostile parties, and that the people will become accustomed on a permanent basis to the rule of the present-day majority parties."[44]

These views were quickly challenged by Albert Vögler, who as party treasurer and spokesman for the industry of the Ruhr wielded considerable influence in the DVP. Vögler favored Graefe's proposal for a "National Bloc" and argued that the party's goal should be a Socialist-free government, not a coalition with the SPD.[45]

Vögler's argument was totally unacceptable from Stresemann's standpoint. He explained why in a letter to another DVP colleague: "I cannot really imagine that there are people in responsible political positions who think . . . that we would do well to drive the Social Democrats back into a permanent and irresponsible opposition and thus force them over into the camp of the Independents and the Bolsheviks."[46] Lest it should appear that he favored a government in which the DVP would be subordinate to the Social Democrats, he clarified his position on cooperation with them: "The goal for which we must strive is the elimination of the dominant influence of the Social Democrats, if possible through a cabinet in which the middle-class parties preponderate."[47] Once the SPD was forced to work with a strong bloc of non-socialist parties, he argued,

[44] *Nachlass*, 3091/6935/140029f., letter of 23.1.1920.
[45] *Nachlass*, 3091/6936/140297ff., minutes of Managing Committee, 4.3.1920.
[46] *Nachlass*, 3091/6935/140077, letter to Krüger, 4.2.1920.
[47] *Ibid.*

its more extreme elements would split off and join the Independents, leaving only those who were willing to accept sound and constructive policies. In this connection, he was hopeful that prolonged cooperation with the other parties would eventually lead the SPD to drop its Marxist class-conflict ideology and become a non-doctrinaire workers' party similar to the British Labour Party.[48]

In spite of Vögler's opposition, Stresemann had little trouble obtaining the support of most of the party's leaders for his views. However, he found it much more difficult to put his plans into effect than he had expected. In view of the size of the small DVP delegation and the strength of the Weimar Coalition (reconstituted in November 1919, with the entry of the DDP into the Bauer cabinet), he saw no possibility of gaining a place in the government during the lifetime of the National Assembly. Instead, he placed his hopes on the elections for the first republican Reichstag, which he expected would be held in the spring of 1920.[49] In view of the DVP's growth during the previous year, he was confident that the elections would greatly increase its parliamentary strength. In addition, it was generally conceded that the widespread dissatisfaction with the peace settlement and with economic conditions would produce significant losses for the Weimar Coalition parties. His hope was that these losses would be large enough to destroy the Coalition's majority, thereby greatly improving his chances of gaining a place in the government for the DVP. There was a serious flaw in his plans, however, for the members of the Bauer cabinet were also aware of the probable outcome of spring elections. They were naturally reluctant to see their parties lose control of the government and so took no steps toward scheduling the new elections.

---

[48] *Ibid.*, 140076. Also, *Nachlass*, 3091/6935/140029, letter to Graefe, 23.1.1920. Also, speech of 18.10.1919, DVP, *Zweiten Parteitag*, pp. 18f. Also, *Nachlass*, 3114/7133/148766, letter to Ambassador Houghton (USA), 4.6.1925.

[49] *Tägliche Rundschau*, 28.1.1920 (No. 50), report on his speech in Frankfurt/Main, 26.1.1920.

The attitude of the Bauer cabinet came as a severe disappointment to the Nationalists as well as to Stresemann and his colleagues, for the leaders of the DNVP had also expected gains from early elections. Throughout January and February the spokesmen of the two parties protested that the National Assembly had been created specifically to adopt a new constitution. As this task had long since been completed, they called for the replacement of the Assembly with the regular legislative body provided for by the Weimar constitution.[50] Their protests had no effect, however, and the cabinet refused to schedule new elections. During late February the indignation of the two parties was still further increased when, as a result of rumors of their intention to nominate Hindenburg for the presidency, the prominent Democratic newspaper *Berliner Tageblatt* proposed a constitutional alteration to provide for legislative rather than popular election of the chief executive. This proposal was obviously aimed at blocking the election of Hindenburg, whose strength lay in his ability to appeal to the people over the heads of the republican parties. The leaders of the DVP and the DNVP regarded it as a cynical attempt to manipulate the country's new governmental structure for partisan purposes. But in spite of their angry protests, the proposal was favorably received by some of the members of the Weimar Coalition parties and there were rumors that it would be put to a vote in the Assembly.[51]

The discontent of the DVP and the DNVP did not escape the attention of General Walther von Lüttwitz, one of the leaders of the group of disaffected Army officers who were soon to launch the Kapp Putsch. On March 4, he met with Heinze and Hergt, the chairmen of the Assembly delegations of the two parties, and suggested that the DVP and DNVP join forces with the dissident officers in the Army. Lüttwitz was primarily con-

[50] See Oskar Hergt's testimony at the Jagow-Prozess (trial of a number of those involved in the Kapp Putsch), 1921, in Karl Brammer (ed.), *Verfassungsgrundlagen und Hochverrat* (Berlin, 1922), pp. 19ff.

[51] Stresemann, *Die Märzereignisse und die Deutsche Volkspartei* (Berlin, 1920), pp. 4ff.

47

cerned with the government's treatment of the armed forces, and especially with its decision to begin compliance with the Allies' disarmament demands by disbanding a number of military units, including two Free Corps brigades under his own command. But apparently in the hope of gaining political backing, Lüttwitz informed the two party spokesmen that the officers wanted not only a revision of the current military policies but also prompt election of a new Reichstag and direct balloting for the presidency. Heinze and Hergt agreed that these were desirable aims, but both rejected the General's suggestion that such demands be presented to the Bauer cabinet in the form of an ultimatum accompanied by an implied threat of armed rebellion. They warned him that their parties would not consent to such an undertaking and promised instead to attempt to alter the political situation by parliamentary means.[52] This promise was upheld by Stresemann and a number of prominent Nationalists at a joint meeting on March 5. Four days later the two parties presented to the Assembly a resolution calling for spring elections and for a reaffirmation of popular election of the President. In spite of their thinly veiled warnings regarding the rebellious mood of part of the Army, the resolution was overwhelmingly defeated by the government parties.[53]

Following the defeat of their joint resolution, the leaders of the DVP and DNVP made no further attempt to lessen the tensions between the dissident officers and the Bauer cabinet which culminated in the outbreak of the Kapp Putsch on March 13. After the rebellion collapsed, the Democratic newspapers *Berliner Tageblatt* and *Frankfurter Zeitung* repeatedly alleged that Stresemann had possessed prior knowledge of the plot and

[52] See the testimony of Heinze and Hergt at the Jagow-Prozess, 1921, in Brammer, *Verfassungsgrundlagen*, pp. 19ff. Also, Walther Freiherr von Lüttwitz, *Im Kampf gegen die November-Revolution* (Berlin, 1934), p. 111.

[53] *Nachlass*, 3090/6932/139643, Stresemann's memorandum on the meeting with the DNVP spokesmen on 5.3.1920. Also, *Verhandlungen* (Assembly), cccxxxii, 4830ff., session of 9.3.1920.

had made this known in a speech to a closed DVP gathering in Hamburg on March 8. No evidence was ever presented to support these charges and Stresemann steadfastly insisted that he had done nothing more than inform a group of party associates at a private dinner of the outcome of the meeting of Heinze, Hergt, and Lüttwitz.[54] It is known that he was acquainted with a number of persons involved in the Putsch, including General Ludendorff and his wartime adjutant, Colonel Max Bauer, both of whom he had hoped to include in the DVP delegation to the next Reichstag.[55] But during much of the period just prior to the beginning of the insurrection Stresemann was absent from Berlin and there is no indication that he was in communication with any of these persons or had any knowledge of their plans. It seems highly probable that he was correct in later saying that he had known no more of the intentions of the officers than he had learned from the reports of Hergt and Heinze. And, as he pointed out, just as much was known by many—including members of the government.[56]

On the morning of the 13th, after hearing of the Putsch and the flight of the Bauer cabinet to Dresden, Stresemann and a number of the other leaders of the DVP hurriedly met to establish the party's policy toward the insurrection and toward the government set up by Wolfgang Kapp, the obscure East Prussian official who had been installed as Chancellor. Although six months earlier Stresemann had pledged before the Assembly that the DVP would reject an attempt to overthrow the re-

---

[54] See *Berliner Tageblatt*, 27.3.1920 (No. 142) and *Frankfurter Zeitung*, 28.3.1920 (No. 237). Also, *Nachlass*, 3089/6928/138839f., letter to Schwabach, 14.4.1920. In his *Nemesis of Power* (London, 1953), p. 73, J. W. Wheeler-Bennett asserts without explanation that Stresemann learned of the plot in Hamburg on March 5. According to Stresemann's papers, he was in Berlin that day attending a meeting with the DNVP leaders, see note 53.

[55] *Nachlass*, 3091/6935/140006f., letter to Ludendorff, 7.1.1920. Also, *Nachlass*, 3088/6922/137895, letter to Bauer, 22.9.1919.

[56] *Nachlass*, 3089/6928/138839f., letter to Schwabach, 14.4.1920. Also, his *Märzereignisse*, pp. 24f. For the information possessed by the government, see Gustav Noske, *Von Kiel bis Kapp* (Berlin, 1920), pp. 203ff.

publican government by means of a Putsch, he and the other leaders of the party did not reject the actions of the insurgents. There was general agreement that their use of force had been regrettable, but at the same time it was also agreed that there had been just provocation as a result of the Bauer cabinet's rejection of the DVP-DNVP resolution a few days earlier. Furthermore, the party's leaders were by no means distressed at what appeared to be the abrupt elimination of the Bauer cabinet and the National Assembly, which they had come to regard as the chief obstacles to their hopes for a change in the political situation.

As for Stresemann himself, there can be little question that he was unwilling to associate himself or his party actively with an illegal assault on the republican government. But an apparently successful rebellion carried out by others was evidently an entirely different matter and he showed himself quite ready to accept its results without protest. The pledge to the Assembly was conveniently forgotten and he joined the rest of the party's leaders in concluding that the situation was similar to November 1918, and that they had no choice except to recognize that a revolution had taken place and a new government had come into being. Neither he nor his colleagues, however, were willing to accept a reactionary dictatorship. Instead, they were hopeful of a quick return to legality, either under the Weimar constitution or a new one that might be drafted to replace it. Because of a lack of information about the rebel regime, they postponed their final decision on the party's policy until a first-hand report on its composition and aims could be obtained. For this purpose, a three-man deputation, consisting of Adolf Kempkes and Oskar Maretzky of the Assembly delegation and Hugo Garnich of the Prussian delegation, was dispatched to talk with Kapp.[57]

When the three emissaries returned from their mission on the

[57] *Nachlass*, 3090/6932/139541f., summary of the meeting by Garnich.

afternoon of the 13th, Garnich and Maretzky reported that they had been very favorably impressed by the Chancellor of the insurgent regime and insisted that he was not a radical reactionary. They urged that the party join in the new government at once so that it would be in a position to influence its policies, a proposal that was promptly seconded by several others. Stresemann, however, adopted a more cautious attitude. He was no less disposed than his colleagues to accept the Putsch and recognize the Kapp regime as the government of Germany, but he was unwilling to give the party's full support to the new cabinet. He had not been convinced by the glowing accounts of Garnich and Maretzky and argued that if the DVP wanted to guard against the establishment of a reactionary regime it could not "go through thick and thin with the new government."[58] Instead, he recommended that the party retain a free hand so that it could oppose the possible adoption of reactionary measures. He felt this would also be desirable from another point of view, for he saw that although the Bauer cabinet had suffered a severe setback it was by no means completely vanquished. If the cabinet should regain power, he realized that the DVP would be left in a highly embarrassing position if it had cast its lot with the Putsch regime. In addition, he felt the party should allow for the possibility of a civil war between the two governments: "We must seek a line which on the one hand will make no difficulties for the new government but which will leave open the possibility of our acting as an intermediary between Dresden and Berlin."[59] In line with these views, his own proposal for the DVP's stand was: "The *faits accomplis* are recognized, but we demand that the present illegal situation be promptly brought into accord with the law."[60]

Although Garnich and Maretzky and a few others continued to favor a full commitment to the Kapp regime, the majority

[58] *Nachlass*, 3090/6932/139549, minutes of the afternoon meeting.
[59] *Ibid.*
[60] *Ibid.*, 139550.

51

of those present supported Stresemann's views. After considerable discussion the following declaration was adopted and released to the press late on the afternoon of the 13th:

"The previous government was unable to gain the confidence of the majority of the people. It opposed every attempt to set up a new government through the constitutional means of new elections and, beyond that, it sought to violate the hitherto existing constitution in order to insure its own power. It therefore bears the responsibility for the fact that the path of organic development, which we endorse, has been departed from. Now a new government has been formed. All of those who want to see the reconstruction of our Fatherland take place in a peaceful, orderly fashion must now demand that the new government give guarantees for the preservation of order, property and freedom to work. The liberal principles of the German People's Party remain unaffected by the upheaval. We therefore demand the quickest possible transformation of the present provisional regime into a constitutional one. We expect the government to conduct without delay new elections to the legislative bodies on the basis of the present free electoral law and so to insure the formation of a constitutional government into which all of those parties will be drawn which are serious about the re-establishment of our economy and the preservation of our national honor. Until that time we must make it our duty, through the cooperation of all Germans, to keep internal strife from bringing about a collapse of our political and economic situation."[61]

The DVP thus followed Stresemann's recommendation, accepting the Putsch and giving the Kapp regime *de facto* recognition, while avoiding an official endorsement of the insurgent regime. The declaration nevertheless leaned heavily in the direction of the Putschists. By designating their regime as "the

[61] *Ibid.*, 139553.

new government" it came close to more than mere *de facto* recognition and accorded them a measure of respectability that was indicative of the party's sympathies. Moreover, it was obviously designed to excuse their assault on the legal government and resorted to open distortion in construing the projected constitutional revision of the presidential election system as an attempt "to violate the hitherto existing constitution." Another important aspect of the declaration was the ambiguous use of the word "constitutional," which left the way open for the fulfillment of the party's demands, either through a restoration of the Weimar constitution or through the adoption of a revised version or a wholly new one.

By the morning of March 14, the second day of the Kapp affair, Stresemann's caution had proved justified, for it had become clear that the Bauer government had in fact survived its initial setback. Most of the members of the cabinet, accompanied by President Ebert, had reached Dresden safely and had managed to keep the rebellion from spreading beyond Prussia. Moreover, the trade unions had proclaimed a general strike of all workers and government officials that was already causing serious difficulties for the insurgents. In view of this changed situation, Stresemann decided that the DVP had gone too far the previous day and that a retreat would be necessary. He was hopeful, however, that it would still be possible to prevent the restoration of the pre-Putsch *status quo* as well as to avoid a civil war, which he feared would divide and destroy the Army, leaving Germany defenseless. When the DVP Managing Committee met on the morning of the 14th, he therefore suggested that the party propose a compromise solution whereby both governments would withdraw in favor of a provisional cabinet of experts, which would take over to hold new elections. His views were accepted by part of the Committee but a sizeable group, led by Maretzky, objected strenuously, arguing that the insurgents held the upper hand and would soon win out. Consequently, it was decided that for the time being the party would do no more than sound out the two contending sides on the possibility of a compromise. For this purpose another deputation was dispatched to Kapp, while Stresemann and several others were commissioned to contact those members of the Weimar Coalition parties who had remained in Berlin.[62]

Because of the confusion and disorganization resulting from the Putsch, Stresemann found it impossible to contact representatives of all the government parties, but his overtures regarding a compromise were favorably received by Eduard Burlage, one of the leaders of the Center.[63] When the Managing Committee reconvened at his apartment on the morning of the 15th, he discovered that Kapp had refused to consider relinquishing or altering his position. In addition, Stresemann learned that two of the DVP men who had talked to the insurgent Chancellor, Maretzky and Fritz Mittelmann, had departed from their instructions. They had not only made no attempt to overcome Kapp's obstinate attitude, but had indicated that they were still hopeful he would win out and even suggested ways in which he might strengthen his hand. As a result, Kapp had offered Maretzky the post of police commissioner in Berlin. The morning papers had quoted sources inside the Putsch regime to the effect that the DVP had decided to support the Kapp government and that one of its spokesmen was about to accept an official position in it.[64]

Stresemann was upset by these developments. But just as disturbing was the report from Heinze, who had returned from Dresden a short time before. He announced that both he and the party's delegation in the Saxon *Landtag* had sided with the Bauer cabinet from the first and that he had himself been instrumental in dissuading General Maercker, who commanded a large volunteer force in Saxony, from obeying Lüttwitz' orders to arrest the fleeing Chancellor and his ministers. Otto Most, a

[62] *Nachlass*, 3090/6932/139554ff., minutes of the meeting.
[63] *Nachlass*, 3090/6932/139562, minutes of Managing Committee, morning of 15.3.1920.
[64] *Ibid.*, 139562ff.

member of the Assembly delegation, then reported that in the Ruhr, also, the DVP leaders had given their backing to the Bauer cabinet.

Faced with a basic split that might easily tear the party apart, Stresemann at first sought to plaster over the differences. Addressing himself to Heinze and indulging in some dubious reasoning, he took the position that both the Saxon organization and the Berlin group had acted correctly, since the situation had looked different in Dresden and in Berlin. In any case, he maintained, the only course now left to the DVP was to proceed with the plan for the compromise settlement which he had put forward the previous day. Heinze, however, wanted a clearer definition of this vague proposal. He insisted that a new government could be formed only under the terms of the Weimar constitution. Forced by Heinze to take a stand, Stresemann indicated that he, too, envisioned the execution of the compromise through a withdrawal of the Bauer cabinet and its replacement by a provisional one named by President Ebert—a stipulation conspicuously absent from his proposal of the previous day. This plan proved generally acceptable and a majority of those present, apparently including Stresemann, agreed that the DVP should claim the Ministry of Economics in the new provisional cabinet.[65]

The only strong objections to this course were voiced by Maretzky, who was still in favor of open support for the Kapp regime. For him, the only question of importance to the DVP was which government was stronger and he was confident that Kapp and his comrades still held the upper hand. Maretzky submitted, though, when it became clear that a defiance of the party leadership would mean the end of his career in the DVP. After the meeting had ended, Stresemann hurriedly announced to the press that the DVP had no connection whatever with the Kapp regime.[66]

[65] *Ibid.*
[66] *Ibid.* Also, see memorandum by Eugen Leidig, DVP deputy in Prus-

But on the afternoon of March 15 Stresemann found it was already too late for his plan. The representatives of the Weimar Coalition parties who had remained in Berlin had grown confident as a result of the increasing effectiveness of the general strike. They therefore refused to consider anything except the restoration of the Bauer cabinet. Also, in an obvious attempt to draw support away from the Putsch regime, they announced that as soon as normal conditions were restored they would propose the prompt election of a new Reichstag, a reaffirmation of popular election of the President, and the immediate replacement of some of the members of the Bauer cabinet.[67]

In the light of this turn of events, Stresemann decided that there was no longer any hope for a compromise between the two governments and that he had no choice except to stage another, and more hasty, retreat. The most that could be hoped for, he concluded, was a negotiated surrender of the Kapp regime that would give the Army units aligned with it an honorable way out and force the Bauer cabinet to agree to the proposals outlined by the Berlin spokesmen of the government parties, thereby preventing a return to the undesirable pre-Putsch *status quo.*[68]

Apparently convinced that there was no time to be lost if anything at all was to be salvaged from the Putsch, Stresemann proceeded without consulting the rest of the DVP Managing Committee and on the morning of the 16th contacted Kapp's Army Chief of Staff, Colonel Max Bauer. As he had been acquainted with Bauer since the war years, he was able to present his views on the situation candidly. The Colonel proved receptive to the suggestion of a negotiated withdrawal and expressed the opinion that both Kapp and Lüttwitz could be brought to resign if suitable terms were arranged. Encouraged by Bauer's

---

sian Assembly who worked closely with Stresemann during the Putsch: *Nachlass,* 3090/6932/139534f.

[67] *Nachlass,* 3090/6932/139536f., Leidig memorandum (see note 66).
[68] *Ibid.*

attitude, Stresemann had this information relayed to Vice-Chancellor Eugen Schiffer of the DDP, who had remained in Berlin as an unofficial representative of the legitimate government.[69] Schiffer was also anxious to bring the Putsch to a quick conclusion. Acting without the approval of the rest of the cabinet, which had moved from Dresden to Stuttgart, he opened negotiations that evening with Major Waldemar Pabst, one of the leaders of the insurrection.[70]

Also on the evening of the 16th, Stresemann received a telephone call from General Lüttwitz, who invited him to come to the Reich Chancellery for a conference. He accepted and a short time later was called for personally by Lüttwitz. The General was still hopeful of buttressing the Putsch regime and during the drive across the city broached the subject of a possible DVP entry into the Kapp cabinet. But when Stresemann indicated that such a step was out of the question he dropped the subject. After arriving at the Chancellery, they were joined by Kapp himself. The determination of the self-styled Chancellor was obviously wavering and he made no effort to conceal the fact that he was ready to consider a withdrawal if suitable terms could be arranged. Lüttwitz, on the other hand, was less yielding. Stresemann made clear his own assessment of the situation and expressed the opinion that a negotiated settlement could be arranged if the insurgents did not insist on unreasonable terms. When he left after an hour's conversation, he felt the prospects were good for the sort of settlement he had in mind. On the morning of the next day, the 17th, however, Stresemann learned that the negotiations between Schiffer and Pabst had come to nothing because of Lüttwitz' determination to extract a long list of concessions from the Bauer cabinet. In addition, when he called at the Chancellery again, the General himself informed

[69] *Ibid.*, 139538f. Also, *Schiffer Papers*, Hauptarchiv, Berlin, Nr. 16, manuscript, "Der Kapp-Putsch," pp. 80f.

[70] On these negotiations, see Harold J. Gordon, *The Reichswehr and the German Republic, 1919-1926* (Princeton, 1957), pp. 120f.

him that Kapp had decided to resign and that he was taking over the insurgent regime as a military dictator until satisfactory terms could be obtained.[71]

After hearing this news, Stresemann proceeded around the corner to the Ministry of Justice, where Schiffer, who was Minister of Justice as well as Vice-Chancellor, had been permitted to remain. There he found a gathering of party leaders. Present were, in addition to Hergt and several others from the DNVP, a number of important spokesmen of the government parties, including the chairman of the Center delegation in the Assembly, Karl Trimborn, as well as two of his colleagues, Johannes Becker and Carl Herold; two representatives of the DDP, former Treasury Minister Georg Gothein and Rudolf Oeser; and two from the SPD, Minister-President Paul Hirsch of Prussia and Prussian Minister of Finance Albert Südekum. The party spokesmen had become alarmed at widespread rumors of an imminent Communist uprising in Berlin and had gathered to discuss the situation. When he found that even the representatives of the government parties were anxious to bring the Putsch to a peaceful conclusion as rapidly as possible in order to head off an outbreak of leftist violence, Stresemann saw a renewed opportunity for a negotiated settlement. He suggested to the party spokesmen that they deal directly with Lüttwitz themselves. This proposal was quickly accepted by the Nationalists, Democrats, and Centrists who were present. The Social Democrats were at first hesitant about actually meeting with the General. They indicated, however, that if the affair could be brought to a close quickly and peacefully their Assembly delegation would probably not reject a negotiated settlement.[72]

With the party spokesmen agreed on negotiations, Stresemann and Martin Schiele of the DNVP went to Lüttwitz and

---

[71] *Nachlass*, 3090/6930/139354ff., letter to the examining magistrate of the *Reichsgericht*, 16.7.1920.

[72] Stresemann, *Märzereignisse*, pp. 18ff. Also, Hergt's Assembly speech, 2.8.1920, *Verhandlungen*, CCCXLIV, 546.

invited him to meet with the politicians. The General, who realized that his support was rapidly melting away, accepted the invitation. Having made this much progress, Stresemann telephoned Schiffer and asked him to take part in the meeting also. The Vice-Chancellor, however, had just been informed by Minister of the Interior Erich Koch-Weser, speaking by telephone from Stuttgart, that the Bauer cabinet would repudiate any negotiations he might enter into with the insurgents. As a result, he refused to take part in the talks himself. He failed, though, to mention the call from Stuttgart and, apparently hopeful of exploiting the projected negotiations, encouraged Stresemann to go ahead with the meeting. Moreover, he made available a room in the Ministry of Justice and agreed to send his Under State Secretary, Curt Joël, as an observer. But at the last minute the whole project threatened to collapse. When Stresemann and Schiele arrived at the Ministry with Lüttwitz and Major Pabst, they discovered that Südekum, who had finally agreed to represent the SPD, had pulled back, deciding he could not negotiate without the consent of his party. As a result of Südekum's action, Gothein, who was to represent the DDP, had announced that he, too, had second thoughts. It thus seemed that there was little purpose in going through with the meeting. The project was rescued, however, when Schiffer, who was following the process of the negotiations closely from the room next door, intervened and persuaded Gothein to take part. The meeting therefore opened with the two insurgent leaders facing Stresemann, Hergt, Gothein, Trimborn, and Joël.[73]

In the course of their talk with Lüttwitz, the four party spokesmen soon discovered that his main concern was to secure amnesty for himself and the others involved in the Putsch. They assured him that they would use their influence to bring their

[73] Stresemann, *Märzereignisse*, pp. 19ff. Also, *Koch-Weser Papers*, Bundesarchiv, Koblenz, Vol. 25, p. 79, memorandum on conversation with Schiffer from Stuttgart. Also, *Gothein Papers*, Bundesarchiv, Koblenz, undated memoir, "Aus meiner politischen Arbeit," pp. 60ff.

respective Assembly delegations to support such a measure. This was not enough for Lüttwitz, who asked whether the Vice-Chancellor could also be counted upon. Since Schiffer had made no secret of his readiness to support a general amnesty during his negotiations with Major Pabst, all four party spokesmen, as well as his own subordinate Joël, believed that he would still be willing to do so. Stresemann and the others therefore assured Lüttwitz that he could count upon the Vice-Chancellor's support, whereupon the General indicated that he was satisfied. With the amnesty settled, the only important question that remained was the timing of the General's withdrawal. At first he insisted that it be postponed for several days, but his position was greatly weakened when two of his subordinates interrupted the meeting to announce that the troops in Berlin were on the verge of mutiny. In the face of this development Lüttwitz agreed to resign at once. Stresemann, Gothein, Hergt, and Trimborn then signed a statement which Joël had prepared. It pledged the party leaders to support an amnesty as well as a number of other measures, the most important of which involved the prompt scheduling of new elections. In addition, it stated that Schiffer would also support an amnesty and Joël expressed the intention of taking the document to the Vice-Chancellor for his signature. In return, Lüttwitz wrote out his resignation and at 3:30 on the afternoon of March 17 the insurrection came to an end.[74]

Stresemann was aware that the agreement between Lüttwitz and the spokesmen of the parties was in no way binding on the Bauer cabinet. Still, he obviously believed that it would be very difficult for the cabinet to claim an unconditional victory after the affair had been terminated by negotiations arranged with

[74] Stresemann, *Märzereignisse*, pp. 20f. Also, Lüttwitz, *Im Kampf*, p. 131. Also, *Nachlass*, 3171/7352/165905, entry in Stresemann's diary, 17.3.1920. Also, *Verhandlungen* (Reichstag), cccxliv, 547, Hergt, 2.8.-1920. Also, *Schiffer Papers*, Nr. 16, manuscript, "Der Kapp-Putsch," pp. 118ff. The document signed by the party spokesmen was later destroyed by Joël, see Schiffer's remarks to cabinet and Interparty Committee, 23.3.1920, quoted in *Koch-Weser Papers*, Vol. 27, p. 27.

the approval of the Vice-Chancellor and participated in by prominent representatives of two of the government parties and an official of the Ministry of Justice. Even if the cabinet tried to do so, he apparently expected that the combined strength of the four non-socialist parties would be sufficient to thwart its attempts. As he soon discovered, he had badly underestimated both the bellicose mood of the victorious Bauer cabinet and the duplicity of Schiffer. The first indication of this came shortly after the meeting with Lüttwitz, when Schiffer would not commit himself to support an amnesty. The final blow was delivered on the next day, the 18th, when the exiled cabinet refused to recognize that any negotiations had taken place and branded Kapp and Lüttwitz and their followers as outlaws. Schiffer hurriedly conformed with the cabinet's stand by announcing that he had known nothing of the talks until they were ended. The Center and Democratic parties also disavowed the negotiations, choosing simply to ignore the roles played by Gothein and Trimborn.[75] With only the DVP and the DNVP left to uphold the agreement with Lüttwitz, it was quickly rendered nugatory. Apparently this was immediately clear to everyone except Lüttwitz and his chief military accomplices, Colonel Bauer and Major Pabst, who were later to bombard an embarrassed Stresemann with letters from their various exiles, charging him with bad faith and demanding immediate action on an amnesty.[76]

From Stresemann's point of view his attempt to arrange a negotiated settlement of the Putsch had ended in complete failure. Instead of keeping the Bauer cabinet from achieving an unconditional victory it had paved the way for just such a tri-

---

[75] Stresemann, *Märzereignisse*, p. 21.

[76] For examples of Lüttwitz' many letters, see *Nachlass*, 3110/7012/143716ff.; 3096/7016/144147f.; 3110/7011/143514ff. For Bauer, *Nachlass*, 3089/6927/138682ff. For Pabst, *Nachlass*, 3117/7169/155730ff. Pabst, under the name of Peters, later became a confidential agent for the Foreign Ministry under Stresemann: Hans W. Gatzke, *Stresemann and the Rearmament of Germany* (Baltimore, 1954), p. 51.

umph. As a result, he found himself and his party in a dangerously exposed position. His frequent visits to the Reich Chancellery during the Putsch had not escaped the attention of the press and his behavior during the insurrection was the subject of widespread suspicion. Even more damaging, though, was the DVP's highly compromising declaration of March 13, which had extended *de facto* recognition to the Kapp regime while roundly attacking the legitimate government. It was no secret that the Bauer cabinet had been shocked by the DVP's stand and intended to demand an accounting. Moreover, the Interior Minister, Erich Koch-Weser of the DDP, had let it be known in Stuttgart that he held Stresemann personally responsible for the declaration, which he regarded as treasonous and was seriously contemplating legal action against him.[77]

Realizing that his political future was in jeopardy, Stresemann hurriedly sought to dissociate himself from the declaration of the 13th. In a letter prepared for distribution to the DVP subsidiary organizations, he claimed to have raised objections to the text of the declaration and to have called for a condemnation of the forceful overthrow of the legal government—neither of which contentions are borne out by the records of the DVP meetings of the 13th.[78]

Then, on the afternoon of the 18th, he met to discuss the party's plight with a group of its spokesmen that included Heinze, Hugo Garnich, Wilhelm Kahl, Paul von Krause, and Jacob Riesser. The product of this meeting was a statement which revealed that Stresemann and his colleagues knew that their conduct could not seriously be defended. It was a deliberately loosely worded document obviously designed to distort the facts and give the uncritical majority of the public the misleading impression that the DVP had rejected the Putsch from the outset. Beginning by once again blaming the Bauer cabinet

---

[77] *Koch-Weser Papers*, Vol. 25, p. 103, diary for 18.3.1920.
[78] *Nachlass*, 3090/6932/139649ff. There is no indication as to whether this letter was ever dispatched.

for the outbreak of the rebellion, though in more moderate terms than those of the first declaration, it continued: "What we had to do in the face of the forcible overthrow of the 13th of March was prescribed for us from the outset by the national and liberal character of the German People's Party. As already emphasized in our statement of the 13th of March, it was impossible for us to leave the path of organic, constitutional development. Accordingly, we must (sic) condemn decisively any violent undertaking directed against the constitution and any use of our troops . . . for an irresponsible undertaking threatening the very existence of the Reich. . . ."[79]

The obvious discrepancy between this declaration and that of the 13th did not escape the attention of the government parties. With good cause, they accused the DVP of an unworthy attempt to falsify the historical record. Having no real answer to these charges, Stresemann and his colleagues sought to confuse the issue. Exploiting the ambiguities of the March 13 declaration, they insisted that the DVP had from the outset demanded the restoration of the Weimar constitution. In addition, they made full use of the split within the party during the Putsch, selecting as their spokesman during the Assembly debate on the affair Heinze, whose active aid to the Bauer cabinet was well known. The much more vulnerable Stresemann, on the other hand, remained conspicuously silent during the debate.[80]

These efforts to explain away the facts would probably have met with no success had it not been for the disruptive events that followed the collapse of the Kapp regime. The most important of these was the clash between the labor unions and the Bauer cabinet. Having demonstrated the effectiveness of the general strike by paralyzing the insurgent regime, the unions refused to terminate it until the cabinet agreed to a number of drastic changes in the structure and policies of the government.

[79] Stresemann, *Märzereignisse*, pp. 27f.
[80] *Ibid.*, pp. 7, 10, 25ff. Also, *Verhandlungen* (Assembly), cccxxxii, 4963ff., debate of 29.3.1920.

Among other things, they demanded a special voice in the formation of cabinets and in the formulation of social and economic policies, as well as the immediate adoption of measures toward the socialization of industry. On March 20 the cabinet submitted to the unions' demands. But some of the more radical workers' organizations insisted that the general strike continue and succeeded in gaining control of a number of the industrial cities of the Ruhr. Finally, troops had to be sent in and only after a number of open skirmishes did the government succeed in re-establishing its authority. These developments evoked reactions of indignation and fear from many quarters and, in spite of the efforts of the Weimar Coalition parties to keep it alive, the question of the DVP's attitude toward the Putsch was soon overshadowed and lost in the rush of events.

Although the Kapp Putsch threatened at first to divide and compromise the DVP, its end effects were unexpectedly beneficial from the standpoint of the party. In spite of considerable grumbling, only a few prominent members, the most important of whom was future Chancellor Wilhelm Cuno,[81] actually broke with the party in protest against its policies during the insurrection. These losses were more than compensated for by the gains it registered at the expense of the DNVP and the DDP as a result of the affair. The Nationalists had at first adopted an official policy toward the Putsch which was very similar to that of the DVP. But since Kapp and several of his associates were members of the DNVP (though not important ones), that party was naturally more closely identified with the insurrection than was the DVP. Consequently, it bore the brunt of the government parties' attacks and lost some of its prominent members as well as the backing of many of the moderate voters who had formerly been aligned with the party.[82] The Democrats, who

[81] *Nachlass*, 3090/6930/139311f., letter to Cuno, 19.7.1920.
[82] On the DNVP and the Putsch, see Werner Liebe, *Die Deutschnationale Volkspartei, 1918-1924* (Düsseldorf, 1956), pp. 51ff. One Nationalist leader, Graef-Anklam, later estimated that the Putsch cost the party at least ten seats in the 1920 elections, *ibid.*, p. 156, note 289.

had steadfastly opposed the Putsch, also suffered. They had offended a large number of their supporters by endorsing the general strike, which for many middle-class voters was far more frightening than the Putsch. Since the DVP was in the fortunate position of being able to benefit from the losses of both the DNVP and the DDP it soon became a refuge for those Nationalists who thought their party had moved too far right and for those Democrats who felt theirs had drifted too far left.[83]

Still another beneficial effect of the Putsch, from the standpoint of the DVP, was the fall of the Bauer cabinet. This took place on March 26, after the Chancellor had encountered difficulties in attempting to meet the unions' demand for the immediate replacement of several members of the cabinet. Bauer's successor was Hermann Müller of the SPD, who quickly set up another Weimar Coalition government. Although no shift in political power was involved, this change proved very advantageous for Stresemann and his colleagues, for the new cabinet decided to hold the spring elections they had hoped for, scheduling them for June 6. In addition, the cabinet definitely ruled out the possibility of a change in the constitutional provision for popular election of the President of the Republic.

✧

The Kapp affair was one of the least creditable episodes in Stresemann's career. While the insurrection appeared to be succeeding, he accepted and even condoned it. When its prospects began to fade, he still sought to exploit it in the interests of his party by attempting to block a return to the unfavorable pre-Putsch *status quo*. Then, after all his efforts in that direction had failed, too, his action in resorting to distortion and misrepresentation demonstrated that he was not above using these less reputable of the politician's tools to extricate himself and his

[83] On the Democrats entering the party, see *Nachlass*, 3089/6928/ 138957ff.; *Nachlass*, 3090/6932/139604f. On the Nationalists, see DVP, *Archiv der Deutschen Volkspartei*, 10.5.1920.

party from a dangerously exposed position. The most important fact revealed by the Putsch, however, was the worthlessness of his earlier pledge to the National Assembly to reject an attempt at a forceful overthrow of the Republic. In explaining his stand to the DVP leadership shortly after the affair he stated his position bluntly: the republican system, itself a product of revolution, had no special claim to legitimacy in his eyes and he therefore felt no obligation to defend it.[84] He thus chose to ignore the all-important fact that the National Assembly, which had adopted the Weimar constitution, was called into being by a free and democratic election, so that the Republic was only indirectly the product of the revolution.

Nor did the collapse of the Putsch and the narrow escape of the DVP bring about any immediate change in his thinking. Afterwards, he also warned the leaders of the party against allowing the reaction against the insurrection to drive them into attaching any "sanctity" to the Weimar constitution. If this were to be the case, he warned that it would have the unfortunate effect of obscuring the fact that "what has come came against our wish and will, while the ideal of our life lies in ruins." Moreover, he made abundantly clear how far he was himself prepared to go to regain that ideal: "No parallels with the happenings of the 13th of March, but if our Lord God and destiny send us a man who, without holding to all the paragraphs of Weimar, builds us a great Germany again, then our party would—so I hope—grant him the same indemnity which the fathers of the National Liberal Party granted to Bismarck."[85]

[84] Speech to the Managing Committee, plus the National and Prussian Assembly delegations, and representatives of the local organizations, 28.3.1920, reprinted in part in his *Märzereignisse*, pp. 31f.

[85] This and the previous remark are quoted in Erich Heinz Schlottner, *Stresemann, der Kapp-Putsch und die Ereignisse in Mitteldeutschland und in Bayern im Herbst 1923* (Frankfurt/Main, 1948), p. 34. Schlottner failed to date this speech but Henry Bernhard, in whose possession he found it, indicated in a letter to the author (8.12.1959) that it was probably a part of Stresemann's speech of 28.3.1920 (see note 84) which was not included in his *Märzereignisse*. This document predates Bernhard's term as Stresemann's secretary and was apparently part of the ma-

As these words reveal, Stresemann was still very much a fellow traveler on the right. He was not a true rightist, for he did not reject democratic parliamentary government altogether and did not share the right's uncompromising refusal to cooperate with the Social Democrats. But like the right, he was far from reconciled to the system established at Weimar.

---

terial he removed from the *Nachlass* during the preparation of Stresemann's *Vermächtnis. Der Nachlass in drei Bänden*, ed. Henry Bernhard (3 vols., Berlin, 1932-1933). Some of this material was turned over to the Politisches Archiv of the Foreign Ministry, Bonn, after Bernhard's death in 1961. This speech, however, was not included. The remainder of Bernhard's papers are in the custody of his son, Rudolph Bernhard of Stuttgart, who has been unable to locate a copy of the speech.

III. THE MAKING OF A
VERNUNFTREPUBLIKANER, 1920-1923

THE SPRING of 1920 provided little breathing space for Germany's politicians. No sooner had the disorders set off by the Kapp Putsch and the general strike been brought under control than the country was plunged into the campaign for the elections to the first republican Reichstag. Stresemann approached this campaign with far better prospects than had been the case at the time of the Assembly elections. The most conspicuous difference was the greatly increased strength of the DVP. In the first fifteen months of its existence the party had made extensive inroads into the popular support of both the Democrats and the Nationalists and the aftermath of the Putsch had served to accelerate this process still further. In addition, a significant number of the former National Liberal provincial newspapers that had supported the DDP in 1919 had been offended by that party's support of the general strike and had switched their allegiance to the DVP. As a result, most observers expected the party to make sizeable gains in the elections. Just as important as these developments was the fact that Stresemann had made use of the period since the disappointing Assembly elections to rebuild the disorganized and truncated party machinery inherited from the crumbling National Liberal Party. The party was thus able to enter the 1920 campaign with a full-scale national organization, staffed by salaried officials in all the electoral districts—a marked contrast to 1919, when it had been completely without branch organizations in nearly a third of the country.

The DVP's financial situation had also improved greatly since the first campaign, primarily because of the establishment of close ties with the heavy industry of the Ruhr. Although Stresemann was by no means opposed to accepting business subsidies, he had not sought this arrangement. It came about during 1919 as a consequence of the debts incurred in the campaign for the Assembly elections. Unable to cover this deficit with the party's regular income, he had obtained assistance after the elections from two of industry's political organizations, the *Kuratorium für den Wiederaufbau des Deutschen Wirtschaftslebens* and the *Kommission zur Sammlung, Verwaltung und Verwendung des Industriellen Wahlfonds*.[1] But in spite of this aid, the chaotic condition of the DVP's organization and the expenses involved in rebuilding it handicapped all attempts to achieve financial self-sufficiency.[2] By October 1919, the national headquarters was left with enough money for only two weeks' operations. The leaders of the party addressed an urgent appeal for additional funds to the *Kommission*, which represented some of the most important industrial firms in the Ruhr. Its general secretary, Johannes Flathmann, a former right-wing National Liberal, replied by announcing that more subsidies would be forthcoming only if the DVP granted places in its next Reichstag delegation to a number of prominent industrial spokesmen, including Hugo Stinnes, reputedly the wealthiest man in Germany. Faced with the possibility of bankruptcy and unable to obtain support elsewhere, Stresemann and the other leaders of the party capitulated to Flathmann and preparations were begun to nominate Stinnes and a number of other industrialists for the Reichstag.[3] But even after this agreement had been made, Stresemann remained apprehensive about associating the DVP with Stinnes, who was regarded as the prototype of the predatory capitalist by the leftist press and parties. Just before the final nominations were to be made, he asked one of the DVP's other industrial

[1] *Nachlass*, 3079/6917/137135ff., letter to Geschäftsführer of the *Kuratorium*, c/o Wilhelm von Siemens, 10.3.1919. Also, *Nachlass*, 3088/6921/137640 and 137704ff., Flathmann, Gen.-Sec. of the *Kommission*, to Stresemann, 12. and 21.3.1919. Also, *Nachlass*, 3088/6921/137724f., letter to Flathmann, 25.3.1919.

[2] See *Deutsche Volkspartei Papers*, Vol. 104a, minutes of Managing Committee, 1.5.1919 and 16.10.1919. Also, *Nachlass*, 3089/6926/138464f., same of 13.9.1920.

[3] *Nachlass*, 3088/6923/138010f., Flathmann to Kuhbier, 31.10.1919. Also, *Dingeldey Papers*, Bundesarchiv, Koblenz, Vol. 86, Flathmann to Garnich, 5.6.1920.

spokesmen, Hans von Raumer, to appeal to Stinnes to withdraw for the good of the party. This appeal, however, was ignored and Stinnes' name went onto the party's list of candidates.[4]

Aside from his misgivings about linking the DVP with the controversial figure of Hugo Stinnes, Stresemann was not pleased about granting the industrialists of the Ruhr an important place in the party. He had often clashed with their spokesmen in the National Liberal Party since they usually had been aligned with the extreme right wing, and he therefore had sought to exclude most of them when the DVP was formed. Moreover, his own close association with light industry had repeatedly brought him into opposition to the iron and steel magnates of the Ruhr, whose desire for high protective tariffs ran contrary to the interests of light industry, which imported many of its raw materials. This long-standing antagonism persisted even after the revolution and was one reason for Stresemann's exclusion from the governing bodies of the powerful new national industrial association, the *Reichsverband der deutschen Industrie*. This organization had been formed early in 1919 by a merger of heavy industry's *Zentralverband der deutschen Industrie* and light industry's *Bund der Industriellen*, of which Stresemann was still an officer. In the weeks prior to the merger he had opposed the move vigorously on the grounds that it would subject light industry to the domination of heavy industry and involve it in battles that were not its own. When the election of officers for the *Reichsverband* took place, he was passed over on the grounds that he was a "professional politician" and no longer primarily a businessman. This charge was not without basis, but it applied with equal accuracy to Alfred Hugenberg and several other politically active businessmen who were elected to high posts.[5]

[4] *Nachlass*, 3159/7395/171736ff., letter to Stinnes, 17.3.1924.

[5] *Nachlass*, 3051/6818/122926ff. and *Nachlass*, 3051/6818/122937ff., Stresemann to *Bund*, 30.1.1919 and 31.3.1919. Also, *Nachlass*, 3051/6818/122944f., *Verband Sächsischer Industrieller* to Stresemann, 12.4.1919.

In spite of his own feelings about the Ruhr industrialists, Stresemann was willing to reconcile himself to their entry into the DVP in return for the subsidies required to build the party into a significant force in German politics. In this respect the arrangement of 1920 did not disappoint him. The party's debts were rapidly eliminated and it was provided with funds sufficient for the reconstruction and expansion of its organization, as well as for an expensive national campaign. In return, a number of those candidacies which virtually assured election went to prominent spokesmen of heavy industry. The most important of these men were Stinnes; Kurt Sorge, a director of the Krupp concern and president of the new *Reichsverband der deutschen Industrie*; Reinhold Quaatz, syndic of the powerful Essen-Mülheim-Oberhausen Chamber of Commerce; Hans von Raumer, a spokesman of the electrical industry; and Helmuth Albrecht, a representative of the potash industry. Standing for re-election was Vögler, who had been forced to resign the post of party treasurer because of his increasingly demanding duties in the Stinnes enterprises.

The heavy industry of the Ruhr was not the DVP's only source of financial support. The party also received smaller subsidies from light industry, banking, and large-scale commerce, and each of these was granted several "safe" candidacies for the 1920 elections. In addition, Stresemann used his influence to obtain nominations for representatives of a number of special interest groups which brought the party support in the form of votes rather than funds. Included among these were the organizations of large-scale agriculture (*Landbund*) and small-scale agriculture (*Bauernbund*), the Christian trade union movement (*Deutscher Gewerkschaftsbund*), the league of government employees (*Beamtenbund*), the organization of independent skilled workmen and artisans (*Reichsverband des deutschen Handwerks*), the organization of non-socialist white-collar workers (*Deutschnationaler Handlungsgehilfenverband*), and the industry-financed, or "yellow," union movement (*Vaterländische Ar-*

71

beitnehmerbewegung). Since most of these organizations were also represented in at least one other non-socialist party, none gave a full endorsement to the DVP. Still, as Stresemann realized, the presence of their spokesmen among the party's candidates greatly increased the number of voters to whom the party could appeal.[6]

Not all of the DVP's candidates were representatives of special-interest groups. Many were simply individuals who commanded respect within their communities and received the nominations of the local DVP electoral district organization. Others were persons who had taken a lead in reorganizing the party after the 1919 elections. Also included were a number of high-ranking military and government officials who had been removed from their positions after the collapse of the old regime. From the Army and Navy came Lieutenant General Karl von Schoch and Rear Admiral Willi Brüninghaus. From the diplomatic corps came Hans von Kemnitz, Baron Kurt von Lersner, and Baron Werner von Rheinbaben. With regard to the composition of the party rank and file, information is scarce. It is known, though, that in 1920 it included such disparate persons as the Göttingen historian Karl Brandi, who played a leading role in drawing up its first platform, the professional anti-Bolshevik Eduard Stadtler, and the renegade Social Democrat August Winnig, who had sided with the Kappists.[7]

By bringing together these various elements in his effort to build the DVP into a viable political party, Stresemann sharply altered its character. Long after 1920, he continued to insist that it was simply a continuation of the National Liberal Party under a new name, but this was more a reflection of his own hopes

[6] See minutes of Managing Committee, 24.8.1919, *Nachlass*, 3088/6922/137865ff. Also, same of 17.4.1920, *Nachlass*, 3089/6928/138884ff. For a recent attempt at an analysis of the leadership of the DVP, see Wolfgang Hartenstein, *Die Anfänge der Deutschen Volkspartei 1918-1920* (Düsseldorf, 1962), pp. 266ff.

[7] See *Nachlass*, 3079/6920/137607; 3097/7019/144598ff.; 3090/6929/139162f.

72

than a serious attempt at analysis. Even at the time of the 1920 campaign, less than half of the party's national spokesmen had been active in the National Liberal organization, and only a third of those had held leading positions.[8] Most of the rest were newcomers who had entered politics for the first time in 1919 and 1920 and for whom the heritage of the old party was of little meaning. Nevertheless, Stresemann, who continued to regard himself as a National Liberal, sought to preserve a continuity between the two parties. He was not inclined to theoretical matters himself, but he opened the pages of his magazine *Deutsche Stimmen* to those members of the party who hoped to provide an ideological basis for its policies by linking it to the traditions of the National Liberal Party. These efforts, which consisted for the most part of vague ruminations about the respective merits of liberalism, democracy, and socialism, had little relevance to the concrete problems facing Germany and became more infrequent as the years passed.[9]

There was, of course, general agreement among the leaders of the DVP on a number of basic points. Among these were the desirability of preserving as much as possible of the private enterprise system and the existing social structure, and the necessity of a revision of the Versailles peace settlement. But the views of the spokesmen of the various interest groups in the party were determined primarily by the aims of those groups and were for the most part without a theoretical basis. This had already been demonstrated in the National Assembly when, to the consternation of Stresemann, Vögler announced in his first speech: "I speak here as the representative of an industry. . . ."[10] The DVP was officially designated a "liberal" party by its own

[8] This is based on the biographies of the successful nominees for the new Reichstag. See Büro des Reichstags, *Reichstag Handbuch, I. Wahlperiode, 1920* (Berlin, 1920).

[9] For examples, see Johannes Jacobi, "Liberalismus und Demokratie," Part I, *Deutsche Stimmen*, 2.5.1920; Part II, *ibid.*, 16.5.1920. Also, Rudolf von Campe, "Liberalismus—Demokratie—Sozialismus," *ibid.*, 30.5.1920.

[10] *Verhandlungen* (Assembly), CCCXXVI, 137 (18.2.1919).

73

proclamations. But despite the survival of the National Liberal group within it, it was not in the tradition of the German *Weltanschauungspartei* and was not united by an ideology. In the words of one of its deputies, Hans von Raumer, it was a party without a *Leitidee*, or unifying idea.[11] Like a number of modern French parties, it consisted largely of representatives of diverse groups, held together only by the personality and ambition of its leader. Perhaps the best designation found for it was the "Stresemann party."[12]

During the 1920 election campaign, the dependence of the DVP on Stresemann was conspicuously evident. He alone among the party's leaders had sufficient national reputation to attract large crowds and capture headlines in all parts of Germany. As a consequence, he was in great demand for speaking appearances on behalf of less well-known candidates. Avoiding a repetition of 1919, when he had been forced to devote all of his efforts to securing his own election, he took a candidacy in a district comprising the western sections of Berlin (officially designated as Potsdam II) that assured him a Reichstag seat and required only a few personal appearances. This allowed him to spend most of the campaign on a speaking tour that took him into virtually every region of the country. The campaign which he conducted was designed to capitalize on the difficulties of the DDP and DNVP by representing the DVP as a rallying point for moderates who had rejected both the Kapp Putsch and the general strike. The party's attacks, however, were directed exclusively at the left as the result of a confidential agreement with the DNVP to concentrate all efforts on weakening the Weimar Coalition while refraining from mutual criticism.[13]

In the campaign, Stresemann and the other leaders of the party joined with the Nationalists in defending the free enter-

---

[11] Letter to the author, 17.6.1958.

[12] Edgar Stern-Rubarth, *Stresemann, der Europäer* (Berlin, 1929), p. 38.

[13] *Deutsche Volkspartei Papers*, Vol. 104c, exchange of letters between headquarters of DVP and DNVP, March 1920.

prise system and in calling for a restoration of Germany's position as a great power in the world. But the position of the DVP was easily distinguished from that of the DNVP, for even while roundly attacking the Social Democrats, Stresemann held to the plan he had set forth in January and made clear the party's readiness to work with them in a coalition government after the elections.[14] In deference to the reaction against the extreme right which followed the Kapp Putsch, he and the other spokesmen of the party carefully refrained from direct criticism of the Weimar constitution. Their platform called for a return to the imperial system of expert ministers, at least with regard to foreign, military, economic, and legal affairs. In addition, it also proposed that a voice in the formulation and adoption of economic legislation be given to the projected national economic council (*Reichswirtschaftsrat*), in which management was to have equal representation with labor.[15] But at the same time they proposed these changes, the party's spokesmen emphasized that they should be made only within the existing constitutional framework. At Stresemann's insistence, the issue of monarchism was avoided altogether, even though the party was officially committed to seek a restoration and campaigned, as did the DNVP, under the black-white-red flag of the Empire.[16]

On the eve of the June 6 elections Stresemann was in a very optimistic mood, but the results of the balloting exceeded even his most hopeful estimates. The DVP emerged almost tripled in size, with 62 deputies, as compared to 22 in the Assembly, while its popular vote increased from 1,345,638 to 3,610,198. Both in terms of number of seats and proportional strength, it had surpassed the size of the National Liberal delegation in the last imperial Reichstag. Smaller gains were registered by the DNVP,

[14] See *Nachlass*, 3089/6928/138897ff., Rauch (Stresemann's private secretary) to Schirmacher-Oncken, 19.4.1920.

[15] "Aufruf der Deutschen Volkspartei," in DVP, *Archiv der Deutschen Volkspartei*, 10.5.1920.

[16] *Nachlass*, 3089/6928/138855, Rauch (Stresemann's private secretary) to Curtius, 16.4.1920.

which went from 44 to 66 seats. The SPD's total dropped to 113 as a result of losses to the Independent Socialists, who capitalized on the quarrel between the labor unions and the Bauer government at the time of the general strike and amassed the sizeable total of 81 seats. The Center was left with only 69 because of the bolt of its Bavarian wing, which entered the campaign as the Bavarian People's Party (*Bayerische Volkspartei* or BVP) and won 19 seats. By far the most severe reversal was sustained by the Democrats, who lost over 3 million votes and 30 seats, returning only 45 deputies to the new Reichstag. The chief beneficiaries of these losses were the DVP and the DNVP, whose gains generally occurred in those districts in which the Democrats' support diminished, with the DVP in most cases receiving the larger share. As a result of the expansion of the DVP's organization, the votes which it received were more widely distributed than in 1919. But all attempts to appeal to the Catholic voters of the south had been in vain and the DVP's strength, like that of the National Liberal Party, remained concentrated in the north.

As Stresemann had hoped would be the case, the election results destroyed the Weimar Coalition government's majority and brought about its resignation on June 8. Three days later President Ebert assigned the task of forming a new cabinet to Hermann Müller, the incumbent Social Democratic Chancellor. Müller attempted to widen the previous coalition by inviting the Independent Socialists to join it, but his efforts ended in failure when they refused to take part in a cabinet which included nonsocialists. After Müller withdrew from consideration the next call to the chancellorship went to the chairman of the DVP delegation, Heinze. His attempt to form a new cabinet was short-lived. In line with the policy Stresemann had set forth, he invited the Social Democrats to join with the DDP, the Center, and the DVP in a new coalition government. This invitation was quickly spurned by the SPD, which refused to participate in a cabinet with the DVP, labeling it a rightist party. On the evening of the 13th, after the Democrats and the Centrists had rejected his proposal of a coalition with the Nationalists, Heinze informed Ebert that he would be unable to form a government and withdrew.

After a week of further negotiations between the parties, a solution was finally found when Konstantin Fehrenbach, a veteran Centrist, formed a government backed by the DDP, the Center, and the DVP. The only serious difficulty encountered in the formation of the coalition arose from the DVP's refusal to agree to a program endorsing the Republic or the constitution. The impasse was finally broken when the DDP and the Center gave in and accepted a program which stated only that the participating parties had agreed to work for the recovery of the country within the framework of the existing constitution. Since the three coalition parties did not command a majority, the cabinet's survival was made possible only by the SPD's decision to "tolerate" it, that is, not to oppose it on essential issues. In so doing, the Social Democrats sought to avoid a crisis that might lead to new elections and further losses to their burgeoning Independent Socialist rivals.

When the members of the new cabinet were chosen during the last week in June, Stresemann was passed over. The public had largely forgotten about his attitude toward the Kapp Putsch, but President Ebert and the SPD had not and they insisted upon his exclusion.[17] Heinze was selected as the DVP's principal representative, serving as both Vice-Chancellor and Minister of Justice. With regard to the rest of the party's share of cabinet posts, Fehrenbach held it to its proposal of a return to the system of expert ministers. He placed the ministries of Economics and the Treasury at the party's disposal and promised that if it would bring a leading figure from the business community into the cabinet he would give it the Ministry of Transport as well. Stresemann hurriedly called a meeting of the industrialists

---

[17] Otto Gessler, *Reichswehrpolitik in der Weimarer Zeit* (Stuttgart, 1958), p. 150.

77

aligned with the DVP, including Stinnes and Vögler, and urged that one of their number enter the cabinet. To his disappointment, they refused to relinquish their business activities. They did, however, nominate as potential expert ministers Ernst Scholz, a prominent career civil administrator and former mayor of Kassel and Charlottenburg, and Hans von Raumer, one of the industrial spokesmen in the new DVP delegation and a former member of the Prussian civil service. Fehrenbach accepted Scholz as Minister of Economics and Raumer as Minister of the Treasury. But since neither was the sort of prominent figure he had been seeking, he concluded that the DVP had not fulfilled the conditions he had set and refused to award it the Ministry of Transport.[18]

In the long run, Stresemann's exclusion from the cabinet redounded to his advantage. It made possible his selection as chairman of the Reichstag's Foreign Affairs Committee, a post which provided him with experience useful in his later career as Foreign Minister. Moreover, it enabled him to succeed Heinze as chairman of the DVP delegation when the latter entered the government. This position, which he retained throughout the next three years, was to prove a key factor in his rise to political power. It made him the party's spokesman both on the floor of the Reichstag and in the Interparty Committee (*Interfraktioneller Ausschuss*), which served as the principal vehicle for behind-the-scenes negotiations between the government parties. By making use of his new position and the increased strength of the party's delegation, he soon won recognition as one of the important figures of parliamentary politics. The new post also reinforced his position within the DVP, for as chairman of the Central Committee, the Reichstag delegation, and the Managing Committee he held the three most important offices in

---

[18] Stresemann, "Politische Umschau," *Deutsche Stimmen*, 14.5.1922 (Stresemann's articles under this title in *Deutsche Stimmen* were signed with the cipher Δ). Also, *Verhandlungen* (Reichstag), cccxliv, 54f., his speech of 30.6.1920.

the party. Later in the year this concentration of power began to attract criticism, and in December he relinquished the chairmanship of the Managing Committee.[19] It was symptomatic of the true distribution of power within the party that as soon as he left this Committee its importance immediately diminished; all important decisions were, in the future, left to the Reichstag delegation and the Central Committee.

After taking over as the DVP's leader in the Reichstag, Stresemann rapidly brought the new delegation under control. His techniques in this regard were interesting, for it was his frequent practice not to attend the beginning of the delegation's meetings but to appear only near their end. As he explained to one acquaintance, Count Harry Kessler, he did this in order to let the deputies "blow off their steam" and thus managed to arrive himself just as they had exhausted their various arguments and were anxious for someone to suggest a solution. "Sovereign disdain for his delegation subjects," was Kessler's reaction.[20] Nevertheless, the technique proved highly effective since it kept him from becoming embroiled in most of the petty disputes within the delegation and set him somewhat apart, and above, the rest of the party's deputies.

One of his first actions as chairman of the delegation was to assert the DVP's independence from the heavy industry of the Ruhr. He had already taken a step in this direction during the campaign by ignoring Flathmann's threat to cut off the subsidies channeled through the *Kommission* unless the spokesmen of heavy industry were given more desirable positions on the party's lists of candidates.[21] A more serious challenge came in early August from Reinhold Quaatz, one of the representatives of the Ruhr in the new DVP delegation. Quaatz insisted that the vital

[19] *Nachlass*, 3171/7352/166034, entry in Stresemann's daily calendar, 14.11.1920. Also, *Nachlass*, 3160/7399/172456, letter to the *Leipziger Neueste Nachrichten*, December 1924.
[20] Harry Graf Kessler, *Tagebücher, 1918-1937* (Frankfurt/Main, 1961), p. 232, entry for 25.6.1920.
[21] *Nachlass*, 3089/6927/138646ff., Flathmann to Stresemann, 4.5.1920.

importance of the coal and steel industries entitled their spokesmen to special representation in the executive committee of the
party's Reichstag delegation and in the committees of the legislature. Furthermore, he served notice that if these claims were
not recognized by the DVP, the industrialists of the Ruhr might
feel compelled to seek representation elsewhere. In answer to
Quaatz, Stresemann adopted the position he was to maintain
throughout the rest of his career. He agreed that the coal and
steel industries formed a vital sector of the economy and indicated that the DVP would consult them on questions involv-
ing their interests. But in spite of the party's dependence on the
subsidies of heavy industry, he refused to grant the spokesmen
of the Ruhr any special privileges beyond the representation in
the delegation which they had already won. Since he had the
great majority of the delegation behind him on this question, he
had no difficulty in defeating Quaatz, who hastily withdrew his
demands.[22]

The formation of the Fehrenbach cabinet represented a refu-
tation of Stresemann's January prediction that no government
would be possible without the participation of the Social Democrats. But he was by no means displeased at being thus contra-
dicted by events. His goal had been a reduction of the power of
the left and the new cabinet represented a sharp shift to the
right. Not only was the SPD completely excluded but the
more conservative elements in both the DDP and the Center
were more strongly represented than were the left wings of those
two parties. "Who among you," Stresemann asked the DVP
Party Congress in December 1920, "would have thought in
1918 that such a government would even be possible two years
after the revolution?"[23] He, it was clear, was among those who
had never imagined it.

Although he was gratified by the shift to the right, Stresemann

[22] *Nachlass*, 3090/6929/139093ff., memorandum on delegation meeting, 4.8.1920.
[23] *Deutsche Stimmen*, 14.12.1920, p. 830.

did not alter his views on the necessity of cooperation with the Social Democrats. When the formation of the new rightward-oriented government set off a wave of truculent overconfidence within the DVP, he cautioned his colleagues against the temptation to embark upon a militant anti-socialist line aimed at perpetuating the SPD's exclusion from the cabinet. Such a policy, he warned, would backfire and drive the SPD into the arms of the Independents and the Communists, thus reuniting and strengthening the divided socialist camp. Instead, he argued that the government parties should stand ready to accept the Social Democrats into the cabinet but at the same time make clear to them that they could not again lay claim to the position of pre-eminence they had occupied prior to the Reichstag elections. Those elections, he maintained, had bestowed the leadership of Germany on the non-socialist parties, a fact the SPD must be brought to accept.[24]

The Fehrenbach government's eleven-month term of office proved extremely important for the development of Stresemann's thinking, for it did much to reduce his reservations about the republican system. Most importantly, it demonstrated that "Republic" was not necessarily synonymous with "socialism" and that the new system could be used for conservative purposes as well as for those of the left. Although the cabinet had to proceed cautiously because of its dependence on the toleration of the Social Democrats it was able to go a long way toward restoring the pre-war economic *status quo*. A major step in this direction was completed with the removal of most of the price and profit controls—a source of much irritation to the business community—which had been either retained from the war years or newly imposed by the first republican governments. But even more important was the governing coalition's success in side-tracking the various plans for the nationalization of industry held over from the Assembly, all of which were allowed to expire quietly in committees of the Reichstag. The threat of so-

[24] *Ibid.*, pp. 829ff.

81

cialization had been a source of grave concern to Stresemann since the revolution and it was a significant juncture when he confidently announced to the DVP in December 1920: ". . . the time of socialist Germany is past."[25]

Also pleasing to Stresemann was the new government's success in blocking the thoroughgoing purges of the Army and the bureaucracy which had been discussed in leftist circles after the Kapp Putsch. While he had long been an advocate of abolishing the aristocracy's privileged position in the military and in the civil service, he did not want a radical democratization of either. He was therefore relieved when the professionals remained in charge. By late 1920 the altered conditions resulting from the change in governments had led Stresemann to the conclusion that the revolutionary period had failed to realize what he regarded as its worst potentialities. The course of events since the revolution, he told the DVP Party Congress at that time, had in fact ended by leading to "the culmination of the healthy tendencies of the old Germany" and had swept away only those aspects of the past "which were no longer tenable."[26]

The one complication in the otherwise harmonious relationship between the DVP and the Fehrenbach government lay in the realm of foreign affairs. While the entire Reichstag delegation was united behind Stresemann in endorsing the cabinet's domestic policies, a sizeable portion of the party's deputies objected to its handling of the negotiations with the Allies concerning those aspects of the peace settlement which had been postponed at the time of the Versailles Conference. The first round of these negotiations took place at the Spa Conference of July 1920, when the Allies presented their demands for German disarmament, the prosecution of war criminals, and the deliveries of coal. The coal requests were regarded as exorbitant in Germany and the Fehrenbach government attempted to secure concessions through negotiation. But when the Allies presented the government with an

[25] *Ibid.*, p. 830.
[26] *Ibid.*, pp. 830f.

ultimatum, backed by a threat of invasion, calling for immediate acceptance of their demands for coal, the government decided to submit.

Many of the DVP provincial leaders felt that in spite of the Allies' threats the cabinet should have refused to accept such humiliating terms. They insisted that the DVP, which was pledged to seek the restoration of Germany's great power status, could not assume responsibility for the government's submission without losing support to the DNVP, which had defiantly denounced the coal agreement. Consequently, they urged that the DVP resign from the cabinet. Stresemann was also dissatisfied with the outcome of the Conference, but he succeeded in defeating the move for withdrawal by pointing out that it would only lead to the entry of the Social Democrats into the cabinet and a revival of the Weimar Coalition. A formula satisfactory to all was finally found; the party remained in the cabinet while dissociating itself from the Spa agreement and emphasizing the role of Stinnes, who had attended the Conference as an advisor to the German delegation and had caused a minor crisis by openly defying the Allied representatives.[27]

The most important of the matters that had been deferred at Versailles, the German reparations debt, was left unsettled by the Spa Conference because of the inability of the Allies to agree upon a set of proposals. It was not until January 1921, that they informed the German government that it would be expected to pay more than 200 billion gold Mark during the next 42 years. Two months later, at a conference in London, Walter Simons, the Foreign Minister of the Fehrenbach cabinet, rejected these terms. In reprisal, the Allies occupied the industrial cities of Düsseldorf, Duisburg, and Ruhrort on March 8. The German government protested that this action was a violation of

[27] *Nachlass*, 3091/6934/139893ff., minutes of joint session of Reichstag delegation, Prussian delegation, and Managing Committee, 21.7.1920. Also, *Nachlass*, 3090/6929/139031ff., same of 26. and 27.7.1920. Also, "Spa," in DVP, *Archiv der Deutschen Volkspartei*, 4.9.1920.

the Versailles Treaty, but it was powerless to obstruct either the occupation or the erection by the Allies of a tariff barrier between the occupied areas and the rest of the country.

The Allied seizure of the Ruhr cities again raised doubts within the DVP about the advisability of remaining in the Fehrenbach cabinet. Stresemann had seen the potential dangers of the reparations question when the Allied terms were first announced in January. At that time he had sought to strengthen the hand of the government and also to lessen the vulnerability of the DVP to criticism from the Nationalists by creating a national unity-front government which would extend from the SPD on the left to the DNVP on the right. Throughout February and early March Stresemann carried on negotiations in an attempt to bring together such a broad coalition, only to see them break down on the day before the Allied occupation because of the intransigence of the SPD. The DVP was thus left, along with the DDP and the Center, to bear responsibility for the failure of the government's policies.[28] Despite his dissatisfaction with the situation, Stresemann opposed leaving the cabinet. Such a move, he believed, would lead either to a revival of the Weimar Coalition or to new elections, which, because of the weakened condition of the Independent Socialists following the bolt of a quarter of their Reichstag delegation to the Communists at the end of 1920, would probably produce significant gains for the SPD. In either case, he argued, the result would be a return to the leftist domination which had characterized the period following the revolution. Once again, his views prevailed and the party remained in the government.[29]

The patience of the DVP delegation came to an end in late April 1921, when Foreign Minister Simons revealed that the United States had rejected an appeal by the German government for mediation in the reparations dispute. Most of the party's deputies felt that the Foreign Minister's note to the United States

28 See *Nachlass*, 3094/7003/*passim*.
29 *Nachlass*, 3094/7003/142567, memorandum of 9.3.1921.

had been couched in unnecessarily subservient terms and that its rejection was therefore an especially humiliating setback. The DVP, they contended, could not afford to continue to support such policies. But when Stresemann again pointed out the undesirable consequences of withdrawal from the government, it was decided to demand only that both Fehrenbach and Simons be replaced at once. Stresemann promptly relayed this demand to the Interparty Committee of the Reichstag. The other government parties, however, refused to consider it and the Chancellor and the Foreign Minister remained at their posts.[30]

Following the failure of the attempt to oust Fehrenbach and Simons, Stresemann dropped his objections to a withdrawal from the cabinet. This change in his attitude was brought about by a proposal put forward by four of the industrial spokesmen in the Reichstag delegation, Johann Becker, Hans von Raumer, Hugo Stinnes, and Albert Vögler. Meeting with Stresemann at the Hotel Adlon on the evening of April 28, they suggested that the DVP deliberately bring about the fall of the Fehrenbach cabinet in the hope that President Ebert would hold it responsible for the formation of a new government, thus opening the way for a Stresemann cabinet. Stresemann proved very receptive to this proposal. Although the final decision on the DVP's policy was postponed until the arrival of the American answer to a second note from Simons, Stresemann set out at once to lay the groundwork for a cabinet of his own. The purpose of this undertaking was to enable the DVP to remain in the government by bringing to an end the series of diplomatic defeats which had made it increasingly difficult for the party to support the Fehrenbach cabinet. Stresemann was convinced that this could be accomplished only by adopting a stronger line in the negotiations with the Allies. This he hoped to achieve by appointing as his Foreign Minister Count Ulrich von Brockdorff-Rantzau, who was something of a national hero because of his resistance

---

[30] *Nachlass*, 3094/7000/141927, his memorandum on Reichstag delegation's meetings of 23. and 24.4.1921.

to the victors at Versailles. On the domestic scene Stresemann planned no major changes in the policies of the Fehrenbach cabinet and hoped to keep the existing DDP-Center-DVP coalition intact. He realized, however, that a new minority government under his leadership could not expect the cooperation which the Social Democrats had extended to Fehrenbach. Therefore, he gained a promise of support from the Nationalists by agreeing to give them a voice in the composition of his projected cabinet.[31]

At first it appeared that these plans would succeed. On May 4, after the United States had refused Simons' second plea for mediation, the DVP brought about the fall of the Fehrenbach cabinet by withdrawing its support. The Social Democrats then rejected President Ebert's proposal that they enter the government and it seemed highly likely that Stresemann would be called to the chancellorship. His candidacy, however, encountered an unexpected obstacle in the form of an Allied note that arrived in Berlin on May 5, just a day after the resignation of the old cabinet. The note was essentially an ultimatum and announced that the entire Ruhr industrial region would be occupied unless Germany agreed to recognize a reparations debt of 132 billion gold Mark within six days. This naturally raised doubts about the feasibility of a Stresemann government, since it was hardly possible to inaugurate a cabinet dedicated to firmer resistance to the Allies by accepting such terms. Nevertheless, Stresemann was determined not to lose his bid for the chancellorship so easily. On May 8 he presented a face-saving solution to the Interparty Committee. He made it clear that he could not form a cabinet if it would have to accept the ultimatum unconditionally but announced his readiness to do so if the impact of the Allied terms on the public could be reduced by a few concessions from London and Paris. Moreover, he indicated that

[31] See his memorandum on the events of 24. to 29.4.1921, *Nachlass*, 3094/7000/141928ff. Also, letter to Schwabach, 18.5.1921, *Nachlass*, 3094/7001/142140.

he was prepared to seek such concessions by means of a personal inquiry to the British government.[32]

Since no other solution had been found, the Interparty Committee approved his proposal. On the morning of the following day, May 9, he asked the British Embassy in Berlin to transmit four questions to London. The most important of these were concerned with the effect of an acceptance of the ultimatum on ending the occupation of Düsseldorf, Duisburg, and Ruhrort, and with the British attitude toward German claims in Upper Silesia, which was soon to be partitioned between Germany and Poland.[33] The whole undertaking was doomed to failure from the outset, however, for the British Foreign Office was intent on an unconditional victory with regard to the reparations question. It therefore delayed the answer to his inquiry until after the Reichstag vote on the ultimatum had been taken. As a result, on the afternoon of May 10, with the Allied deadline only hours off, Stresemann was forced to indicate that the DVP would vote against acceptance and withdraw his name from consideration for the chancellorship.[34] Ebert then assigned the task of forming a new government to Josef Wirth of the Center, who hastily put together a new cabinet of Social Democrats, Democrats, and Centrists. Late on the evening of the 10th the new government secured the support of a majority of the Reichstag for acceptance of the Allied terms.

Two days later Stresemann called on the British Ambassador, Lord D'Abernon, for the replies to his four questions. The Ambassador described the encounter in his diary: "As I read out one answer after another, it was evident that the communication from London was of profound importance to German politics. It appeared to me that what was going through S.'s mind

[32] *Nachlass*, 3094/7001/142147ff., letter from Dingeldey, 20.5.1921. Also, *Deutscher Geschichtskalender*, xxxvii (A), Part 1, 563.

[33] A paraphrase of his inquiries is printed in D'Abernon, *An Ambassador*, I, 164f.

[34] See his speech to the Reichstag, 10.5.1921, *Verhandlungen* (Reichstag), cccxlix, 3631f.

was the reflection that, had the answer—so unexpectedly favourable in its tenor—been received forty-eight hours sooner, there would not have been a Wirth Cabinet, but a Stresemann Cabinet."[35]

The Foreign Office had in fact provided just the sort of concessions he had sought, promising pressure on the French to bring the occupation of the three Ruhr cities to an end and pledging "due regard" for German claims in Upper Silesia. But by holding up their reply, the British had made these concessions meaningless.

Stresemann's disappointment at the collapse of his bid for the chancellorship was further increased by the exclusion of the DVP from the new government. The Fehrenbach cabinet had thoroughly convinced him of the soundness of his decision to take the party into the government and he had hoped that it would be possible to prevent the formation of a leftist-oriented cabinet in spite of the ultimatum crisis. Even while leading the great majority of the DVP Reichstag delegation in voting against acceptance on May 10, he made it clear that the party was ready to share the responsibility for meeting the Allied terms if the ultimatum were accepted. Despite this gesture, the DVP was offered only the token representation of one ministerial post in the new cabinet. When he demanded full parity with the other parties the DVP was excluded altogether.[36] The result was a revival of the Weimar Coalition, hardly a desirable development from Stresemann's standpoint, especially in view of the fact that the new Chancellor, Wirth, was a member of the extreme left wing of the Center Party. But since the new cabinet enjoyed the support of only a minority of the Reichstag, he was hopeful of checking its leftward orientation by gaining admission for the DVP at an early date. During the remainder of May, he extended the party's toleration to the government. Then, in early June he proposed that the DVP be added to the cabinet to provide a

[35] D'Abernon, *An Ambassador*, I, 169.
[36] See his "Politische Umschau," *Deutsche Stimmen*, 3.7.1921.

stronger basis for negotiations with the Allies. To his disappointment, this proposal was promptly rejected by the Social Democrats, who saw no reason to surrender several ministerial posts. Even without such a concession, they realized that the government could count on the tacit toleration of the DVP since Stresemann wished to avoid a crisis that could lead to new elections and bring them sweeping gains at the expense of the crumbling Independent Socialist Party.[37] Thwarted in his attempt to win a place in the government for his party and without prospect of altering the situation, Stresemann decided in mid-June to drop his political activities temporarily and take the lengthy rest his physician had for some time been recommending.

During most of the summer of 1921, the German political scene was remarkably quiet, but the calm was abruptly shattered by the assassination of Matthias Erzberger on August 26. Since the latter stages of the war, Stresemann had been one of the sharpest critics of the controversial leader of the left wing of the Center and had not concealed the fact that he held him responsible for a large share of the misfortunes that had befallen the country in 1918 and 1919. But in spite of his objections to Erzberger, his reaction to the assassination left no doubt that he was genuinely appalled by the use of murder as a political weapon. At a DVP rally in the Ruhr in mid-September he made clear his views on the subject: "Whoever believes that political influence can be exercised through force and murder has nothing to do with us, he stands outside the law. Whoever spills human blood must have his own blood spilled. There are people who believe they can obstruct our further political development by reaching for a dagger or a revolver. In this connection, I shall make no secret of the fact that regardless of the person I do not in any way endorse the notion that so-called 'lofty motives' should reduce the punishment of persons who commit murder."[38]

[37] *Nachlass*, 3109/6999/141760f., his memorandum of 4.6.1921.
[38] *Nachlass*, 3109/6996/141167, speech at Lüdenscheid, 18.9.1921. In her recent biography of Stresemann, Annelise Thimme unaccountably

At the close of this speech, ironically, he was himself the target of a poorly aimed pistol shot fired by a would-be assassin.[39]

The Erzberger murder proved to be a significant event in Stresemann's career, for it led him to make an important alteration in the policy of the DVP. When the assassination took place, many of his doubts and apprehensions about the Weimar system had already been removed by the work of the Fehrenbach cabinet. He looked back on the period since the 1920 elections as a time of stabilization and recovery; he was hopeful that the trend could be continued and that the DVP would soon again be in a position to influence the government's policies. Viewed from this perspective, the Kapp Putsch seemed to him a reckless and unfortunate escapade that had impeded the process of stabilization by setting off the leftist uprisings of the spring of 1920 and strengthening the radicals within the socialist camp.[40] He was therefore very concerned about the effects of the Erzberger assassination. Since it, like the Kapp affair, had been carried out by rightist extremists he feared that it, too, would set off a swing to the left. There was no imminent danger of an armed leftist uprising similar to that of 1920. However, there was a strong possibility that the reaction against the right that followed the assassination would drive the Center and the DDP into a firm alliance with the SPD and, in addition, bring about a reconciliation between the Social Democrats and the rump Independent Socialist Party. He saw that if this should happen the result could be a protracted period of leftist government and a long exile from the cabinet for the DVP.[41] In the hope of preventing such a shift to the left, he decided to try to counteract the widespread notion of a rightist plot against the Republic by

states that after the assassinations of both Erzberger and Rathenau, he sought to defend the murderers and placed the major blame for what had happened on the murdered men themselves, *Stresemann*, p. 43.

[39] *Nachlass*, 3109/6996/141181.

[40] See his "Erzberger," in *Deutsche Stimmen*, 4.9.1921.

[41] See his articles, "Politische Umschau," in *Deutsche Stimmen*, 4. and 11.9.1921.

having the DVP repudiate the extreme right and move a step closer to the new system.

Putting this decision into effect at once, he publicly denounced the assassination on behalf of the DVP and announced that the party not only recognized the Weimar constitution as the legally established basis of government but would defend it against all illegal attacks. This was substantially the same pledge he had given the Assembly in 1919, but this time it was backed by the conviction of experience. As immediate evidence of the party's good faith, he gave its support to President Ebert's emergency decree of August 29, which empowered the government to employ exceptional measures against organizations and publications attacking the Republic and those identified with it. He did this, however, only after indicating that this action involved no change in the DVP's monarchist position and receiving the President's assurances that the government's extraordinary powers would be used against extremists of the left as well as of the right.[42]

Early in September he made still another conciliatory gesture toward the republican parties by openly dissociating the DVP from the DNVP. The Nationalists had opposed the President's emergency decree and at a Party Congress in Munich on September 1, their leader, Oskar Hergt, ruled out the possibility of cooperation with the Social Democrats and called upon the DVP to join with the DNVP in forming a new party of the right. In answer to Hergt's proposal, Stresemann rejected the idea of a party of the right and, taking up the position adopted by his colleague Wilhelm Kahl, announced that the DVP should not be referred to, along with the DNVP, as a rightist party. As a substitute for Hergt's plan, he called for a bloc of the middle, to be made up of the moderate parties, among which, he indicated, the Social Democrats should be included.[43]

[42] See his "Vor wichtigen Entscheidungen," in *Vossische Zeitung*, 28.8.1921 (No. 404). Also, his memorandum on conversation with Ebert, 31.8.1921, *Nachlass*, 3109/6997/141422ff.

[43] See his "Politische Umschau," *Deutsche Stimmen*, 18.9.1921. Also, *Nachlass*, 3109/6997/141449f., letter to Tillmanns, 7.9.1921.

The response to these policies was swift and favorable. Both the DDP and the Center were impressed by the attitude of the DVP and spared it in their attacks on the rightist circles which had instigated the assassination. Even more important was the reaction of the Social Democrats. At their Party Congress at Görlitz in mid-September they accepted Stresemann's overtures and voted by an overwhelming majority to open negotiations aimed at bringing the DVP into the government. This decision came while the Reichstag and Prussian Landtag delegations of the DVP were holding a joint policy meeting in Heidelberg. In response to the Social Democrats' action, the question of a new government was at once placed on the agenda. Against the opposition of the industrialist Albert Vögler and a few other Reichstag deputies who had never become reconciled to cooperation with the SPD, the delegations voted to accept Stresemann's proposal of a Great Coalition of the middle, which would extend from the SPD on the left to the DVP on the right.[44]

Because of the altered attitude of the Social Democrats, Stresemann was hopeful that the DVP would soon regain its place in the government, but he let it be known that he would not be available for a ministerial post. In the opinion of Lord D'Abernon, the explanation for this was that he would settle for nothing less than the chancellorship and had decided to wait for it to become vacant. "Unquestionably a big man, and he knows it," was the Ambassador's verdict.[45] All of Stresemann's precautions regarding his own position were unnecessary, for his optimism about the party's early re-entrance into the government proved to be premature. Even after consenting in principle to cooperate, the DVP and the SPD had to reach agreement on the specific issues which the new cabinet would have to face and this proved to be a difficult process. At first, the negotiations were held up by disagreements on fiscal policy. The DVP insisted on a larger

[44] See his "Politische Umschau," *Deutsche Stimmen*, 2.10.1921. For the opposition, see *Nachlass*, 3159/7396/171784ff.
[45] D'Abernon, *An Ambassador*, I, 208.

proportion of indirect taxes, which would distribute the burden over the whole population, while the SPD favored direct taxation aimed specifically at large concentrations of property and capital. These differences were not insurmountable and some progress toward an agreement was made during late September and early October.[46] But once again, just as at the time of his bid for the chancellorship in May, Stresemann's efforts were frustrated by a development in the realm of foreign affairs. On October 20 the League of Nations announced that virtually all of the industrial areas of Upper Silesia, including many which had voted to remain with Germany, would be awarded to Poland. The leaders of the DVP, as well as the rank and file of the party objected vigorously to this decision. When the Wirth cabinet resigned in protest against it, Stresemann proposed a national resistance front, consisting of the SPD, the DDP, the Center, and the DVP, which would reject the terms of the partition. But his proposal was ignored by the leaders of the government parties, who felt there was no alternative to acceptance. Unwilling to associate the DVP with such a decision, he withdrew from the discussions concerning the new government. The result was the formation of another Weimar Coalition cabinet under Wirth on October 25.[47]

Even after the Upper Silesian crisis, Stresemann continued to hope that the DVP would be able to gain re-entry into the government. In Prussia, where foreign affairs did not complicate matters, a Great Coalition cabinet was set up in early November. Stresemann was confident that after a short time the party's indignation at the acceptance of the League's decision would subside sufficiently to allow a similar arrangement in the Reich. During November he therefore sought to avoid open clashes

[46] *Nachlass*, 3109/6996/141263ff., minutes of Managing Committee, 3.10.1921.
[47] *Nachlass*, 3093/6992/140622f., his letter to Ebert, 25.10.1921. Also, "Die Grosse Koalition, Oberschlesien und die Deutsche Volkspartei," in DVP, *Archiv der Deutschen Volkspartei*, 4.11.1921.

with the new minority Wirth cabinet. Then, early in December, at a Party Congress in Stuttgart, he urged the DVP to work for national solidarity by seeking a Great Coalition government. He stipulated, however, that this would be possible only if the other parties agreed to end what he regarded as their policy of submissive fulfillment of the Allies' demands and adopted a firmer line in dealing with the victorious powers.[48]

In contrast to earlier congresses, his recommendation was not unanimously accepted, for the confusing course the party had followed since May had aroused opposition in a number of quarters. A group which the press labeled at the time of the Congress as the right wing (led by the industrial spokesmen Quaatz and Vögler and two Reichstag deputies from Hamburg and Bremen, Walther Dauch and Alfred Gildemeister), opposed the whole idea of cooperation with the Social Democrats and advocated closer ties with the Nationalists.[49] Criticism of another sort was forthcoming from a group referred to as the left wing. Among the leaders of this group were Fritz Kaiser, the chairman of the DVP delegation in the Saxon Landtag, and three members of the Reichstag delegation, Heinze, Frau Katherina von Oheimb, and Siegfried von Kardorff, the latter a former leader of the old Free Conservative Party who had broken with the DNVP after the Kapp Putsch. They criticized Stresemann for bringing about the fall of the Fehrenbach cabinet and demanded an immediate and unconditional re-entry into the cabinet.[50] Although the appearance of these two wings attracted much publicity at the time, neither was strong enough to diminish the loyalty to Stresemann of the bulk of the Congress, which was made up of representatives of the party's local organizations. As a result,

[48] See his speech to the Congress in *Deutsche Stimmen*, 18.12.1921.
[49] See "Stresemanns Stuttgarter Sieg," *Vossische Zeitung*, 2.12.1921 (No. 567). Also, *Nachlass*, 3111/7124/147061, a memorandum on Quaatz, 1924.
[50] See his "Politische Umschau," *Deutsche Stimmen*, 11.12.1921. Also *Nachlass*, 3093/6995/141107ff., excerpts from the stenographic record of the Congress.

his proposal of a Great Coalition was adopted by an overwhelming majority.[51]

At the time of the 1921 Party Congress, Stresemann broadened his journalistic activities in an effort to strengthen the DVP and took on what was to prove to be a troublesome burden. Since the founding of the party, one of its most conspicuous weaknesses had been the lack of a nationally influential party newspaper to rival the *Vorwärts* of the SPD, the *Germania* of the Center, the *Berliner Tageblatt* and *Frankfurter Zeitung* of the DDP, and the *Kreuzzeitung* of the DNVP. During the first years of the Republic the DVP had generally received the editorial support of the independent Berlin *Tägliche Rundschau*, a paper whose circulation was not large but which commanded a sizeable following in business circles. In September 1921, however, the owners of the *Rundschau*, who had never been entirely pleased with this political line, dismissed their editor, Heinrich Rippler, who belonged to the DVP, and replaced him with an editor associated with the DNVP. As a result, the DVP was left without the backing of a single paper in the capital. In an effort to correct this situation, Stresemann persuaded a group of the party's business supporters to underwrite the launching of a new Berlin daily under his direction. The first edition of the paper, *Die Zeit*, appeared on December 1, coinciding with the opening of the Party Congress. Edited by Rippler, *Die Zeit* professed to be independent, but Stresemann soon made it, like his magazine *Deutsche Stimmen*, into a *de facto* organ of the DVP and frequently contributed political articles to it himself. Contrary to his hopes, *Die Zeit* failed to develop a large circulation. Although it gained considerable prestige from his use of it as a sounding board while he was a member of the government, the paper was never able to hold its own financially. For several years he managed to keep it alive on laboriously gathered business subsidies and sizeable contributions of his own. But in

[51] See "Die Politik der Deutschen Volkspartei nach Stuttgart," in *Nationalliberale Correspondenz*, 6.12.1921.

June 1925, he gave up the venture in disgust and disposed of the debt-ridden paper altogether.[52]

By the middle of January 1922, it seemed that the Great Coalition was at last to be realized. Central to this development was the removal of the troublesome fiscal issue through a compromise between the DVP and the governing Weimar Coalition parties on the tax schedule for the coming year. In the course of the negotiations that produced this agreement, Chancellor Wirth led Stresemann and his colleagues to believe that he intended to widen the minority cabinet in the near future by admitting the DVP. This set off a round of speculation within the party concerning ministerial posts and revealed that Stresemann had reversed his stand of the previous fall and was ready to accept a place in the cabinet. The Reichstag delegation wanted him to aim for the Ministry of the Interior, with its extensive administrative apparatus and patronage opportunities. His own preference, though, was the Foreign Ministry, which Wirth had not filled when reshuffling his cabinet in October.[53]

Just as the prospects seemed brightest, the entire Great Coalition project abruptly collapsed. This sudden turn of events was triggered by the appointment of Walther Rathenau as Foreign Minister on January 31. Since Wirth had not consulted them about this appointment, the DVP leaders regarded it as a breach of faith in view of the Chancellor's earlier assurances that they would have a voice in the realignment of the cabinet. Coupled with signs that the government parties were having second thoughts about the conditions the DVP had posed in the tax compromise, the appointment led the party's leaders to conclude that there was no basis for a coalition.[54]

[52] See Heinz Starkulla, "Organisation und Technik der Pressepolitik des Staatsmannes Gustav Stresemann 1923 bis 1929" (dissertation, Munich, 1951), pp. 46ff.

[53] *Schiffer Papers*, Nr. 1, Heft 1, p. 105, diary entry on conversation with Stresemann. In the typed and revised version of his diary now in the Hauptarchiv, Schiffer dated this as 17.2.1922. Internal evidence, however, indicates that the conversation actually took place in January.

[54] *Schulthess' Europäischer Geschichtskalender*, LXIII, 14f.

During the spring of 1922, the prospects for the DVP's re-entry into the government did not improve. The chances seemed in fact dimmer than ever. The SPD and the rump Independent Socialist Party were on the verge of a *rapprochement* and, as a result, the Social Democrats were inclining to the idea of widening the Wirth cabinet by adding the Independents instead of the DVP. But in spite of this unpromising situation, the DVP followed a cooperative policy toward the government throughout the spring. It gave the cabinet its full backing on the Rapallo Treaty with Russia and, after another round of negotiations, joined with the coalition parties in passing a new tax schedule.

On June 24, 1922, the politics of the Republic were again marred by violence when Rathenau was assassinated by a band of rightist fanatics. Although Stresemann had always respected the new Foreign Minister, their relations had been strained since the revolution of 1918, for Rathenau was one of the foremost advocates of state economic planning and a member of the left wing of the Democratic Party. But upon hearing of the assassination, Stresemann promptly and unequivocally denounced it and called for immediate action against the organization behind it. In addition, he publicly deplored the anti-Semitism involved in the rightist campaign of vilification that had preceded Rathenau's murder. In this regard, his strong feelings were based in part on personal experience, for he was himself a target of anti-Semitic attacks inspired by rumors that the family of his wife, the former Käthe Kleefeld, was partly Jewish.[55]

Politically, Stresemann viewed the Rathenau assassination as a repetition of the Erzberger affair of the previous summer. Shortly afterwards he lamented to a fellow party member: "Political work often seems to me to be a labor of Sisyphus. Whenever one has rolled the stone up far enough so that one can believe in a

[55] See his "Politische Umschau," *Deutsche Stimmen*, 2.7.1922. For a report on the anti-Semitic attacks on him, see *Nachlass*, 3094/7003/142488f. Stresemann's son Wolfgang has stated that there was no foundation to these rumors, which were later seized upon by the Nazis: conversation with the author, 2.2.1962.

97

stabilization of the general situation, then some fanatic plunges us into a new misfortune."[56] Because of the *rapprochement* of the Social Democrats and the Independents, he regarded the danger of a shift to the left as even greater than it had been the previous summer. In the hope of preventing such a development, he decided to adopt the same course he had followed after Erzberger's death and conspicuously dissociate the DVP from the assassination, while supporting the emergency measures of the government.[57]

This policy proved more difficult to carry out than he had anticipated. In addition to another presidential decree similar to that issued after Erzberger's death, the Wirth cabinet called for the adoption of a special law for the protection of the Republic which would remain in effect for five years. This measure, which reached the floor of the Reichstag on July 5, provided the government with sweeping powers to combat agitation against the Republic and its officials. Even after a number of its more stringent provisions had been removed in committee, Stresemann felt that the proposed bill was unnecessarily harsh. But despite his objections, he urged the DVP delegation to support the measure. A margin of two-thirds was required for passage, since the bill impinged on the rights guaranteed by the constitution, and if the DVP joined the Communists and the Nationalists in the opposition it appeared certain that the government would be defeated. Stresemann wished to avoid such a development at all costs, for the Wirth cabinet had served notice that if the protection law was rejected it would resign and promptly call new elections. Such a turn of events would, in his opinion, expose the DVP to the charge of having blocked an attempt to combat terrorism and cost it the support of many moderate voters. Moreover, the increasing seriousness of the inflation that had been developing since the end of the war made an election a dangerous risk in his eyes. With a slogan of "Against the murder organizations

---

[56] *Nachlass*, 3096/7014/143928, letter to Becker, 10.7.1922.
[57] *Ibid.*, 143927.

and for cheaper bread," he feared that the socialists might be able to gain an absolute majority of the Reichstag and thus take over the leadership of the country for an indefinite period to come.[58]

His decision to support the protection bill met with strong opposition in the DVP Reichstag delegation. Many of the deputies felt that it was impossible for a monarchist party to accept such an outspokenly republican measure. In his opinion, this was the same kind of "sentimentality," or exaggerated concern for abstract principles, that had led the DNVP astray. He called instead for a policy of *Realpolitik* that would aim at the achievement of immediate and concrete goals. If the DVP wished to avert a resurgence of the left, he insisted, it had no choice except to avoid new elections by voting for the protection bill.[59] With regard to its republicanism, he was able to provide a solution that was acceptable to a large part of the DVP delegation as well as to the government parties. In order to do so, however, he had to move closer to the Republic than ever before. Following Erzberger's murder, he had pledged the DVP to recognize and defend the republican constitution, but without any indication as to how long the pledge was to remain in effect. During the debate on the protection bill, he led the DVP in adopting a new position that clarified this somewhat, though still not completely: "The dispute over the form of government must be put aside during our Fatherland's time of distress. We are of the conviction that the reconstruction of Germany is only possible within the framework of the republican constitution."[60]

This additional concession to the new system was obviously designed to enable the DVP to vote for the protection measure while retaining its monarchist principles, but it also coincided with Stresemann's own personal views. While he had not aban-

[58] *Nachlass*, 3096/7014/143999ff., letter to Crown Prince Wilhelm, 21.7.1922.

[59] *Nachlass*, 3096/7014/144014f., letter to Böckelmann, 21.7.1922.

[60] Resolution of the Reich Committee, 9.7.1922, printed in DVP, *Archiv der Deutschen Volkspartei*, 15.8.1922.

doned the hope of an eventual restoration, he had become convinced that it would be out of the question for some time to come and had confided to Count Harry Kessler as early as March that he saw no possibility "in the foreseeable future."[61] Thus, although the aftermath of the Rathenau murder forced him to make his position public, and so to move another step closer to the Republic, he had not adopted that position simply in response to the political situation created by the murder.

In his campaign to bring the DVP behind the projected bill, Stresemann had the full support of the left wing of the delegation, which had generally supported his policies since the early part of 1922. But in spite of his exertions on behalf of the bill, he was unable to gain the backing of the whole Reichstag delegation. On July 18 when the final vote was taken, 23 DVP deputies, led by the right wing, absented themselves or abstained, while 3 voted against the measure. Still, his efforts had not been in vain, for he succeeded in mustering 36 votes for the bill, more than enough to secure its passage.

His policy on the protection law was quickly vindicated when, on the day following its adoption, the Democratic and Centrist Reichstag delegations joined with the DVP in forming an Alliance of the Middle (*Arbeitsgemeinschaft der Mitte*) which committed all three delegations to consult with one another on important issues. This unexpected development was the result of a quarrel between the government parties which had begun in early July when the Social Democrats demanded that the Independent Socialists be admitted to the cabinet. The Democrats and the Centrists gave their consent at once but only on the condition that the DVP also be brought in to balance the influx from the left. The Social Democrats flatly rejected this proposal and on July 15 announced the formation of a parliamentary alliance with the Independents. Four days later, after the passage of the protection law, the DDP and the Center retaliated by

[61] Kessler, *Tagebücher*, p. 281.

forming their alliance with the DVP. This arrangement pleased Stresemann greatly since it represented a significant breach in the unity of the Weimar Coalition. Moreover, he believed that it ensured his party's re-entry into the government at an early date. A merger between the Social Democrats and the Independents was expected at any time and the Democrats and Centrists had let it be known that when it took place they would demand that the DVP be admitted to the cabinet to compensate for the increased strength of the SPD.[62]

When the union of the two socialist parties was finally consummated in late September 1922, Stresemann's high hopes for the Alliance of the Middle were somewhat dampened. Just as they had indicated they would, the Center and the DDP promptly asked that the DVP be admitted to the government. The Social Democrats, however, refused. They argued that the expansion of their party had given the Wirth government a firm majority and therefore no further additions to the cabinet were necessary. Rather than provoke a crisis, the other two government parties let their demands drop for the time being. Moreover, they raised no objections when the SPD reopened the issue of the presidency by calling for an immediate election.

Ever since the Kapp Putsch, this issue had been simmering quietly in the background of the Republic's politics. Following the Reichstag elections of 1920, it had been generally assumed that a presidential election would soon be held. At that time Stresemann tried to revive the candidacy of Hindenburg, but because of the reaction against the right set off by the Putsch, the Field Marshal requested that his name not be entered. Seeking a substitute behind whom all the non-socialist parties could unite, Stresemann then proposed former imperial Chancellor von Bülow, for whom he had high personal regard.[63] However, this suggestion encountered stiff opposition from within the other

[62] See his letters to Stinnes, 21.7. and 3.8.1922, *Nachlass*, 3096/7015/144079ff. and 144109.

[63] *Nachlass*, 3089/6926/138473, minutes of Managing Committee, 13.9.1920.

parties and it was dropped. The non-socialist parties were unable to agree upon another candidate and the SPD was in no hurry to face an election so soon after their heavy losses in the elections to the first Reichstag. The whole matter was thus put aside in the fall of 1920, with all the parties tacitly agreeing to leave Ebert in the office on a provisional basis. By the time the Social Democrats revived the question in 1922 their absorption of the Independents had greatly improved their position. With the non-socialist parties still lacking a unity candidate, they obviously expected that Ebert would easily win the seven-year term provided for by the constitution. Feeling it was pointless to postpone the issue any longer, the Center and the DDP at first raised no objections to the election. Stresemann, however, was determined not to see the SPD handed control of the presidency until 1929 and brought pressure to bear on the Center and the DDP. Unwilling to endanger the new Alliance of the Middle, the two gave in and blocked the legislation necessary to call the election. This produced a stalemate that was resolved in October when the DVP and the government parties agreed to extend Ebert's term until 1925.[64]

After his success in mobilizing the Alliance to block the presidential election, Stresemann began during October to press the Center and the DDP to renew their efforts to bring the DVP into the government. At first the efforts of the two parties were frustrated by Chancellor Wirth. A member of the left wing of the Center, he was not displeased at the prospect of continuing at the head of the newly expanded Weimar Coalition and sought to delay a decision on the DVP. Finally, in November his own party and the DDP indicated that they would withdraw their support if the DVP was not admitted. When the SPD, largely in deference to the newly readmitted Independents, refused once again to consider such a move, Wirth was forced to dissolve his cabinet on November 14.

[64] See his "Politische Umschau," *Deutsche Stimmen*, 20.10.1922.

At first, Stresemann believed that the fall of the Wirth cabinet might bring him a call to the chancellorship. For the second time he began considering the steps he would take if he were given a chance to form a new government. But his hopes were balked by the President, who named as Chancellor the man Stresemann himself had intended to appoint as his Minister of Economics: Wilhelm Cuno, head of the Hamburg-America shipping line and a member of the DVP until the Kapp Putsch.[65] Cuno's appointment led to a week-long government crisis, for he quickly came into conflict with the parties. He set out to form a Great Coalition, but as a non-party man he hoped to choose his ministers without submitting to the usual bargaining among the parties regarding the distribution of the various cabinet posts. When the parties nevertheless presented their demands, a paralyzing stalemate developed, with the Chancellor-designate and the parties holding stubbornly to their positions. Coming as it did in the midst of the steadily worsening inflation, this apparent breakdown of parliamentary government produced a wave of criticism of the republican system. Moreover, it provided additional impetus for the outbreak of speculation about dictatorship which had been set off in rightist circles during October by the successful Fascist revolution in Italy.

Stresemann was greatly disturbed by the reaction to the crisis. Despite his misgivings about the particular form it had been given in the Weimar constitution, he had never questioned the basic principle of constitutional parliamentary government and he hoped to see it preserved even if the monarchy should be restored. The new attack on the existing system was therefore also an attack on his own position and he quickly took issue with it. In an article in his magazine, *Deutsche Stimmen*, he made clear his views on the subject: "A great many circles in Germany have, with an unusual unanimity, already decided in favor of dictatorship. To be sure, they have no dictator and do not even know how things will develop, but they see in dic-

---

[65] *Nachlass*, 3097/7019/144661f., letter to Dingeldey, 4.12.1922.

tatorship the only thing that can help us. Mussolini's victory in Rome, which was regrettable from Germany's standpoint, is acclaimed by them. Herr Hitler holds rallies in Munich which are allegedly attended by 50,000 persons. The urge toward new things is unmistakable. Many perhaps believe that it is possible to bring about the shift to the right which they desire by means of a movement that makes parliamentarianism contemptible. They forget one thing, that it has repeatedly been those who stood the farthest right who have, through their policies, brought about the strongest shifts to the left. The Communists and the right radicals will knock each other's heads in if we try to get rid of the childhood illnesses of the new German parliamentarianism through an operation that costs the patient his life instead of trying the perhaps by no means hopeless course of curing the illness itself."[66]

With regard to this illness, he maintained that it was by no means fundamental and predicted that the long string of weak minority governments and crises could be brought to an end if the parties were willing to show a bit more flexibility. In any case, he argued, under the circumstances the only alternatives to the existing system at the moment were a dictatorship of the right, similar to that of Italy, or of the left, similar to that of Russia. He left no doubt about his own point of view which was that both of these were unacceptable and that under the circumstances Germany would be wisest to retain the existing republican system.[67]

The government crisis was finally resolved on November 21 when Cuno put together a non-coalition cabinet. He drew his ministers from the parties of the Alliance of the Middle and included two men from the DVP: Heinze, who again took over the dual posts of Vice-Chancellor and Minister of Justice, and Johann Becker, one of the Ruhr spokesmen, who was named Minister of Economics. Since the Alliance controlled only a mi-

[66] "Politische Umschau," 5.12.1922.
[67] *Ibid.*

nority of the Reichstag, the new cabinet was at first dependent on the toleration of the Nationalists. They later opposed it on many points, however, and it survived only because of the Social Democrats' decision to drop their initial oppositional stance and grant it their toleration.

At first Stresemann was very doubtful about the capabilities of the new Chancellor. Shortly after the cabinet's installation he confided his views to a party colleague: "Cuno causes us great concern. He is not the strong man he passes for. We must therefore not identify ourselves too closely with him."[68] By the end of 1922, however, his doubts had been dispelled by the Chancellor's decision to ignore strong Allied pressure and persist in his demands for a moratorium on reparations.[69] When this action, plus several defaults in coal and timber deliveries, led to the French-Belgian occupation of the Ruhr in January 1923, he gave his full backing to Cuno's policy of passive resistance.

During the first half of 1923, Stresemann played a leading role in supporting the government's defiance of the French. Since all the republican parties were united behind that policy, this served to diminish still further the gap that separated him from them. Furthermore, his activities on behalf of the resistance effort greatly enhanced his own political reputation. In this connection, his work as chairman of the Reichstag's Foreign Affairs Committee since 1920 proved of great value. It had acquainted him with the officials of the Foreign Ministry and brought him into frequent contact with the Berlin diplomatic corps. Especially important in the latter regard were his good relations with the British Ambassador, Lord D'Abernon, whom he had come to know quite well since their encounter at the time of his bid for the chancellorship in May 1921. By making use of the information about the diplomatic situation which he gathered from these various sources, he quickly won recognition as one of the Reichstag's best informed and most articulate critics of French policy.

[68] *Nachlass*, 3097/7019/144662, letter to Dingeldey, 4.12.1922.
[69] *Nachlass*, 3097/7113/145031, letter to Uebel, 8.1.1923.

Although he was sometimes critical of the Cuno cabinet's foreign policy, he usually cooperated closely with it and occasionally delivered attacks on the French which the government wished to see made but for which it did not want to assume responsibility.[70] As a result of his generally recognized position as one of the foremost spokesmen of the German position in the Ruhr dispute, the foreign press frequently quoted his remarks and gave prominent display to interviews with him, all of which further increased his stature at home.[71] In domestic politics he was an outspoken advocate of national solidarity against the French. He helped to bring the Social Democrats behind the government by endorsing their demand for the taxation of the capital goods of industry and by joining them in calling for a speedy termination of the inflation, which had reached runaway proportions as a result of the paralysis of the industries of the Ruhr.[72]

Largely because of the new prominence which these activities brought him, there were persistent rumors during May 1923, that Stresemann would be called in to replace Cuno, who had failed to make any progress toward a solution of the crisis.[73] But in spite of his long-standing ambition to head a cabinet, he was not at all anxious to take over the chancellorship at that time since the circumstances were hardly propitious, with French troops in the Ruhr and inflation out of control.[74] Therefore, when the DDP and Center delegations threatened to withdraw their support from the cabinet during the third week of May, he threw

[70] See *Nachlass*, 3098/7115/145429f.; *Nachlass*, 3098/7115/145482.

[71] *Times* (London), 3.3.1923, p. 10; *New York Times*, 8.3.1923, p. 1; *Manchester Guardian*, 22.2.1923, p. 14, interview; *Le Temps* (Paris), 28.2.1923, p. 1.

[72] See his "Vom Rechte, das mit uns geboren," *Deutsche Stimmen*, 5.2.1923. Also, his "Politik und Wirtschaft," article for *Die Zeit*, 15.5.1923, *Vermächtnis*, I, 64.

[73] *Nachlass*, 3098/7115/145502f., letter from Prince von Isenburg, 8.5.1923. Also, *Nachlass*, 3098/7115/145401f., letter to Schweighart, 9.5.1923.

[74] *Nachlass*, 3098/7115/145504, letter to Prince von Isenburg, 14.5. 1923.

his full support to the Chancellor and found a compromise solution that brought the two delegations back into line.[75]

By the beginning of August there was renewed speculation that he might soon replace Cuno, for the government's position had deteriorated steadily during the summer.[76] The Social Democrats were growing increasingly impatient at the cabinet's failure to cope with the runaway inflation and were seriously considering withdrawing their support. The Chancellor, on the other hand, was himself disappointed at the failure of his efforts and no longer concealed his readiness to relinquish his post. In addition, a part of the press was insisting that if the republican government failed to find a solution quickly there would be no alternative except to call in a dictator to handle the situation with a firm hand.[77]

In view of these developments, Stresemann concluded that it would be virtually impossible to avoid a change of government. Unwilling to see the chancellorship elude him for the third time, he decided to try to set up a Great Coalition cabinet if he should be called upon to replace Cuno. He was hopeful, however, that a government crisis could be staved off at least until the results of the Cuno's cabinet's appeal to the British for mediation in the stalemate with the French became known. It was expected that the British reply would be in the negative and he was anxious to spare a new government the embarrassment of beginning its term of office by announcing another diplomatic setback.[78] Consequently, when Cuno further weakened the position of the cabinet by delivering a pessimistic address to the Reichstag on August 8, he sought to avert an immediate crisis with a speech of his own the following day.

[75] See his notes on meeting of the Alliance of the Middle, 22.5.1923, *Nachlass*, 3098/7116/145546f. Also, his diary notes, *Vermächtnis*, I, 65.

[76] See his "Politische Umschau," *Deutsche Stimmen*, 5.8.1923.

[77] Stresemann found articles of this sort in the rightist press, particularly the papers *Der Westen* and *Deutsche Zeitung*, see *Nachlass*, 3098/7117/145840, letter to Leidig, 3.8.1923.

[78] *Nachlass*, 3098/7117/145814f., letter to Jänecke, 1.8.1923.

His speech to the Reichstag on the 9th of August proved to be a significant one. In it he firmly aligned himself with the defenders of the Weimar system. He began by endorsing the policies of the Cuno cabinet and was more optimistic than the Chancellor about the prospects for an agreement with the French and for a solution to the problem of inflation. Then he took sharp issue with those who were speculating about an experiment with the untried, and in his opinion highly dangerous, idea of a dictatorship. Although he was still unwilling to endorse the existing system as the best government for Germany on a permanent basis, he revealed that he had come to the conclusion that the country had been fortunate to escape from the revolution with a constitutional parliamentary republic: "In the period from November 1918 to August 1919 an important domestic struggle was . . . fought out in Germany which the German so easily forgets. . . . At that time the issue was whether we would go the way of the dictatorship of the proletariat or return to the idea of constitutional government. The victory of the constitutional idea in this struggle gave us the basis for a possible consolidation of the German situation."

Moreover, he made it clear that he felt the attempts to unseat the new regime had been distinctly against the best interest of the country as a whole: "Without political murder and secret conspiracies we would be a great deal further along in this consolidation of our political situation." Finally, he called upon all the parties to rally to the support of the existing system and warned: "He who today attacks the state as it is, casts us back into the conditions that existed in the period before the establishment of this constitutional basis."[79]

At first it seemed that the government would survive the August crisis in spite of Cuno's pessimism. Contrary to the expectations of many, the Social Democrats did not oppose the emergency fiscal legislation which the Chancellor placed before

[79] *Verhandlungen* (Reichstag), CCCLXI, 11778.

the Reichstag and on the 10th, the cabinet secured the passage of its entire program. Stresemann was relieved at this turn of events and concluded that the crisis had been postponed.[80] He had to revise this opinion quickly, however. On the same day that the Reichstag adopted the new fiscal legislation the Berlin printers went on strike and cut off the supply of paper currency which the government had been using to meet its obligations during the inflation. Faced with this new complication, Stresemann brought the DVP delegation to adopt a resolution to support Cuno as long as he wished to remain as Chancellor, but to seek a Great Coalition government, headed by a non-socialist, if his cabinet fell.[81]

The final blow to the Cuno cabinet came with the announcement on August 11 of the British failure to bring the French and Belgians to adopt a conciliatory attitude toward the German government's reparations proposals. This development apparently led the Social Democrats to conclude that the cabinet's plight was hopeless, for they promptly withdrew their support from it. Cuno, deciding it would be futile to attempt to remain in office against the opposition of the SPD, resigned on the morning of the 12th. In an effort to avoid a lengthy governmental crisis, President Ebert conferred with the leaders of the moderate parties later in the day and asked their advice about a successor to Cuno. Largely on the strength of the speech he had delivered to the Reichstag three days earlier, Stresemann was the unanimous choice of the moderate parties, including the SPD. Ebert promptly accepted the recommendation of the parties and on the evening of the 12th he commissioned Stresemann with the task of forming a cabinet. Working late into the night and throughout the next day, the latter hurriedly conducted the inter-party negotiations necessary to put together a new government. Then, at 7:30 on the evening of August 13th, less than twenty-

[80] Stresemann, *Vermächtnis*, I, 76, diary entry for 9.8.1923.
[81] *Nachlass*, 3159/7394/171264f., memorandum on the meeting of the Reichstag delegation, 10.8.1923.

four hours after he had first been summoned by the President, he announced that he had succeeded in forming the Republic's first Great Coalition cabinet and was officially appointed Chancellor by Ebert.[82]

✧

The years between the Kapp Putsch and Stresemann's assumption of the chancellorship in August 1923, are crucial for an understanding of his career. It was during this period that his views underwent the change that determined the course of his subsequent political activity. In early 1920, as the Putsch clearly revealed, he was quite willing to accept an illegal overthrow of the Republic, whereas three and a half years later he was prepared to step in and actively defend it. This alteration in his position was not the result of a sudden conversion, or "Damascus," as some writers have argued, though with widely differing theories as to when and why this supposedly occurred.[83] Nor can it be dismissed as simply the result of an opportunistic acceptance of the new circumstances, as has lately been suggested.[84] It was, instead, the product of a genuine, though gradual, revision of his attitude toward the new system that eventually brought him to the conclusion that it was the best political solution available under the circumstances.

Because of the subjective aspects of this process of revision, it can probably never be charted precisely. It is possible, however, to isolate three important phases. The first of these resulted from Stresemann's discovery at the time of the Fehrenbach cabinet that the Republic need not be revolutionary and could be used just as effectively by the defenders of the *status quo*

[82] See his memoranda on these events, *Vermächtnis*, I, 79 and 88. Also, "Regierungswechsel Cuno-Stresemann," article in DVP, *Archiv der Deutschen Volkspartei*, 15.8.1923.

[83] See Görlitz, *Stresemann*, p. 117; Olden, *Stresemann*, pp. 151ff.; Antonina Vallentin, *Stresemann, Vom Werden Einer Staatsidee* (Leipzig, 1930), pp. 40ff.

[84] A. Thimme, *Stresemann*, pp. 40ff.

as by reformers. From his standpoint, this thoroughly vindicated his earlier decision to take the DVP into the government and led him to hope that it would be possible for Germany to have a period of moderate government and economic recovery within the framework of the new system. In addition, it convinced him that the Kapp Putsch had been an unfortunate setback in the process of recovery. In this way the first phase set the stage for the second, which came with the assassinations of Erzberger and Rathenau. Fearing that these rightist excesses would, like the Putsch, set off shifts to the left, he decided that the non-committal attitude he and his party had previously adopted toward the Republic was no longer sufficient. At the time of Erzberger's death, Stresemann agreed to recognize the constitution as the legitimate basis for government and promised once again to defend it against illegal attacks, though with more conviction than at the time of his earlier pledge. Then, after Rathenau's murder, he made a further concession and announced that the DVP would put aside the issue of a restoration of the monarchy until after the country's recovery was complete. During the final phase of the revision of his attitude, which began in late 1922 at the time of the formation of the Cuno cabinet, he came to the important conclusion that the crisis of the new system was also the crisis of constitutional parliamentary government. If it fell, he realized, the result could only be a dictatorship of the right or the left. He therefore decided that it was necessary to put all lingering doubts aside and take an active part in the defense of the Republic.

With Stresemann's acceptance of the new system, that period of his career came to an end which Erich Koch-Weser of the Democratic Party was aptly to label his *Sturm- und Drang-zeit*.[85] There can be little doubt that he was glad to leave this period of his life behind him. It had been a time of uncertainty and groping, during most of which he had been repeatedly cast in the uncongenial role of negative and defensive opposition. It

[85] *Koch-Weser Papers*, Vol. 36, p. 111, diary for 4.4.1927.

had also been a time of danger; at the time of the Putsch, he had come very close to leaving the path of legality and had so imperiled his own future and that of his party that he had felt compelled to resort to the unsavory technique of obscuring the facts of the case. The course he had followed since the formation of the Fehrenbach cabinet, on the other hand, had made him the respected leader of a responsible party, with a voice in the affairs of state and influence over the course of events. But in spite of the undeniable advantages which this change of course brought him, and the opportunities it opened to him, it would be a mistake to attribute the change solely to personal ambition. The decisive factor was his hard-won realization that cooperation within the new system offered the only means of achieving those political ends which he regarded as the most desirable for Germany: the preservation of as much of the old social and economic order as was possible under the new circumstances, the recovery of economic prosperity, and the restoration of national power and prestige.

This realization had come slowly in his case, and, as a result, his accommodation to the Weimar system is more difficult to chart than that of the scores of adherents of the Empire who had quickly made their peace with the Republic after the revolution, in many cases overnight. But this made his acceptance of the new order no less genuine than theirs. Indeed, it might in a sense be regarded as more genuine for having been more laboriously won. Strictly speaking, his acceptance was not without reservation, for even as he assumed the chancellorship he remained a monarchist. His hopes for a restoration, however, had been moved far into the indefinite future and were no longer a serious factor in his thinking. He had become, in short, what his venerable colleague in the DVP, Professor Wilhelm Kahl, later referred to as a *Vernunftrepublikaner*, a republican in mind though not in heart.[86]

[86] *Vermächtnis*, I, 327.

To most of his contemporaries, as well as to most historians who have dealt with it, Stresemann's progress from opponent to defender of the Weimar Republic was to remain something of a mystery. The essential point, however, was immediately obvious to the perceptive editor of the *Berliner Tageblatt*, Theodor Wolff, who had played a leading role in driving him out of the Democratic Party five years earlier. In giving his paper's endorsement to Stresemann's candidacy for the chancellorship on August 13, Wolff wrote: "Only a few German politicians, and still fewer of those Germans who dabble in politics, have learned as much from the events of the past as he has."

IV. CHANCELLOR OF THE
REPUBLIC, 1923

ON THE AFTERNOON OF August 14, 1923, Stresemann mounted the podium of the Reichstag for the
first time as Chancellor of the Republic. After briefly
paying tribute to his predecessor, he presented his
Great Coalition cabinet. Of the new ministers, four were drawn
from the SPD, three from the Center, and two each from the
DDP and DVP. He named no one to take over the Foreign
Ministry, announcing that he would administer that portfolio
himself until a suitable appointment could be made.

Dispensing with the usual governmental program, he followed
the presentation of the new cabinet with a short, forceful speech
in which he emphasized the critical state of affairs. "Programs
will not get us far," he declared, "unless measures for recovery
are taken as rapidly as possible." As the first steps in that direction, he promised energetic efforts toward an improvement of the
economic situation and a resolution of the Ruhr impasse. But
lest the French assume that the change of cabinets was a sign
of weakness, he made it clear that he intended to continue Cuno's
policy of passive resistance. In an obvious attempt to dispel
any doubts about his own loyalty to the Republic he alluded to
the recent talk of a dictatorship and warned: "Whoever believes
that present conditions give him the right to band together with
political cohorts and undertake assaults upon the state and its
constitution will, wherever he may stand, come into conflict
with the unyielding will of the state to oppose this violence with
all its strength." He then closed with an appeal for unity and a
reaffirmation of his faith in the country: "The only people who
are lost are those who give themselves up. We have the right to
believe in Germany's future and we have the duty to safeguard
it."[1]

[1] *Verhandlungen* (Reichstag), CCCLXI, 11839ff.

114

Late on the afternoon of the 14th the new cabinet passed its first test when the Reichstag adopted a motion of confidence by a vote of 239 to 76. This victory was somewhat marred by the fact that 19 DVP deputies and 53 of the 171 members of the SPD delegation absented themselves from the balloting. The dissident Social Democrats were for the most part former Independents who had been opposed from the start to the decision of the majority to work with the DVP. The bolt of the DVP deputies, on the other hand, was an unexpected development. On the previous day only two members of the delegation's right wing, Reinhold Quaatz and Albert Vögler, had opposed Stresemann's plans for a Great Coalition. But at that time the composition of the new cabinet was still uncertain. When the rest of the right wing discovered at the Reichstag on the 14th that the SPD was to control four ministries, including the important Ministry of Finance, there was a hurried, and for the new Chancellor embarrassing, exodus from the Reichstag chamber.[2]

The call to the chancellorship was for Stresemann the achievement of a goal of more than two years' standing and he welcomed the chance to take over the reins of government. He confided to his son Wolfgang that he expected it would be "fun" to deal with the difficulties of his new office and told Lord D'Abernon, "Bismarck said: 'If you have to jump a ditch you must fling your heart over first.' Well, I have flung my heart over, and I trust that both the horse and rider will also get to the other side safely."[3] But in spite of this optimism, he was well aware of the seriousness of the situation and was convinced that his cabinet would be Germany's last constitutional government if it failed to solve the problems facing the country.[4]

As he recognized, his cabinet's survival depended upon the

[2] *Nachlass*, 3111/7124/147063, memorandum, "Betrifft: Geheimrat Dr. Quaatz."

[3] The remark to his son is quoted from a 1953 speech by the latter in A. Thimme, "Gustav Stresemann, Legende und Wirklichkeit," p. 310. For the remark to D'Abernon, see his *An Ambassador*, II, 237.

[4] *Vermächtnis*, I, 111, memorandum of 7.9.1923. Also, Gessler, *Reichswehrpolitik*, p. 250.

115

success of the first real attempt at collaboration between the SPD and the DVP. He thus made every effort to avoid any friction within the government that might strengthen the hands of the groups in both parties that opposed the Great Coalition. As the DVP's other representative in the cabinet he chose Hans von Raumer, a spokesman of the electrical industry who enjoyed the confidence of the SPD because of his part in arranging the 1918 agreement which had formed the basis for relations between industry and the trade unions since the revolution.[5] Also, in conducting the cabinet meetings, Stresemann was careful to be as nonpartisan as possible and occasionally sided with the SPD ministers against his own party colleague. When impasses developed, he avoided open clashes by urging that the differences be settled in private conversations, a technique that almost invariably produced a solution. As a result of his adroit leadership, the Great Coalition cabinet was a smoothly functioning reality within a few days of its formation and it seemed that the speculation about the bankruptcy of the Weimar system had been premature.[6]

The members of the new cabinet quickly came to the conclusion that their most urgent problem was the eight-month-old Ruhr stalemate. Until it had been resolved, they were agreed that it would be impossible to combat the runaway inflation, since the hundreds of thousands of idle workers in the Ruhr could be supported only by printing unbacked paper currency. There was general agreement within the cabinet that acceptance of French Premier Raymond Poincaré's demand for an unconditional termination of passive resistance would be a severe, and perhaps fatal, blow to the prestige of the new government. But it was also agreed that Germany's capacity to resist was limited. From the outset, Stresemann was convinced that resistance

---

[5] *Vermächtnis*, I, 144.

[6] See the minutes of the cabinet meetings in Germany, Alte Reichskanzlei, *Kabinett-Protokolle*, microfilm, National Archives of the United States (hereafter cited as AR, *Kabinett*), reels 1748 and 1749.

could be continued only until the beginning of cold weather, when the shortage of coal would be felt throughout the country.[7] With the approval of the cabinet he therefore launched a rapid-fire campaign aimed at wringing at least a few concessions from the French so that the end of resistance would not come as a complete German surrender. In conversations with the French Ambassador, Pierre de Margerie, and in public declarations, Stresemann indicated that Germany was ready to end its resistance, give the Allies a mortgage on part of its economy, and guarantee the western boundaries established at Versailles. In return he asked only that the French restore normal economic conditions in the Ruhr immediately and promise an eventual evacuation of their troops.

These proposals drew no response from the stubborn Poincaré, who realized that time was on his side and remained firm in his refusal to negotiate until all resistance was at an end. Stresemann's last hope was England. He knew that many British officials, including the Foreign Secretary, Lord Curzon, had disapproved of the French-Belgian venture from the beginning. During late August and early September, he remained hopeful that London might bring pressure upon Poincaré to end the stalemate. This hope vanished abruptly on September 19, when the British Prime Minister, Stanley Baldwin, ended the speculation about England's attitude by publicly endorsing Poincaré's position. On the following day Stresemann asked for and received the cabinet's permission to begin laying plans for the end of passive resistance.[8]

In an effort to lessen the impact of the decision to end resistance, he carefully prepared the way for the official announcement. In his public statements he began to minimize the significance of the resistance struggle and to emphasize the fact that Germany would never surrender its sovereign title to the Ruhr. To prepare the occupied areas for the announcement, he dis-

---

[7] AR, *Kabinett*, reel 1748/frames 756435ff., meeting of 23.8.1923.

[8] *Vermächtnis*, I, 128. Also, AR, *Kabinett*, 1748/756765ff., meeting of 20.9.1923.

patched Wilhelm Sollmann, the Social Democratic Minister of the Interior, to explain the government's intentions to the local officials and community leaders. Then, on September 24 and 25 he summoned to Berlin the Minister-Presidents of the federal *Länder*, representatives of the occupied zone, as well as spokesmen of various business and professional groups. After explaining the government's position, he succeeded in securing their endorsement of the impending step. Finally, on the 26th, he and the rest of the cabinet joined with President Ebert in announcing the termination of resistance.[9]

Largely because of the thoroughness with which Stresemann had prepared the way, the announcement of the end of passive resistance was received calmly throughout Germany despite the vociferous protests of various rightist groups, including the DNVP. Only in Bavaria, where the *Land* government was controlled by the conservative Bavarian People's Party, were there serious reverberations. The Munich authorities immediately indicated their disapproval of the national cabinet's decision by declaring a state of emergency and appointing Gustav von Kahr, a leader of the right wing of the BVP, as General Commissar, with virtually dictatorial powers.

Confronted with this challenge from the second largest of the federal *Länder*, Stresemann and his ministers decided to answer the Bavarians with a national state of emergency that would place extraordinary powers in the hands of Minister of the Army Otto Gessler. President Ebert readily agreed to this plan and on the 26th he issued an emergency decree under Article 48 of the constitution. The cabinet then contended that a national state of emergency took precedence over that of a *Land*. The Bavarians refused to concede this point, however, and continued to insist that Kahr was legally the supreme authority within their territory. When neither side would retreat, an acrimonious dispute developed between Munich and Berlin.[10]

[9] *Vermächtnis*, I, 133ff.
[10] *Ibid.*, 131f.

Stresemann's acceptance of responsibility for the termination of passive resistance was one of his greatest services to the Republic. There can be little doubt that if the same step had been taken by a Chancellor identified with the left, the consequences would have been more serious. As it was, the decision was roundly attacked in conservative and nationalistic circles. But Stresemann's close identification with the cause of German nationalism and his record of opposition to the demands of the Allies made it difficult to represent the government's action as simply another humiliation imposed upon the country by "internationalist" and "cosmopolitan" leftists. As a result, the attacks of the rightists found little public support.

For Stresemann, the decision to give in to the pressure of the French involved an important political sacrifice. Since the revolution, one of his cardinal principles had been to hold the DVP aloof from the agreements forced upon Germany by the Allies, even though he was often convinced that there was no way to avoid accepting them. His aim had been to keep the DVP free from any taint of "fulfillment" and so enable it to compete successfully with the DNVP for the votes of the large nationalistic sector of the German electorate, which was defiantly opposed to the acceptance of any of the victors' demands. In September 1923, he could have resigned when it became clear that further resistance was futile. But rather than risk a serious government crisis he took the burden of ending the struggle upon himself, even though he realized it would hurt the DVP in the next elections. Tested by that most accurate gauge of a politician's worth, responsibility, he had shown himself capable of putting the good of the country above partisan considerations and had displayed what he himself later referred to as "the courage to be unpopular."[11]

After ending the resistance to the French, Stresemann expected that it would at last be possible to negotiate a settlement of the Ruhr and reparations questions. But he had failed to

[11] *Ibid.*, 208.

119

take into consideration the resourcefulness of Poincaré, who refused to deal with the Berlin government and sought to arrive at separate reparations agreements with the industrialists of the occupied areas. At first, Stresemann tried to keep the industrialists from entering into negotiations with the French. But since the government could not continue to subsidize the chronic unemployment of the Ruhr indefinitely, he was forced to allow them to begin talks with Paris with regard to at least a temporary *modus vivendi.*[12] After many delays these talks finally produced the so-called MICUM (*Mission Interalliée de Contrôle des Usines et Mines*) Treaty between the Ruhr industrialists and the French-Belgian occupation authorities. This agreement, which was signed on November 23, provided for a temporary regulation of the reparations question until April 15, 1924.

With a final settlement of the dispute with France apparently out of the question for the time being, the cabinet turned to domestic problems. There was full agreement that sweeping measures were urgently needed to deal with the deteriorating economic situation. But in view of the known differences between the SPD and the DVP in economic matters, it was also agreed that it would be a mistake to attempt to put the government's program through the Reichstag, which had reconvened on September 27, after a six-week summer recess. At the suggestion of the Social Democratic Minister of Finance, Rudolf Hilferding, the cabinet therefore decided to ask the chamber to pass a general enabling act and then adjourn, leaving the cabinet to govern by decree. The members of the cabinet then quickly drew up an enabling bill and submitted it to the Reichstag delegations of the coalition parties.[13] It proved acceptable to all except the Social Democrats, who announced on October 2 that they would oppose the bill unless it was rewritten to deny the cabinet the authority to suspend the eight-hour workday law.

[12] AR, *Kabinett,* 1748/756895ff., meeting of 1.10.1923. Also, *Vermächtnis,* I, 158ff.

[13] AR, *Kabinett,* 1748/756875ff., meeting of 30.9.1923.

The SPD ministers had been willing to accept a suspension of the workday measure, at least for essential industries, but a majority of the party's deputies regarded the law, which had been adopted in November 1918, as one of the major social achievements of the revolution. They were thus unwilling to see it even partially suspended.[14] The prevailing view within the DVP, on the other hand, was that the limitation on the workday had been a severe handicap to Germany's economic recovery. Stresemann shared this view, regarding the measure as "the most foolish" of the revolutionary laws.[15] He therefore offered no opposition when the party's Reichstag delegation indicated on the afternoon of the 2nd that it would insist that the cabinet be empowered to suspend the workday law. With the fate of the government in the balance, most of the next day, October 3, was devoted to various attempts at a compromise between the DVP and the SPD. Both delegations held firm, however. Late on the evening of the 3rd Stresemann therefore announced that since it had proved impossible to agree on the text of an enabling act, he had no alternative except to dissolve the cabinet.[16]

When he reported the collapse of his cabinet to President Ebert on the night of October 3, Stresemann was again commissioned with the task of forming a new government. With the SPD apparently determined to refuse any concessions on the workday issue, he decided not to try to revive the old cabinet. The only other possibility of a majority government lay to the right, in a coalition with the DNVP. This was also unacceptable to him, since he felt that such a sharp shift to the right would be interpreted as a repudiation on his part of the Great Coalition idea. With the possibility of a majority cabinet thus ruled out, he decided to attempt to set up a minority government by filling the posts of the former Social Democratic members of the

[14] *Ibid.*, 756951ff., meeting of 2.10.1923.

[15] *Nachlass*, 3159/7396/171803, Stresemann to the DVP Party Congress, 30.3.1924. Also, *Vermächtnis*, I, 141, memorandum of 3.10.1923.

[16] AR, *Kabinett*, 1749/757003ff., third meeting of 3.10.1923.

cabinet with expert ministers who were aligned with, but not active in, the DNVP. In that way he hoped to gain the backing of the rightist party without actually bringing it into the government.[17]

While he was ready to govern with a minority cabinet, Stresemann was not willing to consider a departure from the Republic's constitutional framework. This course was proposed to him by Baron Werner von Rheinbaben, a member of the DVP delegation whom he had chosen as his State Secretary in the Reich Chancellery. Rheinbaben insisted that the only effective way to deal with the situation was to dissolve the Reichstag and govern Germany by decree, with the President's cooperation if possible or without it if necessary. When the crisis had been ended, he argued, the Reichstag could then be reconvened to ratify the government's actions with an indemnity act. Through Colonel Kurt von Schleicher, the ubiquitous political representative of the Army, Rheinbaben was in contact with the Chief of the Army Command, General Hans von Seeckt, and he indicated that the Army could be counted upon to support a decisive attempt to deal with Germany's problems. Much to his disappointment, however, the Chancellor would have nothing to do with his plans, explaining that he was too *parlamentarisch* to undertake any such venture. Thereafter, Stresemann's attitude toward his subordinate cooled noticeably and in mid-October he forced Rheinbaben to resign his official post.[18]

Stresemann met with little success in his attempt to set up a minority cabinet. His offers of ministerial posts were rejected by a number of the persons he had hoped to bring into the cabinet, the most prominent of whom was Otto Wiedfeldt, a former director of the Krupp concern who was currently Ambassador to Washington. In addition, the DNVP dealt a severe blow

[17] *Vermächtnis*, I, 327f., his article for the *Kölnische Zeitung*, 29.4. 1924.
[18] Werner Freiherr von Rheinbaben, *Viermal Deutschland, 1895-1954* (Berlin, 1954), pp. 188ff. Also, *Seeckt Papers*, Institut für Zeitgeschichte, Munich, microfilm reel 15, Stück 72, letter from Rheinbaben, 16.10.1923.

to his plans by announcing on October 4 that it would refuse to back any cabinet which he headed.[19] From the outset he had not been enthusiastic about the prospect of a minority government and in the face of these disappointing developments he responded readily when the two leaders of the DDP, Erich Koch-Weser and Carl Petersen, offered on the 5th to attempt to arrange a compromise that would make it possible to revive the Great Coalition.[20]

Negotiations were launched at once, and after long hours of bargaining, the spokesmen of the four parties reached an agreement in the early morning hours of October 6. The non-socialist parties agreed to exclude the authority to regulate the length of the workday from the enabling act. In return the SPD agreed to allow the passage of regular legislation that would temporarily suspend the eight-hour day while confirming it as the normal standard.[21] On the basis of this compromise, Stresemann presented to the Reichstag a slightly altered version of his Great Coalition cabinet on the afternoon of October 6. Two days later the chamber granted him a firm vote of confidence and on October 13 the coalition pushed the enabling act through by the necessary two-thirds margin.

The second Stresemann cabinet was faced with a number of difficult problems. In the Rhineland there was an outbreak of French-encouraged separatist agitation aimed at the creation of an independent buffer state. The importance of this development, however, was greatly diminished when the majority of the Rhenish population showed no interest in the separatist movement. Much more serious was the dispute between the national government and the Bavarian authorities which had begun in September and which worsened sharply in mid-October. At that time the Munich government blocked the efforts of Army Minister Gessler to fire the chief of the Bavarian branch of the

---

[19] *Vermächtnis*, I, 145.
[20] Rheinbaben, *Viermal*, p. 191.
[21] *Vermächtnis*, I, 145f., editor's note.

Army, General Otto von Lossow, for refusing to ban the *Völkischer Beobachter,* the newspaper of the Nazi movement, which, along with several other radical, right-wing groups, was backing the Bavarian government. The Munich officials then sharpened the dispute still further by extracting a special oath of allegiance from the Bavarian units of the Army, an act that represented a direct challenge to the authority of the Berlin government. In addition, the new General Commissar, Kahr, roundly attacked the Great Coalition cabinet, charging that it was subservient to the Marxist left.

In early October the cabinet was presented with still another problem when the Social Democrats formed coalition *Länder* governments with the Communists in Saxony and Thuringia. These governments, both headed by Social Democrats, adopted a very lenient policy toward leftist agitation. As a result, Communist activities were greatly stepped up in both regions. In Stresemann's opinion, the developments in Saxony and Thuringia were far more disturbing than the dispute with Munich. He regarded the Communists as the hirelings of a foreign power and believed, as was in fact the case, that their moves in the two *Länder* were aimed at preparing the way for a Bolshevik revolution in Germany. In order to frustrate their designs he was quite willing to make use of the full power of the state at the slightest provocation.[22]

With the exception of such groups as the Nazis, on the other hand, he regarded the Bavarians as loyal, if misguided, Germans. To his way of thinking this excused much, for he was convinced that "it is the duty of the national government to pursue the path of conciliation to the last as long as it is a case of Germans on the one side and Germans on the other."[23] Although

[22] Stresemann-Bernhard, "Das Kabinett Stresemann, IV," *Deutsche Stimmen,* 5.2.1924. (One of a series of articles he wrote in collaboration with his private secretary, Henry Bernhard, and published under the latter's name; see Bernhard's explanation, *Vermächtnis,* I, 85.)

[23] *Vermächtnis,* I, 209, speech in Halle, 11.11.1923. Also, Stresemann-Bernhard, "Das Kabinett Stresemann, IV," *Deutsche Stimmen,* 5.2.1924.

the Bavarians were obviously violating the constitution, he felt that the seriousness of their offense was greatly reduced by the fact that their aim was apparently the recovery of the federal prerogatives they had enjoyed under the imperial constitution, and not the destruction of the Republic.[24] In any case, he ruled out the possibility of police action against Munich on practical grounds. He genuinely doubted, first of all, that the Army would obey an order to fire on the Bavarian troops and the rightist organizations aligned with them. But even if the troops should prove loyal, he feared that the Bavarians were strong enough either to secede or to set off a civil war that would greatly weaken Germany.[25]

In contrast to Stresemann's views, Minister of the Army Gessler and the Social Democratic members of the cabinet felt the government should immediately challenge the defiant Bavarians. They called upon the cabinet to hale the Munich authorities into the Republic's supreme court and to prepare to send in troops if they refused to yield. Determined to avoid an open break with Munich, Stresemann strongly opposed these proposals. As a substitute line of action, he suggested that the cabinet seek a settlement of the affair through the mediation of the Reichsrat, which consisted of representatives of the various *Länder* governments. In a long and stormy session on October 22 he won the support of the majority of the cabinet for this plan, and the proponents of a harder line also agreed to go along with it. When the Reichsrat took up the problem on the 24th, however, it was unable to close the gap between Munich and Berlin.[26]

[24] *Vermächtnis*, I, 229f., speech to DVP Central Committee, 18.11. 1923.
[25] See his letter to the Crown Prince, 23.7.1923, *Nachlass*, 3099/7119/ 146066ff. Also, Stresemann-Bernhard, "Das Kabinett Stresemann, IV," *Deutsche Stimmen*, 5.2.1924. Also, his remarks to the cabinet, 2.11.1923, AR, *Kabinett*, 1749/757581.
[26] AR, *Kabinett*, 1749/757283ff., meeting of 22.10.1923. Also, *ibid.*, 757434ff., meeting of 26.10.1923.

The failure of the attempt to arrange a settlement with Bavaria was quickly overshadowed by developments that shifted attention to the threat from the left. On October 23 and 24 the Communists carried out an abortive insurrection in Hamburg, and in the following days, there were insistent rumors that a similar uprising was being planned in Saxony. In view of this turn of events, Stresemann decided it would be necessary to depose the new Saxon government, which had stubbornly refused to take measures against armed red bands that had clashed with Army units on a number of occasions since the SPD-Communist coalition had taken office. He regarded such a move as the potential key to the national government's predicament and hoped it would not only snuff out the threat of a Communist revolution but also facilitate a settlement with Munich. An important factor in the unyielding attitude of the Bavarian authorities was, in his opinion, their apparently genuine belief that his cabinet was operating under Marxist pressure. Since he knew he could rely upon the Army to deal summarily with the Communists, he was hopeful that decisive action in Saxony would force the Bavarians to revise their opinion of his government and adopt a more conciliatory attitude. On the other hand, if the cabinet did not act, he feared that the Bavarians might take matters into their own hands and launch an invasion of Saxony and Thuringia, thus plunging the country into a civil war.[27]

Convinced that the situation required swift action, Stresemann joined with Gessler on October 27 in asking the cabinet to authorize the deposition of the Saxon government. This request was immediately approved by all the members of the cabinet except the Social Democrats. They, too, agreed that something had to be done, even though only a few days earlier, before the Hamburg insurrection, they had steadfastly maintained that there was no danger of a Communist uprising. They were extremely re-

[27] Stresemann-Bernhard, "Das Kabinett Stresemann, IV," *Deutsche Stimmen*, 5.2.1924. Also, AR, *Kabinett*, 1749/757445 and 757450, meeting of 27.10.1923.

luctant, however, to sanction the removal of a legally constituted *Land* government, and especially one headed by a member of their own party. In the face of the united opposition of the rest of the cabinet they finally agreed by way of compromise that the Chancellor should urge the Saxon government to resign voluntarily and indicate that it would be removed from office if it refused to do so. The cabinet then approved the text of a message to Erich Zeigner, the Social Democratic Minister-President of Saxony, in which he was instructed to give his answer before the end of the next day, October 28.[28]

When Zeigner had failed to reply satisfactorily by the morning of the 29th, Stresemann decided to proceed with the removal of the Saxon cabinet. But he apparently feared that the Social Democrats would refuse at the last minute to go through with the actual deposition and so avoided informing the cabinet of his decision until the afternoon of the 29th. By that time he was able to confront his ministers with a virtual *fait accompli*. At his request, President Ebert was preparing an emergency dissolution decree under the almost unlimited powers given him by Article 48 of the Weimar constitution. In addition, his party colleague Rudolf Heinze, whom he had appointed Reich Commissar in charge of carrying out the decree, was already on his way to Dresden, where the Saxon units of the Army had been placed at his disposal.

When Stresemann revealed this situation to the cabinet, the Social Democratic ministers protested with some justification that he had exceeded his authority in taking such steps without consulting the cabinet. They were alarmed at the idea of using the Army against the Saxon authorities and called for an attempt at a settlement that would not involve force. Stresemann defended his actions by contending that he had done nothing that was not a necessary consequence of the course of action agreed upon on the 27th by the entire cabinet, including the SPD ministers. This argument failed to move the Socialists, but

[28] AR, *Kabinett,* 1749/757450f., meeting of 27.10.1923.

it was endorsed by all of the non-socialist ministers, who were unwilling to see the whole elaborate operation interrupted by the last-minute misgivings of the SPD. Stresemann was therefore able to issue the final deposition order in the name of the majority of the cabinet. It was carried out later on the afternoon of the 29th by Heinze, who seized the undefended *Land* capital with a superfluous display of military pomp. Two days later, on October 31, relatively normal conditions were restored in Saxony when a new cabinet consisting solely of Social Democrats was approved by the Landtag.[29]

The Social Democrats objected strenuously to the cabinet's action in forcing the Zeigner government out of office. Realizing, however, that it would be futile to try to reverse the action, the SPD Reichstag delegation demanded that the government at least take similar measures against the still defiant Bavarian government. Stresemann, determined to avoid a clash with the Munich officials, strongly opposed such a course. It would only lead, he argued, to a civil war and a possible partition of the country. His viewpoint was endorsed by the other non-socialist ministers, including Gessler, whose previous confidence about the loyalty of the Army in the event of a struggle with Bavaria had been shattered by the discovery that Field Marshal von Hindenburg had let it be known that he sympathized with the Bavarians.[30] Gessler not only urged that the Social Democrats' demands be rejected but insisted that their departure from the government would be a desirable development. Only such a break with the left on the part of the cabinet, he argued, could keep the Bavarians from opening military actions against Thuringia during the coming week.[31]

[29] AR, *Kabinett*, 1749/757503ff., meeting of 29.10.1923. Also, *Vermächtnis*, I, 187ff.

[30] At a meeting of the non-socialist ministers on 2.11.1923, Gessler reported that he had tried to get the support of *ein grosser Mann in Hannover*, but that he stood on the side of the Bavarians. See AR, *Kabinett*, 1749/757585.

[31] *Ibid.*

Stresemann was far less pleased than Gessler at the prospect of an SPD exit from the cabinet. The Great Coalition was a goal he had been working toward since 1921 and he had become firmly convinced that it offered the best means of stabilizing Germany's political life. He was thus extremely reluctant to see it sacrificed. Nevertheless, he was ready to sacrifice it if the SPD stood in the way of a peaceful settlement with Bavaria, which he regarded as the paramount necessity of the moment. He conceded Gessler's point that it would be easier to reach an agreement with Munich if the Social Democrats were not in the government, but he was unwilling to see them simply driven out, realizing that such an action would make a revival of the Great Coalition difficult. He therefore insisted that the SPD be given a chance to back down on its demand regarding Bavaria.[32] When the cabinet took up the matter on the afternoon of November 2, however, the Social Democratic ministers held firm. After the rest of the cabinet refused to yield, they resigned, dissolving the Great Coalition for the second time.[33]

The withdrawal of the Social Democrats placed Stresemann in a difficult position. His cabinet was not only left without a parliamentary majority but also lost the exceptional powers provided for by the enabling act of October 13, which had been designed to lapse when the composition of the government changed. An immediate effect of this drastic reduction in the strength of the cabinet was a renewed outbreak of speculation about a dictatorship. It was soon no secret that a number of influential persons and groups associated with the right, including the DVP industrialist Hugo Stinnes and the leaders of the DNVP, were favorably disposed to a solution of that sort. There seemed, in fact, to be a well-developed plan, calling for the establishment of a three-man *Direktorium*, the leading candidates being Kahr, the Bavarian General Commissar, Friedrich Minoux, a banker

[32] *Ibid.*, 757586. Also, 757581, remarks to meeting of 2.11.1923, 1 P.M.
[33] *Ibid.*, 757575ff., meeting of 2.11.1923, 1 P.M.

closely connected with the Stinnes enterprises, and Ambassador Wiedfeldt, formerly an official of the Krupp concern.[34]

This speculation was particularly ominous in view of the fact that the Republic's parliamentary machinery was in grave danger of paralysis. With both the SPD and DNVP in opposition, the remaining rump cabinet was apparently destined to fall when the Reichstag reconvened from the recess it had imposed upon itself following the passage of the enabling act. Since a new government would be impossible without the backing or toleration of either the SPD or the DNVP, it seemed quite possible that the result would be a stalemate that might force the President to accept some sort of dictatorial solution, especially since the tense Bavarian situation appeared to rule out any possibility of new elections. Apparently with this in mind, Ebert authorized the Chief of the Army Command, Seeckt, to sound out Ambassador Wiedfeldt confidentially about the possibility of heading a government.[35] In the meantime, without mentioning the overture to Wiedfeldt, he asked Stresemann to try to hold his faltering cabinet together.

Stresemann at once accepted this commission. As a first step he decided to fill the vacant posts in the cabinet with conservative independents and, if possible, at least one representative of the Bavarian People's Party, a move aimed at facilitating a settlement of the dispute with Munich. This step, however, would not alter the basic problem arising from the government's lack of a parliamentary majority. He therefore planned, with Ebert's approval, to stave off a crisis as long as possible by indefinitely prolonging the Reichstag recess, which only the President or a petition of one-third of the chamber could bring to an end.[36]

---

[34] AR, *Kabinett*, 1749/757564f. and 757600ff., Stresemann's reports on 1. and 5.11.1923. For a rather exaggerated account of these developments, see G.W.F. Hallgarten, *Hitler, Reichswehr und Industrie* (Frankfurt/Main, 1955), pp. 29ff.

[35] *Seeckt Papers*, reel 15, Stück 73, letter to Wiedfeldt, 4.11.1923. Nothing came of this overture. Wiedfeldt delayed his answer until 24.11.1923 and then rejected the idea: *ibid.*

[36] AR, *Kabinett*, 1749/757600ff., meeting of 5.11.1923.

Stresemann secured the rump cabinet's approval for his plans on November 5, but he quickly encountered strong opposition from within his own party. Most of the members of the DVP Reichstag delegation had neither shared nor understood the change of outlook he had undergone since 1920. As Stresemann had moved closer to the Republic and to the republican parties, an increasing number of disappointed deputies had gravitated to the oppositional right wing while he himself had become identified with the party's smaller left wing. By the time he took office as Chancellor, as the vote of confidence for the first Great Coalition cabinet revealed, nearly one-third of the Reichstag delegation was aligned with the right wing. During the first months of his chancellorship, the strength of the opposition group increased steadily. A contributing factor in this development was the election of Ernst Scholz to the position of delegation chairman—a post Stresemann was forced to give up in order to enter the government. Scholz had first gained prominence in the party when the industrialists recommended him for the post of Minister of Economics in 1920. He was a coldly arrogant, yet colorless figure who represented no direct threat to Stresemann's position as party leader. But whereas Scholz had previously been considered a member of the neutral middle group, he soon showed that he sympathized with the right wing on many points. With the delegation meetings under his direction, and with Stresemann usually absent because of his governmental duties, the opposition was therefore able to obtain a much better hearing for its point of view than had previously been the case.

Another cause of the growing strength of the DVP opposition group during Stresemann's chancellorship was the decision to end passive resistance. Many of the party's deputies were extremely reluctant to agree to such a capitulation to French pressure, especially when it had to be carried out by a DVP Chancellor. In the end, Stresemann succeeded in gaining the support of a majority of the deputies, but the right wing was able to capitalize on the dissatisfaction within the delegation to strengthen its position.[37] Much the same thing happened in the wake of the deposition of the Saxon government. Many of the DVP deputies had expected that the removal of Zeigner's cabinet would lead to a new government in which the DVP delegation in the Saxon Landtag would play an important role. There was thus much disappointment when Stresemann, hoping to soften the blow for the Social Democrats, used his influence to prevent such a swing to the right, with the result that the new Saxon cabinet was drawn solely from the ranks of the SPD.[38]

Even more important than these developments was the growing dissatisfaction of the spokesmen of agriculture and heavy industry in the DVP with the economic policies of the Great Coalition cabinet. The agricultural group in the Reichstag delegation was for the most part aligned with the conservative *Landbund*, which was also strongly represented in the DNVP. Its president, Karl Hepp, was a member of the DVP delegation and he and other *Landbund* spokesmen objected strenuously to the government's attempts to regulate food prices during the inflation. In addition, they were offended by its rejection of the proposal by the DNVP economist, Karl Helfferich, that the Reich adopt as a new currency a *Roggenmark*, based on the value of rye—an arrangement that would have been highly advantageous to the farming interests.[39]

The opposition of the spokesmen of heavy industry to Stresemann's policies was not new. Since the rejection of their bid for a special voice in the party's affairs in 1920, they had clashed with him on a number of occasions. The most heated of these had come in 1921, when Stresemann successfully resisted their demand that the DVP press for the transfer of the country's railways from the national government to private business.[40] It was

[37] *Nachlass*, 3159/7394/171326ff., delegation meeting of 25.9.1923.
[38] See the minutes of the delegation meeting of 6.11.1923, 4:15 P.M., *Nachlass*, 3159/7394/171442f. Also, Roland Thimme, *Stresemann und die deutsche Volkspartei 1923-1925* (Lübeck & Hamburg, 1961), p. 20.
[39] AR, *Kabinett*, 1748/756838ff., remarks of Stresemann and Raumer, 26.9.1923. Also, *Vermächtnis*, I, 201.
[40] *Deutsche Stimmen*, 18.12.1921, his speech to the Party Congress.

only after the formation of the Great Coalition, however, that relations reached the breaking point. The source of the trouble was the so-called demobilization laws which the revolutionary government had enacted in 1918. These measures, which included the eight-hour workday and a program of unemployment insurance, subjected the economy to numerous, though by no means drastic, controls in order to protect the working man during the transition to peacetime conditions. To the DVP heavy industry group, though, the laws were an unsound and dangerous violation of the principles of free enterprise and one source of the country's slow recovery. Its spokesmen had never ceased to protest against them and with the elevation of their party leader to the chancellorship they concluded that the time had come to restore the less confining economy of the prewar era.[41] To their disappointment and anger, most of their demands were ignored by Stresemann, who was determined not to weaken his government by offending the SPD unnecessarily. They did gain one concession when Stresemann supported them on the eight-hour day, but this was largely offset by the slow progress toward its repeal. Moreover, they were angered anew when his cabinet used its powers under the October enabling act to issue decrees providing for compulsory and binding arbitration of labor-management disputes and for government regulation of industrial cartels.[42]

For the members of the DVP opposition group the basic fallacy of Stresemann's policy lay in his cooperation with the Social Democrats. As long as the SPD was in the government they felt it would be impossible to follow what they regarded as sound economic policies. Therefore, during the first months of Strese-

[41] *Nachlass,* 3159/7394/171304ff., minutes of the delegation, 12.9. 1923; *ibid.,* 171326ff., same of 25.9.1923; *ibid.,* 171432ff., same of 5.11.1923.
[42] *Dingeldey Papers,* Vol. 58, Otto Thiel to Dingeldey, 18.6.1931. Also, Vereinigung der deutschen Arbeitgeberverbände, *Geschäftsbericht 1923 und 1924* (Berlin, 1925), pp. 299ff. Also, Rudolf K. Michels, *Cartels, Combines and Trusts in Post-War Germany* (New York, 1928), pp. 43ff.

mann's chancellorship they repeatedly urged, both in private and in public, that the party withdraw from the Great Coalition.[43] But in spite of the growing strength of the right wing, they were never able to muster enough support to effect such a move. The resignation of the Social Democratic ministers at the beginning of November was thus a welcomed release for them. They objected strongly, however, when Stresemann announced his intention to continue at the head of the remaining minority cabinet. Such a minority government, they were convinced, would eventually be forced to depend on the toleration of the SPD and would therefore have to frame its policies with that party's views in mind. This, they felt, would be essentially the same thing as a Great Coalition. As a substitute solution, they favored the formation of a majority government by adding the DNVP to the remaining DDP–Center–DVP coalition to form a *Bürgerblock*.[44]

Scholz, the new delegation chairman, shared the views of the right wing and on November 5 he called the party's deputies together to discuss the possibility of a coalition with the DNVP. He revealed that with Stresemann's consent he had talked to the Nationalist leaders Oskar Hergt and Count Kuno von Westarp on the previous day. Hergt, he reported, had expressed the view that the DNVP could be brought to serve under Stresemann only in a "supra-parliamentary" cabinet in which the right was heavily represented. In addition, the Nationalist leader had indicated that his party would consent to such an arrangement only if it was agreed from the outset that Stresemann was to serve as Chancellor solely on a temporary basis. As his replacement, Hergt had mentioned Ambassador Wiedfeldt and suggested that Stresemann might be awarded the latter's post in Washington when the change took place. In spite of this discouraging con-

---

[43] *Nachlass*, 3159/7394/171337ff., memorandum of DVP Reichsgeschäftsstelle, 3.10.1923.

[44] *Nachlass*, 3159/7394/171430f., "Illusionen," article by Reinhold Quaatz in *Der Tag*, 4.11.1923, a representative sample of the right wing's views.

versation, Scholz remained confident that the Nationalists could be brought into a parliamentary coalition. He insisted that if Stresemann officially invited the DNVP delegation to join the government it would not refuse. Backed by the support of the right wing, he proposed that the delegation ask the Chancellor to issue such an invitation.

In the midst of the discussion of Scholz's proposal, Stresemann, arriving late, entered the DVP caucus room. He angrily announced that he had no intention of issuing an invitation to the Nationalists and indicated that he considered Hergt's terms unacceptable. He also made it clear that he regarded the Nationalists' goal of a "supra-parliamentary" government as simply a euphemism for dictatorship. Even if it should be possible to bring the DNVP to enter a parliamentary regime, he maintained that it would be impossible to assemble a Reichstag majority for such a cabinet since both the DDP and the Center had indicated that they would refuse to work with the Nationalists. He appealed to the opposition group to leave the formation of the new cabinet to him and warned that he was "fed up with the dog's life" which their "intrigues" had forced upon him. Referring to rumors that armed nationalistic bands in various parts of the north were preparing to make common cause with the Bavarians and rise against the government, he emphasized the gravity of the situation and asked the delegation for its loyal backing. Then, alluding to the flight of the Bauer cabinet at the time of the Kapp Putsch, he made clear his own position: "If the bands should force their way into Berlin—I shall not go to Stuttgart, . . . they will have to shoot me down at the place where I have a right to sit."[45] This explosive outburst appeared to overwhelm the opposition and aside from a stubborn demand by Hugo Stinnes for an extension of the government to the right there was no further resistance from the deputies.

The DVP delegation was not the only quarter from which

[45] The minutes of this meeting are in *Nachlass*, 3159/7394/171432ff., (an abridged version is in *Vermächtnis*, I, 195ff.).

Stresemann's decision to continue with his rump cabinet was challenged. Also on November 5, General von Seeckt called upon President Ebert. Seeckt, who was secretly in favor of a *Direktorium* and hoped to play a prominent role in such a government, tried to prevail upon Ebert to install a rightist cabinet that would be able to come to an understanding with the Bavarians and the nationalistic groups that sympathized with them. When he encountered the President's unyielding opposition on this point, the General suggested that at least Stresemann be replaced. Ebert asked if he would be willing to repeat his request directly to the Chancellor. When he indicated his readiness to do so, the President sent him, along with Gessler, who had also been present, to Stresemann. Upon arriving, Seeckt explained his position with no loss of words: "Herr Chancellor, it is impossible to carry on the struggle under you. You do not have the confidence of the troops." In reply Stresemann asked: "Are you withdrawing the Army's support from me?" But before Seeckt could answer, Gessler interrupted to announce: "Herr Chancellor, only I can do that." When Seeckt remained silent the Army's brief venture into politics was ended.[46] Apparently because of the General's curious lack of determination at the crucial moment of this interview, Stresemann failed to realize that Seeckt had political ambitions and had sought to wrest control of the government from him. He concluded that the General only meant to suggest that another non-party cabinet along the lines of Cuno's might be better able to deal with the situation. Later, he was to inform Lord D'Abernon that he had regarded Seeckt as "quite trustworthy" during his chancellorship.[47]

---

[46] Gessler, *Reichswehrpolitik*, p. 299. He errs in dating the episode on 3.11.1923. At the DVP delegation meeting of 6.11.1923, it is repeatedly referred to as having taken place on the 5th (see below, pp. 137f.). Seeckt's biographer incorrectly has Schleicher relaying this message to Stresemann on the 5th, Friedrich von Rabenau, *Seeckt. Aus Seinem Leben, 1918-1936* (Leipzig, 1940), p. 265.

[47] D'Abernon, *An Ambassador*, III, 56. See also *Nachlass*, 3159/7394/171448f., Stresemann's report to DVP delegation, 6.11.1923. Rabenau states, but without proof, that Stresemann knew of Seeckt's ambitions

At first it seemed that Stresemann's stormy appearance before the delegation on the 5th had brought the opposition into line, but it soon became apparent that his difficulties with the DVP were just beginning. When the delegation reassembled on the morning of the 6th, again in his absence, the right wing took up the attack. Leading the assault were Alfred Gildemeister of Bremen, and Julius Curtius of Baden, two of the most outspoken leaders of the opposition group. They charged that Stresemann was attempting to suppress the will of the party and asked that the delegation bypass him and commission Scholz to negotiate directly with the DNVP delegation. Curtius even went so far as to propose that Stresemann be asked to resign as party chairman. In view of the violence of these attacks, the leaders of the left wing, Siegfried von Kardorff and Albrecht Morath, prevailed upon Scholz to adjourn the meeting until later in the day, when Stresemann had indicated he could appear to defend himself. But when the delegation reconvened on the afternoon of the 6th, the Chancellor had again been delayed and the right wing continued its offensive. Karl Hepp of the *Landbund*, Otto Hugo and Reinhold Quaatz of the Ruhr group, and Carl Piper of Hamburg all joined in the attack, demanding immediate negotiations with the DNVP regardless of Stresemann's attitude.[48]

With the opposition offensive rapidly approaching the stage of open revolt, two members of the right wing, Baron Kurt von Lersner and Oskar Maretzky, decided the time had come to resort to heavy weapons. They therefore informed the delegation of conversations they had had earlier in the day with Seeckt. The General apparently regretted not having pushed his own revolt more aggressively the day before and had decided upon another attempt at felling Stresemann, this time by pro-

(*Seeckt*, p. 365). In his memoirs, Gessler intimates that he knew of the General's aims (*Reichswehrpolitik*, pp. 274ff.), but it seems more likely that he reinterpreted the affair in the light of the Seeckt documents in Rabenau's biography.

[48] For the minutes of 6.11.1923, see *Nachlass*, 3159/7394/171437ff. (an abridged version is in *Vermächtnis*, I, 198ff.).

137

viding ammunition for the opposition group within the DVP. Seeckt had announced, the two deputies reported, that on the previous day he had told Stresemann to his face that his position as Chancellor had become untenable and had demanded that he resign. Since there had been no previous disclosure of the Stresemann-Seeckt encounter, this report stunned the delegation. Even Stresemann's most loyal defenders expressed doubt about the possibility of his continuing as Chancellor, for Seeckt's remarks, as presented by Lersner and Maretzky, seemed to indicate that the Army was openly opposing him. Constitutionally, of course, the Army had no right to interfere in the politics of the Republic, but the thought of opposing the will of the military was seemingly beyond the grasp of the DVP deputies.[49]

Fearing a precipitous move on the part of the delegation, several of Stresemann's loyal supporters demanded more evidence about Seeckt's remarks. Scholz promptly telephoned Stresemann and Gessler, both of whom flatly denied that Seeckt had demanded Stresemann's resignation on behalf of the Army. Incensed at the tactics of the right-wing leaders, Stresemann then hurried to the meeting himself and gave his version of what had taken place. The General, he said, had expressed only the purely personal opinion that a new non-party cabinet might be able to find a bloodless solution to the problem of the rebellious right more easily than his own. In no case, he insisted, had Seeckt withdrawn the confidence of the Army. Since this account tallied closely with that of Gessler, an eyewitness, the opposition was left with no reply. As for the right wing's proposal of negotiations with the Nationalists, Stresemann announced that he had just learned in a talk with Hergt that the DNVP was definitely not interested in serving under him in a parliamentary coalition. Then, having also made his position clear on several less important questions, he abruptly left the meeting.[50]

---

[49] *Ibid.*

[50] *Ibid.* Also, *Seeckt Papers*, reel 19, Stück 88, Lersner to Seeckt, 7.11. 1923, a letter which confirms Lersner's account of Seeckt's disclosures to him.

This brief appearance effectively offset the temporary advantage the opposition had gained from the reports of Lersner and Maretzky. When the proposal to bypass Stresemann and negotiate directly with the DNVP delegation was put to a vote only a minority of the delegation supported it and the measure was defeated. The right wing, however, persisted, maintaining that the true attitude of the DNVP delegation could never be known until it had been officially and publicly invited to join the government. One of their spokesmen, Reinhold Quaatz, also charged that Stresemann had not fully heard the opposition's point of view. To avoid further conflict it was finally agreed to send to the Chancellor a deputation consisting of the chairman, Scholz, a representative of the right wing, Curtius, and a representative of the left wing, Carl Cremer.[51] On November 7 these three informed Stresemann of the divergent viewpoints within the delegation. Again he refused to issue an invitation to the DNVP. But in a gesture aimed at restoring unity he indicated he would not object if the delegation approached the Nationalists independently regarding the possibility of their entry into the government.[52]

By making this concession, Stresemann unwittingly opened the way for a rebellion that threatened for a time to deprive him of the support of the DVP delegation. He evidently assumed that the right-wing leaders would admit defeat if they discovered for themselves that the DNVP was unwilling to accept him as Chancellor or to take part in a parliamentary coalition. They were much more determined than he realized, however, and were quite willing to agree to his replacement as Chancellor and to the formation of a "supra-parliamentary" regime in order to get the Nationalists into the government. When the delegation met on the morning of November 9, again in his absence, to discuss the details of the pending negotiations with the DNVP, they lost no time in making their views known. Led by Gildemeister and

[51] *Nachlass,* 3159/7394/171449.
[52] *Nachlass,* 3159/7394/171467, Scholz's remarks to the delegation, 9.11.1923.

Maretzky, they introduced a declaration inviting the DNVP to join the government, but omitting any mention of Stresemann. This omission was quickly detected by the left wing, which introduced a motion altering the declaration to stipulate that Stresemann must remain as Chancellor.

A few days earlier the left wing's motion would probably have been backed by a majority of the party's deputies, but by the time of the meeting on the 9th the situation had taken an unexpected turn that greatly improved the position of the right wing. During the previous night, Adolf Hitler, with the support of General Ludendorff, had attempted unsuccessfully to force the Munich authorities to launch a march on Berlin and had then undertaken an armed insurrection aimed at overthrowing both the Bavarian and Reich governments. With the outcome of this development still in doubt at the time of the DVP delegation meeting, the right wing was able to exploit the situation by arguing that the time had come to strengthen the government by bringing in the DNVP at once, regardless of Stresemann's views. This argument was apparently not without effect on the middle group of deputies who held the balance between right and left and who usually supported Stresemann. The motion to revise the declaration was rejected, 20 to 22, with several abstentions. Realizing that they could not block the passage of the right wing's declaration, some of the left wing, led by Kardorff, sought to capitalize on the fact that it said nothing explicit about sacrificing Stresemann and voted with the right wing in an effort to confuse the issue. As a result, the declaration was adopted by a vote of 31 to 15.[53]

The leaders of the right wing were jubilant at the outcome of the meeting of the 9th. Even though nearly a third of the party's deputies had been absent, they were confident they could carry off a full-scale revolt that would repudiate Stresemann's policies and reorient the DVP to the right. But in attempting to exploit the victory they had won over the left wing, they over-

[53] *Nachlass*, 3159/7394/171465ff., minutes of 9.11.1923.

reached themselves. Shortly after the end of the delegation meeting, Alfred Gildemeister provided the press with an account of the session which made it appear that the DVP had already jettisoned Stresemann.[54] This unauthorized action offended Scholz, who had refused to go along with the right wing's attempt to undermine Stresemann. In a statement published in the morning papers of the 10th he gave his full support to the Chancellor and dismissed the defeat of the left wing's motion as the result of an "accidental majority." Moreover, since the Nationalists had released an announcement on the afternoon of the 9th which reiterated their refusal to accept Stresemann as Chancellor, he indicated that from the DVP's point of view the question of their entry into the government was closed.[55]

Scholz's statement represented a severe setback for the opposition, but an even more devastating blow came later on the 10th, when he called the delegation together to defend his action. This meeting took place in quite a different atmosphere from that of the previous morning, for in the meantime the Hitler Putsch had been quickly and successfully squelched by the Bavarians and there was no longer a threat of imminent crisis. Presented with Scholz's *fait accompli* under these altered circumstances, most of the middle group of deputies who had sided with the right wing or withheld their votes on the previous day decided to support Stresemann. The opposition was thus reduced to a minority again and the short-lived revolt was terminated. But the leaders of the extreme right wing refused to admit defeat. As the meeting closed, one of their spokesmen, Karl Hepp, angrily announced that the unity of the delegation was at an end.[56]

Stresemann was unable to take part in the struggle within the delegation because of the Munich crisis, which required his

[54] *Nachlass*, 3159/7394/171463, DVP press release, 9.11.1923. Also, remarks of Scholz and Gildemeister to delegation, 10.11.1923, *Nachlass*, 3159/7394/171474f.

[55] *Nachlass*, 3159/7394/171471, text of Scholz's statement.

[56] *Nachlass*, 3159/7394/171474ff., minutes of 10.11.1923.

presence at the Chancellery. When he first learned of Hitler's plot, late on the evening of the 8th, he immediately summoned a hurried emergency cabinet meeting at which President Ebert presided. Fearing a general rightist onslaught upon the government, the cabinet drew up and released a proclamation denouncing the Putsch and calling for the support of the public. Then, apparently still unaware of Seeckt's political ambitions, Stresemann and the rest of the cabinet agreed to a proposal put forward by Gessler which transferred to the General the exceptional powers that had been given to the Minister of the Army by the emergency decree of September 26.[57] With the quick suppression of the insurrection on the 9th, however, the crisis evaporated and the government was never forced to face a rightest revolution. Moreover, the ludicrous failure of the would-be dictator, Hitler, effectively discredited the speculation about a dictatorial regime at the national level—at least for the time being.

Stresemann later discussed the Bavarian affair in one of a series of articles on his chancellorship written in collaboration with his private secretary, Henry Bernhard, and published under the latter's name in early 1924. At that time he asserted that his policy had been predicated on the expectation of just such a development as Hitler's Putsch. He had been confident from the outset, he maintained, that the alliance between the particularistic, conservative Bavarian government and the nationalistic, radical groups such as the Nazis could not last long. His plan, he reported, had been to maintain a hands-off attitude until "the Bavarian lions" began to fight among themselves.[58] It is, of course, possible that he may have followed such a line of thought

[57] *Vermächtnis*, I, 204f., editor Bernhard's notes. The papers of the Reich Chancellery do not contain a copy of the minutes of this cabinet meeting. Rabenau (*Seeckt*, p. 375) has Stresemann "flying about in extreme agitation" during the meeting, but Gessler, one of the participants, contradicts this, maintaining that the session took place in a calm and collected atmosphere, see his *Reichswehrpolitik*, p. 274.

[58] Stresemann-Bernhard, "Das Kabinett Stresemann, IV," *Deutsche Stimmen*, 5.2.1924.

during the Bavarian affair, but if that was the case it is strange that he failed to mention it during the meetings of the cabinet, when he was often extremely hard-pressed to defend his position against the Social Democrats.

But whatever the reasoning behind it, his policy of non-intervention in Bavaria and firm action against the Communists in Saxony and Thuringia (where they were forced out of the cabinet on November 6), had in fact brought about the clash between Hitler and the Bavarian government. As he had hoped, the assault on the Communists served to convince the Bavarian authorities that his cabinet was not subservient to Marxist pressure and also demonstrated to them its control over most of the Army. In addition, the withdrawal of the SPD from the government removed still another obstacle. During the first week of November, there were rumors in Munich to the effect that the dominant clique, headed by General Commissar Kahr, had concluded that the time had come for an agreement with Berlin.[59] Alarmed by the prospect of an end to the crisis, Hitler, who was bent on the overthrow of the national government, decided to attempt his desperate Putsch and ended by destroying the tenuous alliance which had made the Bavarian question such a serious threat to the Republic. Deprived of the armed strength and popular support which its radical allies had provided, the Munich government was forced to adopt a less defiant attitude. The result was a gradual process of reconciliation which was completed early in 1924.

Although it was one of the most burdensome problems of his chancellorship, the Bavarian issue allowed Stresemann to fulfill a long-standing promise. For several years he had been in communication with the Hohenzollern heir apparent, Crown Prince Wilhelm, and had even made a pilgrimage to the latter's exile residence in Holland in the fall of 1920. While most observers found the Crown Prince a weak and unimpressive figure, Stresemann was left with a "deep impression of his humane

[59] Gordon, *The Reichswehr and the German Republic*, p. 242.

143

personality."[60] This may be explained in part by the fact that he had a pronounced weakness for royalty, and especially for the Hohenzollerns. But another important factor was the attention lavished upon him by the Crown Prince at the time of his visit to Holland, a gesture of intimacy well calculated to impress a man of Stresemann's humble origins.[61] This friendliness on the part of the Prince, which was in sharp contrast to the former Emperor's practice of refusing even to speak to politicians, is not difficult to fathom. He wished to re-enter Germany as soon as possible and found in Stresemann one of the few men in government circles who was willing to help him. The Prince quickly gained a loyal supporter, even though at the time it was of little practical value to him, since Stresemann was in no position to aid him effectively. When the latter took over the chancellorship in August 1923, however, the Prince lost little time in reminding him of his promises of support. But with the Ruhr stalemate in the balance, Stresemann was unwilling to risk provoking the Allies by readmitting the Prince and decided to postpone the matter.[62]

Following the end of passive resistance, foreign policy was no longer such an obstacle to the Prince's return, but there remained the difficult task of securing the consent of the republican parties in order to avoid endangering the Great Coalition. Finally, the Bavarian government provided Stresemann with a solution by indicating to the Prince that he could re-enter Germany across one of the borders it controlled. There was actually little chance of his accepting this invitation in view of the adverse reaction it might cause in Prussia, where the Hohenzollerns' main strength

[60] *Nachlass*, 3171/7352/166007f., his diary entries on the visit to Holland, September 1920. For further information on Stresemann's relations with the Crown Prince, see Paul Herre, *Kronprinz Wilhelm* (Munich, 1954), pp. 177ff. Herre places Stresemann's trip to Holland in the fall of 1921, following an error in a memorandum written by the latter in 1924, see *Vermächtnis*, I, 223.

[61] *Nachlass*, 3171/7351/165763f., memorandum on the trip by Stresemann's private secretary, Friedrich Rauch, 23.9.1920.

[62] *Vermächtnis*, I, 219f.

lay. Nevertheless, Stresemann decided to exploit the opportunity. On October 24 he urged the cabinet to allow the Prince to return at once and intimated that there was a real danger that he would go to Bavaria. Anxious to deprive the Munich regime of an important boost to its prestige, the cabinet, including the Social Democratic ministers, approved his proposal with the stipulation that the Prince refrain from all political activity.[63] Although Stresemann undoubtedly still hoped that the Prince might one day play a role in an eventual restoration, his views had undergone important changes since he had first offered his support in 1920. He, too, was opposed to any outbreak of monarchist agitation, feeling that it would only impede Germany's recovery by adding to the political divisions that had weakened the country since the war. He therefore indicated to the Prince that he stood firmly behind the cabinet's stipulation regarding political activity.[64]

The last and perhaps most important achievement of Stresemann's chancellorship was the stabilization of the currency. Because of the long paralysis of the Ruhr industrial region and the government's reliance on the printing press to meet its own expenses, the old Mark had become almost worthless, standing at nearly a trillion to the American dollar. Under his direction, however, the cabinet was moving toward a solution. At the time of the formation of his second cabinet in October, he had appointed Hans Luther to replace the Social Democratic Finance Minister, Rudolf Hilferding, who had been unable to decide upon a course of action and so was under fire from both the DVP and his own party. Luther, a career administrator and a political independent who had served ably as Minister of Food and Agriculture under Cuno and in the first Stresemann cabinet, proved to be a wise choice. He plunged into his difficult task at once. By October 16, only ten days after his appointment, he had provided the cabinet with an interim solution calling for

---

[63] AR, *Kabinett*, 1749/757302f., cabinet minutes, 23.10.1923.
[64] *Nachlass*, 3099/7118/145925ff., letter to the Prince, 24.10.1923.

the issuance of a new currency, the *Rentenmark*, to be backed, at least in theory, by a mortgage on the country's agricultural and industrial resources. Using the special powers granted it by the enabling act of October 13, the cabinet immediately authorized his plan. During the next month, the new Finance Minister, assisted in the final stages by the banker Hjalmar Schacht, prepared to put the reform into effect. Finally, on November 15 the first issues of the *Rentenmark* appeared and the liquidation of the long and costly inflation began.

The most serious difficulties arising from the currency reform involved the occupied areas of the Rhineland and the Ruhr. At first the cabinet expected it would be possible to introduce the new currency into the occupied areas, but early in November the French made it clear that they would not allow such a move. Another complication arose when Finance Minister Luther refused to guarantee the stability of the new *Rentenmark* if the government continued to meet the astronomical costs of unemployment compensation in the occupied areas, where economic activity was still far below normal as a result of the months of passive resistance. If the cabinet continued to pour aid into those areas, Luther argued, the French would sabotage the new currency by draining off the German government's financial resources through what he described as the "hole in the west."[65]

Although they did so reluctantly, Stresemann and the rest of the cabinet decided on November 9 to limit the currency reform to the unoccupied areas and to suspend the national government's unemployment payments in the occupied zones. They regarded their decision as a calculated risk, based on the assumption that any advantages it might give to the French-inspired separatist movement would, in the long run, be offset by the re-establishment of the economic health of the rest of the country. Moreover, they planned to try to turn the tables on the French by blaming them for the hardships that would be imposed on the population of the occupied areas, a propaganda

[65] Hans Luther, *Politiker Ohne Partei* (Stuttgart, 1960), p. 180.

move which they hoped would result in British pressure for an end to the occupation.[66]

While it is true that the cabinet's plan involved granting the occupied territories temporary financial autonomy, there is no factual basis for the recent allegation of Konrad Adenauer, who was at the time Lord Mayor of Cologne, that Stresemann planned to sever those territories from the Reich and allow the establishment of a *de facto* independent state.[67] Stresemann made it abundantly clear at all times that he would never agree to the formation of an independent or autonomous Ruhr-Rhineland state, or even to severance of any part of the area from the Prussian *Land*. Moreover, Adenauer, contrary to his later version of the affair, recognized the necessity of financial autonomy. As Adenauer reports, he and the other spokesmen of the Ruhr and the Rhineland did protest against the cabinet's policies, but he does not mention that their objections had to do only with the proposed suspension of the national government's unemployment payments in their part of the country—a move that would have placed the entire burden on the local authorities. Nor does he mention that he and the other spokesmen of the occupied areas accepted the cabinet's policy when Stresemann and Luther agreed to compromise and continue these payments temporarily and on a reduced scale.[68]

While Stresemann was clearing up the difficulties arising from the currency reform, a new attack on his cabinet was being prepared, this time by the Social Democrats. Since that party's exit from the government there had been a struggle within its delega-

[66] AR, *Kabinett*, 1749/757711f., cabinet minutes, 9.11.1923. Also, Luther, *Politiker*, p. 180.

[67] See the memorandum prepared by Adenauer for his authorized biography, *Konrad Adenauer*, by Paul Weymar (Munich, 1955), pp. 120ff.

[68] AR, *Kabinett*, 1749/757738f., Stresemann's report to the cabinet on the meeting with representatives of the occupied zone, 12.11.1923. Also, *ibid.*, 1750/757766ff., his report to the cabinet on 13.11.1923. Also, *ibid.*, 1750/757799f., minutes of meeting of the cabinet with representatives of occupied zones, including Adenauer, 17.11.1923. Also, Luther, *Politiker*, pp. 178ff., 199ff.

tion between those who wished to allow the minority cabinet to remain in office and those, led by disgruntled deputies from Saxony, Thuringia, and Bavaria, who wanted to bring it down by throwing the party's 171 votes to the opposition. In the second week of November the latter group emerged as the majority and gained control of the delegation. Since this placed more than the requisite one-third of the Reichstag at their disposal, they were able to force President Ebert, who had sided with the minority, to schedule a new session of the chamber.[69]

At first Stresemann was hopeful that he could mollify the SPD by terminating the state of emergency imposed upon Saxony and Thuringia after the ouster of the Communist ministers. He had to abandon this plan, however, when it met with the opposition of Seeckt, who was still in possession of the extraordinary powers granted him on November 8.[70] Determined to save his cabinet, Stresemann then planned to confront the Social Democrats with the threat of new elections unless they dropped their intention to fell the government. But here he also encountered opposition, this time from Ebert, who refused to grant him a dissolution decree. The President's explanation was that it would be impossible to carry out an election with so much of the country under foreign occupation. Stresemann accepted this explanation as sincere and adequate.[71] Its accuracy, however, appears questionable in view of the fact that Ebert had granted him a dissolution decree in order to force the SPD into line on the enabling act of October 13, when just as much of the country had been under occupation. At the time, Lord D'Abernon suspected that the President's attitude was dictated by a desire for "a more amenable Chancellor and one less out of sympathy with the views of an old-fashioned Socialist of the Ebert type."[72] In addition, there were rumors to the effect that here, too, Seeckt had been busy

[69] AR, *Kabinett,* 1749/757737, Stresemann's remarks to the cabinet, 12.11.1923.
[70] *Seeckt Papers,* reel 26, Stück 281, Blatt 51.
[71] D'Abernon, *An Ambassador,* II, 274.
[72] *Ibid.*

behind the scenes and had used his influence to affect the President's decision.[73] A more likely explanation than either of these is that Ebert simply felt the situation was basically different from that of October. At that time the SPD had been in the government and he could be confident that a dissolution decree would force the dissidents into line and would thus never have to be used. In November, on the other hand, the party was out of the cabinet and in an angry mood, so that there was no guarantee that the majority would not defy the decree and thus force him to go through with the elections.

Balked in his other plans, Stresemann considered avoiding a call for a vote of confidence when the Reichstag convened. Such a move would force the opposition parties to present no-confidence motions. Since the SPD and the DNVP would probably refuse to unite behind one motion, the opposition would thus be split and none of the no-confidence measures would gain a majority. This plan was quickly rejected by the other members of the cabinet, who pointed out that even if the government survived the initial round of votes by such a stratagem it would be almost certain to fall on some other issue in the near future.[74] Reluctantly, he reconciled himself to the prospect of defeat and when the SPD made clear its intention to oppose the government as soon as the Reichstag session began, he decided to call the issue by asking for a vote of confidence.

The Reichstag reconvened on November 20, and on the 22nd Stresemann appeared before it. He defended the policies of his government and asked the chamber to adopt the confidence measure. But regardless of the fate of his own cabinet, he called upon the parties to think of the country's welfare and to avoid a paralyzing crisis. The parliamentary system was, he admitted, "going through all the childhood illnesses that a completely new system must go through in any country." But even though the

[73] Remark of Maretzky, relayed to Stresemann by Naumann, letter of 5.12.1923, *Nachlass*, 3159/7395/171547ff.

[74] AR, *Kabinett*, 1750/757825, meeting of 19.11.1923.

system was admittedly not perfect, he cautioned against any temptation to indulge in experiments with other types of governments: ". . . one should not forsake something—I won't say the good, but rather the existing—until it has been demonstrated that there is something better available to replace it. I believe that Bolshevism of the Russian type or the Fascism that has been created under a completely different sun in Italy by a highly gifted statesman are not models that could suddenly replace this system in Germany without tearing Germany to pieces. Our German body politic is feverishly ill and cannot stand the quack treatment of a new civil war."

In addition, he called upon the extremes of both right and left to give up any notion of a revolution: "Let us be clear about one thing: a solution through force could have no permanence. It could be feasible temporarily, but not permanently. There is hardly a country anywhere that is so divided by political, economic and social differences. Only by bridging these differences can our recovery be permanent." He also made clear his own views as to the proper course of action: "Not restoration and not counterrevolution, but rather evolution and reconciliation, these must be the guiding principles of our politics."[75] His eloquence had no effect on the Social Democrats, however, and when the confidence measure went before the chamber on the evening of the 23rd they united with the DNVP to defeat it, 156 to 231. Later that evening, after serving as Chancellor for one hundred and three days, Stresemann submitted his resignation to the President.[76]

❖

Stresemann's brief chancellorship stands as one of the high points of his entire career. Faced with a series of grave threats to the Republic, both from without and within, he acted with resolution and boldness and managed to preserve the unity of the country and the integrity of the constitution. Moreover, by

[75] *Verhandlungen* (Reichstag), CCCLXI, 11294f.
[76] *Vermächtnis*, I, 244f.

pushing through the long-needed currency reform he laid the basis for the eventual stabilization of the German economy.

Although the importance of these achievements has generally been recognized, the record of Stresemann's chancellorship has repeatedly been subjected to criticism by historians. The principal target of these attacks has been his handling the Saxon and Thuringian situations in one way, and the Bavarian in another. It betrayed, according to the usual line of attack, a double standard toward the left and the right and so endangered the cause of German democracy. The existence of a double standard in the cases in question is undeniable. Stresemann himself openly admitted his willingness to be more indulgent toward the defiant Bavarian authorities, though not the Nazis and other extremist groups, than toward the Communist-infiltrated governments of Saxony and Thuringia. The criticism, however, ignores the possibility that this was a legitimate double standard and that there was in fact an important difference between defiance of the central government by the conservative, particularistic Bavarians and the entrance of a foreign-controlled subversive party into the governments of Saxony and Thuringia. In any case, as has been shown here, the double standard has been exaggerated as a determinant of the line Stresemann finally adopted toward the Munich authorities. The decisive factor was his conviction that the conservative orientation of the Army made it impossible to depend on its loyalty in an open clash with the rightist Bavarians, a point which even Minister of the Army Gessler was eventually forced to concede. Finally, this line of criticism does Stresemann injustice in that it also overlooks the fact that his aim in dealing with the threats from both the left and from the right was never other than to preserve the existing parliamentary Republic, the indispensable prerequisite for further democratic development in Germany.

An important aspect of Stresemann's chancellorship which has been neglected is the effect his term of office had on his own political outlook. Most important in this regard is that by calling him to the chancellorship the Republic had bestowed far greater honors upon him than he had ever hoped for during the imperial era. Even during the last phase of the Empire, when a few parliamentarians were named to some of the lesser ministerial posts, he had consistently refused to allow his name to be placed in consideration. The reason for this was his lower-middle-class background, which he feared might subject him to the ridicule of the dominant aristocratic circles at the imperial court.[77] Under the Republic, this constraining factor was eliminated and less than five years after the establishment of the new system he was called to its highest active political office. Although there is no evidence that he ever commented on this aspect of the transition from Empire to Republic, it is difficult, especially in view of his obvious ambition and desire for political pre-eminence, to escape the conclusion that it served to weaken his remaining emotional ties to the old regime and strengthen his allegiance to the new one.

Another important point that has been overlooked is that Stresemann's chancellorship altered his position within the political circles of the Republic. At the time he assumed office he had, as a *Vernunftrepublikaner*, aligned himself with the Weimar system and moved very close to the position of the republican parties. But because of the memory of his days of fellow-traveling with the right he was nevertheless regarded with a certain amount of suspicion by many republicans, particularly those on the left. In the course of his term as Chancellor this anomalous situation was quickly remedied, for his responsibilities brought him directly into collision with the oppositional right. The most striking aspect of this was the wide gap which opened between him and the Nationalists as the result of his decision to end passive resistance and their complicity in the various schemes aimed at establishing a dictatorial regime. He made no secret of his disgust with the DNVP's intransigence and irresponsibility

[77] See Eugen Schiffer, *Ein Leben für den Liberalismus* (Berlin, 1951), p. 112.

and its leaders reciprocated by leveling at him the same vitriolic attacks they customarily bestowed upon those who accepted the unpleasant realities of Germany's situation and sought to take realistic steps to improve it. Just as important as the rupture with the Nationalists was the final destruction of his former uncritical esteem for the two foremost symbols of the oppositional right, Ludendorff and Hindenburg. This bitter disillusionment took place during early November, when, in the midst of his efforts to preserve the unity of Germany and stave off civil war, he learned to his dismay that Hindenburg had tacitly sided with the rebellious Bavarian government and that Ludendorff had joined the rabble-rousing Hitler in launching a Putsch aimed at overthrowing his own cabinet.

With these developments, Stresemann's break with the right was at last complete and this fact did not escape the attention of the republicans of the Center, the DDP, and the SPD. Not the least of those to notice it was President Ebert, whom Stresemann had come to respect greatly in the course of their close cooperation during his term in office and whose complete confidence he had won by his loyal defense of the Republic. When he heard of his party's action in bringing down the cabinet on the 23rd, Ebert made no effort to conceal his feelings and hurled an angry and prophetic reprimand at the SPD leaders: "The reasons why you have felled the Chancellor will be forgotten in six weeks, but you will feel the effects of your stupidity for the next ten years."[78]

[78] *Vermächtnis*, I, 245. According to the editor's note, this remark was relayed to Stresemann by a Social Democrat.

153

V. THE PARTY LEADER AND THE
FOREIGN MINISTER, 1924

AFTER the defeat of his government on November 23, Stresemann remained as Chancellor on a caretaker basis for another week. His term of office officially came to an end on the 30th, when Wilhelm Marx of the Center formed a coalition government backed by the DDP, the Center, the DVP, and the Bavarian People's Party. The new cabinet was essentially a slightly revised version of the previous one, with most of the ministers remaining at their posts. At the insistence of the DDP and the Center, which were anxious to preserve a continuity of foreign policy, Marx assigned the Foreign Ministry to Stresemann, who had administered it on a provisional basis throughout his own term as Chancellor.

Since the new government did not command a majority in the Reichstag, its installation was made possible only by the toleration of the SPD. The Social Democrats were unwilling to enter the cabinet because of the still unsettled Bavarian affair, yet they wished to avoid driving the middle parties into an alliance with the DNVP. Although they had felled almost exactly the same cabinet a week earlier in order to chastise Stresemann, the Social Democrats also voted to give the government sweeping emergency powers—including the power to suspend the controversial eight-hour workday—until the middle of February.

Stresemann was well pleased with the Marx government. The new Chancellor, a mild-mannered, taciturn former judge from the Rhineland, relied heavily on his advice during the deliberations of the cabinet and made no effort to reverse the policies he had initiated during his own term of office. Even more important, Marx refrained from interfering with his conduct of foreign policy. While still Chancellor, Stresemann had launched Germany on a course of conciliation with the Allies by urging that the Ruhr-reparations impasse be broken through a resumption of German payments on a scale to be determined by impartial experts. In the last weeks of his term of office, this policy had begun to produce results, for after long hesitation the French finally agreed to an assessment of Germany's reparation capacities by a group of international financial experts. Stresemann regarded this development as an important turning point and was therefore gratified when Marx gave him a free hand to carry his policy to completion.[1]

During the first months of 1924, Stresemann's attention was occupied mainly by the international experts' inquiries and other foreign policy matters. But at the same time he also had to contend with a new assault from the right wing of the DVP. Following his clash with the Reichstag delegation in November, he had secured the approval of the Central Committee for his policies. At that time he appeared to have thoroughly subdued the opposition.[2] Its position was suddenly improved, however, when the SPD felled his cabinet. This development embittered many of the decisive middle group of DVP deputies against that party and thus made them more receptive to the right wing's argument that the DVP should seek allies to the right. Anxious to capitalize on the new mood of the delegation, the right wingers returned to the attack. They directed their fire at the Central Committee, challenging its authority to impose policy decisions on the Reichstag deputies, who, they pointed out, were designated by the constitution as independent representatives of the people.[3] At a meeting of the DVP delegation on January 12 they called upon the deputies to make their own policy and proposed a resolution designed to reorient the DVP sharply to the right. This resolution denounced the SPD, ruled out any possibility of a revival of the Great Coalition, and pledged the DVP to seek the inclusion of the Nationalists in the government.[4]

[1] See the minutes of the Marx cabinet, AR, *Kabinett*, reels 1750, 1751, 1752, 1753.

[2] *Vermächtnis*, I, 226, meeting of 18.11.1923.

[3] *Nachlass*, 3159/7395/171536ff., Gildemeister to Stresemann, 8.12. 1923.

[4] *Nachlass*, 3111/7124/147061f., memorandum, "Betrifft: Geheimrat Dr. Quaatz." Text of the resolution: 3159/7395/171626f.

Stresemann strongly objected to this resolution. He, too, was angry that the Social Democrats had toppled his cabinet and agreed that the current domination of the SPD by its left wing made a renewal of cooperation impossible.[5] Still, he was not willing to go as far as the DVP deputies and set the party on a doctrinaire anti-socialist course by ruling out even the possibility of an eventual return to the Great Coalition. In his opinion, the experiment in cooperation with the SPD had proved its worth during his chancellorship in spite of its vicissitudes. Even on the day of his fall he had announced that he regarded such cooperation "indispensable" for the political health of the country.[6] Equally objectionable to him was the unqualified pledge to bring the DNVP into the government. He was not opposed to an attempt to work with the Nationalists, but his experiences as Chancellor had left him extremely skeptical about the possibility of bringing them to cooperate constructively.[7]

Since his views on both the SPD and the DNVP were well known, the right wing's resolution amounted to a direct challenge. But in spite of his opposition, the feeling against the SPD was so strong within the delegation that the resolution was adopted at the meeting of January 12. The right wing was deprived of a complete victory, however, for Stresemann succeeded in bringing the deputies to submit the resolution to the executive committee of the delegation for final formulation. There his supporters prevailed and on January 21 the resolution was effectively emasculated. The revised version ruled out cooperation with the SPD, but only for as long as its left wing continued to dominate the party. Similarly, it retained the pledge to seek the admission of the DNVP to the government. But in line with his views it stipulated that this would be possible only if the Nationalists agreed to a constructive program and accepted the

---

[5] *Nachlass*, 3106/7165/154896, his article for *Die Zeit*, 8.12.1923.

[6] *Vermächtnis*, I, 246.

[7] *Nachlass*, 3159/7395/171540ff., letter to Gildemeister, 10.12.1923.

principle that the constitution was to be altered solely by legal means.[8]

Stresemann found nothing unacceptable in this revised text of the resolution and it was released to the press. But lest even this watered-down version create the impression that the DVP had turned against the SPD and toward the right, he qualified it still further in his public statements and thus made clear his own views on the part the DVP should play in the Republic's politics. He took issue with those who wanted the DVP to adopt a more consistent course and insisted that the party would do Germany no service if it aligned itself with the left or the right and held stubbornly to either position. "The art of statecraft in a divided nation," he said, explaining his position on one occasion, "can be nothing other than the politics of compromise, the bringing together of whatever forces are at the moment capable of propelling things forward."[9] The proper role for the DVP, in other words, was to take its place beside the Center as a middle party, free from all ties to the right or the left, but willing to work with either as the circumstances demanded.

The majority of the party's deputies accepted the revised version of the January 12 resolution and Stresemann's formulation of the DVP's place in the Republic's politics. The right wing, however, objected angrily. The result was the formation of an opposition organization within the party under the name National Liberal Union (*Nationalliberale Vereinigung*). For the most part, the leadership of this organization consisted of the same group of deputies who had taken part in the attacks on Stresemann's policies during his chancellorship. In all, twelve members of the Reichstag delegation were involved. The most active of these were Alfred Gildemeister, who was aligned with conservative business interests in Bremen, Albert Vögler of the heavy industry group, Baron von Lersner, and Oskar Maretzky.

[8] *Nachlass*, 3111/7124/147061f., memorandum, "Betrifft: Geheimrat Dr. Quaatz." For the text, *Nachlass*, 3159/7396/171768.

[9] *Vermächtnis*, I, 320, speech at Dresden, 22.2.1924.

In addition to Vögler, three other prominent members of the Ruhr group joined the National Liberal Union: Kurt Sorge, Reinhold Quaatz, and Johann Becker, former Economics Minister under Cuno. Also involved in the opposition organization were two spokesmen of the *Landbund*, Karl Hepp and Friedrich Doebrich; an official of the Christian trade union movement, Otto Adams; and two representatives of the conservative business interests of Hamburg, Walther Dauch and Carl Piper. In addition, the Union soon boasted an imposing list of supporters outside the Reichstag delegation. For the most part, its followers came from the ranks of the party's business supporters. It was especially successful in the Ruhr, where it gained the backing of such influential DVP industrialists as Friedrich Flick, Otto Hembeck, and Moritz Klönne, all of whom were associated with the steel industry. In Berlin the new organization was quickly endorsed by two conservative newspapers aligned with the business community, *Der Tag* and the *Börsenzeitung*.[10]

From the outset, the leaders of the National Liberal Union left no doubt that their aim was to wrest control of the DVP from Stresemann and reverse his policies. The organization's first full meeting took place in the Reichstag building on March 26. Its spokesman, Gildemeister, announced that the formation of the Union had become necessary because Stresemann's "personal rule" had resulted in a "party machine" that throttled all criticism within the delegation and from the rank and file. He argued that most of the party was opposed to the line followed by its chairman and dismissed as "manipulation from above" the repeated votes of confidence the latter had received from the Party Congress and the Central Committee, both of which consisted of elected representatives of the local organizations. He rejected Stresemann's designation of the DVP as a middle party and announced that the Union's goal was the formation of an anti-socialist majority government consisting of all "na-

[10] *Nachlass*, 3159/7396/171762ff., a collection of data on the Union.

tionally and economically sound parties." And he left no doubt that such a government would include the DNVP.[11]

Gildemeister's views were echoed by other speakers at the meeting, including Doebrich, Lersner, and the industrialist Klönne. Moreover, Klönne openly demanded that Stresemann resign as leader of the party. All the speakers emphasized that they and the other leaders of the Union considered themselves reformers, not revolutionaries. Although few of them had been active in the National Liberal Party, they insisted that their aim was simply to return to its principles. The DVP, they charged, had been formed in 1918 to oppose the revolution and the SPD, but had been diverted from its original principles by Stresemann, who was seeking to make it part of the left against the will of its members.[12]

Stresemann responded angrily to the formation of the National Liberal Union and to the attacks its leaders made on his policies. He realized that an intraparty struggle might handicap the DVP's campaign for the forthcoming regular Reichstag elections, which had been set for May 4. Still, he decided that the time had come to draw the line against those who wanted to make the party into a pawn of heavy industry or a satellite of the DNVP. This involved a considerable risk, for the party's finances had suffered heavily from the inflation, which had been particularly hard on the propertied middle-class groups that made up much of its membership. It was therefore still dependent on the subsidies of its industrial backers, many of whom had aligned themselves with the National Liberal Union.[13]

At the end of March Stresemann submitted the whole question to the Party Congress and the Central Committee, both of which met at Hanover. In a speech to the full Congress on the 30th he defended the course he had charted for the DVP and took issue with the charge that he had betrayed its principles: "If one

[11] *Nachlass*, 3159/7396/171785ff.
[12] *Ibid.*
[13] R. Thimme, *Stresemann und die deutsche Volkspartei*, pp. 55f.

159

questions the correctness of the policy we have followed from 1920 to 1924, of seeking allies where we could find them, where the most productive work could be accomplished, then I must ask whether the greatest German statesmen . . . have not done the very same. He who elevates principle above all else must lay his wreath not on the monument of Bismarck, but rather on the monument of Eugen Richter. The idea of holding unflinchingly to principle is an aspect of political Philistinism. . . . Bismarck knew how to take things as they were and make allowances for circumstances."[14]

The DVP's goal, he maintained, had never changed. It had been, and remained, the recovery of Germany and the restoration of national solidarity. He then adroitly undercut the opposition group by endorsing the policy set forth in the revised proclamation of January 12, ruling out a coalition with the SPD as long as its left wing was dominant and indicating his readiness to accept a coalition with the Nationalists if they showed a willingness to assume responsibility. When the policy question was put to the vote, the result was a resounding endorsement for Stresemann by both the Central Committee and the Party Congress. The National Liberal Union was condemned and its members were informed that they would be expelled from the party unless they resigned at once from the new organization.[15]

The outcome of the Hanover meetings abruptly terminated the challenge of the National Liberal Union. Half of the deputies who had been active in its formation, including Adams, Becker, Dauch, Gildemeister, Hepp, and Sorge, proved unwilling to face expulsion from the DVP and the probable loss of their Reichstag seats. They meekly complied with the ban on the Union and submitted their resignations. Only three members of the Reichstag delegation, Lersner, Maretzky, and Vögler, elected to remain with the Union and accept expulsion from the party. With the help of funds supplied by Vögler and his associates in the Ruhr steel industry, they entered the Union in the election

[14] *Vermächtnis*, I, 374.   [15] *Ibid.*, 372ff.

campaign in six districts as an independent party. Three other leaders of the Union group, Doebrich, Klönne, and Quaatz, also left the DVP. They joined the DNVP, which awarded them safe candidacies for the Reichstag elections of May 4.[16]

At the same time this exodus was taking place, Hugo Stinnes, reputedly the most powerful of the Ruhr industrialists, also ceased to play a role in the DVP. Stinnes, who was in ill health at the time, had taken no direct part in the formation of the National Liberal Union, although a number of executives connected with his industrial empire had. He had, however, never made a secret of his rejection of the course Stresemann had set for the DVP. In other respects, too, he had been a source of disappointment to Stresemann. Although it was popularly assumed that he was the chief financial backer of the DVP, this was anything but the truth. Upon entering the party he had agreed to contribute 10,000 paper Mark a year and to Stresemann's disgust, he stubbornly held to the original agreement even after the inflation had made that sum worthless.[17] He also proved unreceptive to most appeals for indirect financial help. In 1923 Stinnes answered Stresemann's request for advertising to help subsidize the foundering newspaper, *Die Zeit,* by dryly announcing that his firm needed no additional advertising at the moment.[18] Moreover, he even failed to support the party's policies fully and allowed the *Deutsche Allgemeine Zeitung,* a prominent Berlin newspaper which he controlled, to criticize the DVP freely.[19] He also neglected his duties as a Reichstag deputy, never once addressing the chamber and rarely attending its sessions. But in spite of his almost total disregard for the party and for parliamentary politics in general, Stinnes' reputation as Germany's most notorious monopoly capitalist and his association with the DVP in the mind of the public greatly increased the party's vulnerability to

[16] *Deutsche Volkspartei Papers,* Vol. 105m. Also, *Nachlass,* 3159/7396/171873f.

[17] *Nachlass,* 3096/7018/144517f., letter to Bömers, 19.10.1922.

[18] *Nachlass,* 3159/7394/171293, Stinnes to Stresemann, 31.8.1923.

[19] *Nachlass,* 3096/7015/144079ff., letter to Stinnes, 21.7.1922.

the attacks of the leftist press and parties. In the opinion of the party's left wing he was therefore an unjustifiable political liability.

Stresemann, who admired Stinnes' business abilities but scornfully regarded him as an unmitigated Philistine, had never been happy about having him in the Reichstag.[20] He was thus inclined to sympathize with the left wing's view. With his tacit approval, one of that group's spokesmen, Albrecht Morath, wrote the industrialist in February 1924, asking him, in the interests of the party, not to stand for re-election in May. Stinnes, who, according to another member of the delegation, had "an outspoken aversion" toward Stresemann,[21] angrily accused the party chairman of plotting against him. But since he was in ill health, he was unable to press his case and in late March he withdrew his candidacy.[22] Three weeks later, on April 10, he died at the age of fifty-four.

From the battle with the dissidents in the DVP Stresemann was plunged directly into the campaign for the May Reichstag elections. He was from the outset pessimistic, realizing that the DVP would almost certainly suffer at the polls because of its association with the unpopular, though unavoidable, measures of his cabinet, in particular the termination of passive resistance. "In the trenches of responsibility," he remarked on one occasion during the campaign, "there are more casualties than in the rear lines of the opposition."[23] The chief beneficiary of the election, he predicted, would be the DNVP, which stood to gain the votes of many nationalistic voters who had backed the DVP in 1920.[24]

[20] For his views on Stinnes, see *Nachlass*, 3096/7017/144395f., letter to Kircheisen, 1.10.1922. Also, his draft of an article after Stinnes' death, *Nachlass*, 3112/7127/147505ff.

[21] Rheinbaben, *Viermal*, p. 190.

[22] *Nachlass*, 3159/7395/171663ff., Morath to Stinnes, 9.2.1924. Also, 171736ff., Stresemann to Stinnes, 17.3.1924. Also, 3159/7396/171746ff., Stinnes to Stresemann, 20.3.1924.

[23] *Vermächtnis*, I, 321, speech in Dresden, 22.2.1924.

[24] D'Abernon, *An Ambassador*, III, 56.

In the second week of April the DVP's election prospects were somewhat brightened by the first tangible return on Stresemann's conciliatory foreign policy: the report of the international experts, usually known as the Dawes Plan. This report, which the Marx cabinet promptly endorsed, recommended a solution for the Ruhr-reparations dispute that was generally regarded as favorable to the Germans. On the crucial question of reparations it called for a resumption of German payments, but at a lower level than before and on more favorable terms of transfer. With regard to the Ruhr occupation it left the political question of the evacuation of the Belgian and French troops to be negotiated between the powers but called for a speedy return to the German civilian authorities of all administrative and economic controls. Finally, it provided for an international loan of 800 million gold Mark to speed the recovery of German industry.

Stresemann at once sought to make domestic political capital of this first success of his diplomacy. Although there was a brief flurry of opposition to the Plan within the DVP, he quickly overcame it by confidentially assuring his colleagues that the agreement would end the occupation of the Ruhr.[25] Once he had disposed of this resistance within the party he set about building its campaign around the Plan, using the slogan "Through Work and Sacrifice to Freedom."[26] This approach was especially effective in rallying business support, since the prospect of international credit amounting to 800 million Mark naturally made the Plan highly desirable in many business circles. The response of the heavy industry of the Ruhr to the Plan was overwhelmingly favorable; it was also endorsed by the majority of the members of the influential *Reichsverband der deutschen Industrie*. As a consequence, the gap that had been opened between the DVP and business at the time of the National Liberal Union episode was narrowed—a development which eased the party's financial situation.

[25] *Nachlass*, 3113/7129/147918, diary for 19.7.1925. Also, *Vermächtnis*, I, 457.
[26] *Vermächtnis*, I, 397.

The Plan was far from universally acclaimed, however. In spite of the international credit, the more nationalistic business circles rejected the whole idea of resuming reparation payments and bitterly opposed the Plan. The radicals of the right, led by the Nazi-Racist group, assailed it as "a second Versailles." Only slightly less virulent were the Nationalists, who warned that acceptance of the reparations burden set forth in the Plan and the international controls involved would result in the "enslavement" of Germany. Stresemann rejected these allegations and pointed out that Germany had no choice except to decide between two evils—a continued French occupation of the Ruhr or acceptance of the Dawes Plan. Since the sacrifices it entailed were mainly material, he maintained that the Plan was clearly the lesser of the two evils.[27]

Although it received little attention because of the emphasis on the Dawes Plan, the main domestic plank in the DVP's campaign was the revised resolution of January 12, which ruled out cooperation with the SPD for the time being and pledged the DVP to seek to bring the DNVP into the government. Since he had strong personal doubts about both the wisdom and the practicality of this resolution, Stresemann sought to soften its impact throughout the campaign. It did not, he insisted, affect the DVP's position as a middle party, and neither committed it to a doctrinaire anti-socialist stand nor permanently ruled out the possibility of another Great Coalition. In view of the strength Germany would need to face the difficult decisions ahead, he maintained that it would be shortsighted to draw the political lines of division still tighter than they were. "I regard it as my duty as party man and minister," he said in one campaign speech, "to do all I can to unite the German people for these decisions, and not to force upon them the question: bourgeois or socialist?"[28]

On most other domestic issues the party's position was the

[27] *Ibid.*, 391ff., article for *Die Zeit*, April 1924.
[28] *Ibid.*, 400, speech at Bremerhaven, 30.4.1924.

same as in 1920, but there was a slight shift with regard to the issue of monarchism. Stresemann was again anxious to keep the question of a restoration from becoming a factor in the campaign, because of the divisive effects at home and the possible adverse reaction abroad. But since the more enthusiastic monarchists in the DVP were unwilling to see the party continually sidestep the issue, he agreed to the inclusion in the election platform of a pledge to seek a *Volkskaisertum*. Although this vague commitment to an even vaguer concept represented no real alteration in his position or that of the DVP, the militantly republican *New York Times* immediately sensed a plot and reacted violently in early April with an editorial entitled "Stresemann Joins the Junkers."[29] In view of the possible effect of such adverse publicity on the United States' attitude toward the Dawes Plan and the international loan, Stresemann acted swiftly to allay American suspicions. In a special interview with the *Times* correspondent in Berlin, he explained that the DVP's commitment to the eventual establishment of a constitutional monarchy in no way precluded his loyally serving the Republic. To back up his argument he pointed out that the monarchist Thiers had been the first President of the third French Republic.[30] Throughout the rest of the campaign he and the other leaders of the DVP returned to the position he had adopted after the assassination of Rathenau, maintaining that the reconstruction of Germany could only be carried out within the framework of the Republic.[31]

Although it undoubtedly lessened the severity of the setback, the Dawes Plan could not rescue the DVP from a defeat at the polls on May 4. The result was much as Stresemann had feared it would be. The party received a million fewer votes than in the previous elections and lost nearly a third of its Reichstag seats, emerging with a delegation of only 45. The other principal

[29] *New York Times*, 1.4.1924, p. 20.
[30] *Ibid.*, 5.4.1924, p. 1.
[31] *Vermächtnis*, I, 384, speech at Kiel, 6.4.1924.

government parties, the DDP and the Center, also suffered losses, dropping from 39 to 28 and 68 to 65, respectively. But the most crushing setback was registered by the SPD, which plummeted from 171 to 100. As Stresemann had predicted, the chief victor was the DNVP, which emerged as the most powerful party in the Reichstag, controlling 106 seats. Gains were also scored by the Communist Party and the Nazi-Racist group, which controlled 62 and 32 seats, and by a host of splinter parties. The National Liberal Union was a conspicuous failure, winning only one seat, which went to Maretzky, who joined the DNVP after a futile attempt to set up a "National Liberal Reich Party."

The first result of the elections was the revival, for the first time since 1918, of the question of liberal unity. The impetus came from the badly decimated DDP, whose new chairman, Erich Koch-Weser, had long favored a union with the DVP.[32] The overtures were actually made by two other leaders of the party, Hermann Fischer, the Cologne businessman and Willy Hellpach, head of the strong DDP organization in Baden. Soon after the elections they both approached Stresemann with proposals for a merger. Stresemann, however, refused to consider a fusion. In part, this was undoubtedly due to the fact that the DVP's losses had increased the clamor for a coalition with the DNVP, a move which it was hoped would halt the migration of DVP voters to the right by saddling the Nationalists with responsibility for the unpopular steps the government was so often forced to take. Since a merger with the DDP would complicate this project by tying the DVP to the left, it would clearly have encountered opposition within the party. This was not the only reason for Stresemann's attitude, however. Even more important was his bitterness toward the left-wing Democrats because of the treatment they had accorded him in 1918. He made this plain by indicating that while there could be no merger, the DVP was ready to admit the right wing of the DDP to its ranks. This was

[32] *Koch-Weser Papers*, Vol. 31, p. 1.

naturally unacceptable to the Democratic leaders and they let the matter drop.[33]

In the light of subsequent events, Stresemann's rejection of the Democratic overtures must be recorded as a severe blow to the Republic. Had a united liberal party been formed in 1924, it would almost certainly have been a potent force in rallying support to the new regime and in counteracting the trend toward party fragmentation which was such an important factor in the system's eventual paralysis. In addition, with both the DDP and the DVP staggered by severe losses and united behind the Dawes Plan, and with the DVP's right wing weakened by the withdrawal of some of its leaders, conditions were especially favorable for a merger in May 1924. They were better, in fact, than they had been at any time since 1918 or were to be again during the life of the Republic. It was therefore extremely unfortunate that at such a time Stresemann regarded old animosities and the comparatively minor differences that separated him from the left-wing Democrats as more important than the broad area of agreement which the two parties shared.

On May 15 the cabinet of Chancellor Marx held its first meeting following the sharp reduction of the minority coalition's strength by the elections. Because the SPD was unwilling to enter the government unless the suspension of the eight-hour workday (put into effect under the enabling act of December 1923) was reversed, the cabinet decided it had no choice except to invite the greatly enlarged DNVP to join the government. The Nationalists quickly indicated their readiness for such a step. But at the same time, they demanded the withdrawal of both Marx and Stresemann and the appointment as Chancellor of Admiral Alfred von Tirpitz, former chief of the Imperial Navy and a newly elected DNVP deputy. Furthermore, they served notice that they would press for important revisions in the Dawes Plan.

[33] *Nachlass*, 3160/7397/171989ff., Hellpach to Stresemann, 13.5.1924. Also, *Vermächtnis*, I, 405, "Tagesnotizen" on talk with Fischer. Also, *Nachlass*, 3161/7400/172759; *ibid.*, 3098/7116/145521.

The Nationalists' conditions appalled Stresemann and thoroughly confirmed his doubts about the possibility of bringing them to cooperate within the government. He was naturally angered by their demand for his own replacement and complained to Lord D'Abernon: "In other countries the successful conduct of foreign affairs brings about confidence in the Minister. Here it only produces envy. . . . Events like this . . . make one realize what Bismarck meant when he said, 'I hated all night long.' "[34]

But just as unacceptable, from his standpoint as Foreign Minister, were the Nationalists' attitude on the Dawes Plan and their nomination of Tirpitz, whom the Allies identified with the worst aspects of the old regime. With regard to the Plan, Stresemann was thoroughly convinced that Germany's only hope for a reasonable settlement of the Ruhr-reparations dispute lay in insisting that the experts' proposals be accepted without changes. It was no secret that some French leaders considered the Plan too lenient on Germany and he felt they would welcome a proposal for revision, since that would take the whole question back into the realm of power politics. If this should happen, the French, with their close ties to the British, would have the advantage. As he explained it to a closed meeting of the DVP Central Committee: "Poincaré is just waiting for German reservations. If I make ten reservations, then he will make twenty-five, and he has all the leverage. . . ."[35]

The rest of the cabinet accepted his views on the Dawes Plan and decided to reject the DNVP's terms and break off the negotiations. But the talks were soon begun again when the Nationalists indicated a willingness to compromise, offering as an opening concession to accept Marx as Chancellor if a new Foreign Minister was appointed. Both the cabinet and, to Stresemann's chagrin, the DVP delegation decided that the question of one minister's retention could not be allowed to block the

---

[34] D'Abernon, *An Ambassador*, III, 68.
[35] *Deutsche Volkspartei Papers*, Vol. 105n, p. 33, speech of 6.7.1924.

formation of a parliamentary majority.[36] Confronted with this display of unanimity, he indicated his willingness to withdraw. Still, he was bitterly disappointed at the prospect of having to relinquish his post just as the Dawes Plan negotiations with the Allies were about to enter the decisive stage. He therefore spent several anxious days while Marx conducted talks with the DNVP. In the end, the Nationalists came to Stresemann's rescue by holding firm on most of their demands regarding the Dawes Plan. On June 2 Marx declared the negotiations terminated.[37] That evening the Chancellor formed a new cabinet, consisting mostly of his former ministers, including Stresemann, which was backed by the DDP, the Center, the DVP, and the BVP. Four days later, when the confidence question was put to the new Reichstag, the votes of the small minority coalition, plus those of the SPD and several splinter parties, proved sufficient to override an opposition consisting of the DNVP, the Nazi-Racist group, and the Communists.

Relieved at the outcome of the governmental crisis and anxious to rule out any attempt on the part of the Nationalists to undermine his position during the final Dawes Plan negotiations with the Allies, Stresemann prevailed upon the Marx cabinet to announce that no changes would be made in the government's composition until after the Plan had been put into effect.[38] The cabinet could not, however, completely ignore the Nationalists' evident determination to gain a place in the government. One of the laws necessary to implement the Dawes Plan, a measure providing for international supervision of German railway finances, involved a change in the constitution and so required the backing of two-thirds of the Reichstag. While the government could command a simple majority with the help of the SPD, it could manage the two-thirds margin only with the support of at least part of the DNVP delegation. If the Nationalists voted in a block against

[36] *Vermächtnis*, I, 412ff., his diary notes.
[37] *Ibid.*, 413.
[38] *Ibid.*, 429, his article for *Die Zeit*, 13.6.1924.

the measure, the cabinet's only recourse would be to ask the President to dissolve the Reichstag and call new elections.

In the light of these facts Stresemann reluctantly concluded that the government had no choice except to seek the support of the Nationalists. As Foreign Minister, he regarded the delay that would result from a dissolution as potentially ruinous, since in his opinion the current international situation was uniquely propitious. In England the Conservatives had suffered a setback at the polls the previous December and the first Labour government had taken office under Ramsay MacDonald, whose vigorous opposition to the policies of Poincaré was well known. Even more important, Poincaré had lost his dominant position in France, where the elections of May 11 had led to the formation of a less nationalistic government headed by the Radical Socialist Edouard Herriot. The one drawback in this otherwise favorable situation was, as Stresemann realized, that neither of these two new governments was firmly established. Both were dependent on flimsy coalitions for their support and were thus subject to a decisive defeat at any time. In view of this, he feared that if negotiations were held up until a new Reichstag was elected the diplomatic landscape might not be so favorable when talks were resumed. And if in the interval *Poincarismus* should again come to the fore in France, he felt that all would be lost.[39] In the hope of winning the Nationalists' support, and thus the needed two-thirds margin for the railway bill, Stresemann indicated in mid-June in a newspaper article that their entry into the government could be taken up again after the adoption of the Dawes legislation, but only if they joined with the government in passing the necessary measures.[40] The article had no

[39] *Deutsche Volkspartei Papers*, Vol. 105n, pp. 34ff., his speech to the Central Committee, 6.7.1924. Erich Eyck overlooks this factor, as well as the economic consequences of prolonging the Ruhr occupation, in reproving Stresemann for not having exploited the situation to deal the DNVP a setback at the polls and provide the electorate with a lesson in political responsibility: *Geschichte der Weimarer Republik* (2 vols., Zürich & Stuttgart, 1954–1955), I, 416f.

[40] *Vermächtnis*, I, 429, his article for *Die Zeit*, 13.6.1924.

visible effect on the DNVP, however, which continued to insist upon alterations that would have effectively undermined the whole Plan.

The Nationalists' stubborn stand confronted the government with a perplexing problem, but at the same time it provided Stresemann with a useful diplomatic weapon for the final negotiations regarding the Dawes Plan, which took place at the London Conference during August. Soon after the Conference opened, he requested the promise of a speedy end to the occupation of the Ruhr in return for Germany's resumption of reparations payments. Contrary to his expectations, his request was firmly rejected by the new French Premier, Herriot, who had been bound by his cabinet not to make such a pledge. This development came as a severe disappointment to Stresemann, for from the beginning he had counted on a rapid liquidation of the occupation once the Dawes Plan had been adopted. He had assured the government parties that this would be the case and it was quite possible that a French refusal might set off a revolt, since feeling on the matter was strong, especially within the DVP.[41] For several days it seemed that the issue of the evacuation would produce a stalemate and bring the Conference to an end. The situation was rescued, however, when Stresemann made skillful use of the fact that he had to deal with the recalcitrant Nationalists when he returned from the Conference. He convinced Herriot that he had to have a tangible concession to take home. After a quick flight back to Paris to consult with his cabinet, the French statesman agreed to pledge the withdrawal of all troops from the right side of the Rhine within a year and consented to an immediate evacuation of several areas that had been occupied in 1921.[42] These concessions satisfied the government parties but not the Nationalists. On August 22, a week after the end of the London Conference, their Reichstag delegation met and announced that it would oppose all of the Dawes legislation, including the crucial railway bill.

[41] *Ibid.*, 457.   [42] *Ibid.*, 466ff.

Even in the face of this announcement, Stresemann remained confident that the Nationalists would not wreck the Dawes Plan. It was well known that they were being subjected to heavy pressure on behalf of the measure by a number of special-interest groups. Of these the most important were the Army, which feared a leftist victory at the polls if the agreement was rejected, and industry, which was anxious to see the international loan go through. In view of the influence the Army and industry commanded within the DNVP Stresemann apparently concluded that their efforts would suffice to shift the balance within the rightist party in favor of those who were willing to accept the Plan. Therefore, he showed no interest at first in a proposal submitted to him on August 23 by Julius Curtius and Alfred Zapf of his party's Reichstag delegation. On the basis of information from within the DNVP delegation, the two deputies insisted that the Nationalists could be brought behind the necessary legislation. This could be accomplished, they maintained, if the DVP would agree to demand their admission to the government in the autumn and also to back that demand with a threat to withdraw its own support from the cabinet if the other coalition parties refused to admit them. Evidently convinced that no such step would be necessary to gain the needed DNVP votes, Stresemann saw no reason to endanger his good relations with Chancellor Marx, whom he had only recently dissuaded from reopening negotiations with the Nationalists. On the 24th he informed Curtius and Zapf that the DVP could not consider making any such unilateral commitment behind the back of the Chancellor.[43]

As the final decision on the Dawes legislation approached, the pressure on the DNVP steadily increased. Stresemann apparently contributed to this himself, for his state secretary in the Foreign Ministry, Ago von Maltzan, arranged for a meeting between the American Ambassador, Alanson B. Houghton,

[43] *Nachlass*, 3112/7126/147334f., memorandum on talk with Curtius and Zapf, 24.8.1924.

and three leading Nationalists, Oskar Hergt, Otto Hoetzsch, and Count Kuno von Westarp, on August 24. At this meeting, the Ambassador, while unable to make any official commitment, clearly indicated that the American loans provided for in the Dawes Plan, plus additional private credit, would be forthcoming as soon as the necessary legislation was adopted. He left no doubt, on the other hand, that a rejection would bring the whole project into question in Washington.[44] Still another form of coercion was brought to bear on the Nationalists on the morning of the 27th, when President Ebert announced that if the legislation was not adopted he would dissolve the Reichstag and call new elections. In spite of this mounting pressure, Stresemann's optimism proved to be unfounded. When the legislation came before the chamber for a preliminary vote on the evening of the 27th, the DNVP held firm and the crucial railway bill failed to obtain the needed two-thirds margin.

In the wake of this development Stresemann hastily swept aside all domestic political considerations in a desperate attempt to rescue his foreign policy. Reversing his earlier stand, he gave his approval to the Curtius-Zapf proposal. Accordingly, on the 28th the DVP delegation released an open letter to the Nationalists, pledging support for their admission to the government if they would join in approving the Dawes legislation.[45] In addition, with the approval of the rest of the cabinet, he promised the DNVP that the government would follow the adoption of the Dawes Plan with a renunciation of the war-guilt clause of the Versailles Treaty, both to the German public and to the Allies.[46] These moves weakened the resistance of the Nationalists, but their leader, Hergt, sought still another concession, demanding that the chancellorship go to the DNVP's Count

[44] Felix Hirsch, "Stresemann, Ballin und die Vereinigten Staaten," *Vierteljahrshefte für Zeitgeschichte*, III (1955), 30f.

[45] *Vermächtnis*, I, 559, letter to Campe, 8.9.1924. Also, *Deutscher Geschichtskalender*, XL, Part 2, 200.

[46] *Vermächtnis*, I, 561, telegram to Maltzan, 2.9.1924. Because of the strong reaction of the Allies, the renunciation was never made to them, *ibid.*, 561ff.

Westarp when the party was brought into the government. Since this was unacceptable to both the DVP and the Center his demand was rejected. As a result, Hergt instructed the Nationalist delegation to oppose the Dawes legislation when the final vote was taken.

Stresemann's last-minute moves had, however, produced the desired effect and undermined the unity of the DNVP. On August 29, when the crucial railway bill came before the chamber, 48 Nationalist deputies ignored Hergt's instructions and backed the measure, while 52 opposed it.[47] This gave the bill the necessary two-thirds margin and provided Stresemann with a resounding victory. A day later the final documents necessary to bring the Dawes Plan and the evacuation of the Ruhr into effect were signed in London.

The rescue of Stresemann the Foreign Minister by Stresemann the party leader at the time of the Dawes legislation was not to be an isolated incident. Absorbed in the task of directing Germany's relations with the rest of the world, he was coming increasingly to look at domestic politics in terms of their relationship to his foreign policies. From this it was only a short step to the exploitation of his influential position as a politician in the interests of those policies. As the Dawes episode demonstrated, he had completed that step by the summer of 1924. Only with this in mind is it possible to understand the sharp shift to the right which during the fall of that year turned him into one of the most outspoken advocates of Nationalist participation in the government, leaving most contemporary observers thoroughly baffled.

This turn to the right was by no means simply a consequence of the DVP's pledge of August 28 to the DNVP. For Stresemann that pledge had been nothing more than an unpleasant emergency measure and in early September, only a little over a week after it had been made, he was already thinking of repudiating it

[47] Hertzman, "German National People's Party," pp. 425ff. Also, Liebe, *Die Deutschnationale Volkspartei*, pp. 85ff.

altogether. From the outset, he had been doubtful about the willingness of the Nationalists to cooperate constructively within the government and apprehensive about the inevitable friction which the DVP's support for their entry would cause with its closest allies in the Reichstag, the DDP and the Center. He was also naturally uneasy about the fact that the Nationalists had never rescinded their demand that he be replaced as Foreign Minister. His worst doubts about the DNVP seemed to be confirmed in early September by an attempt on the part of its intransigent right wing to purge the 48 *Ja-sager* who had voted for the Dawes Plan. At this time he seriously considered repudiating the DVP's pledge on the grounds that only a minority of the Nationalist deputies had fulfilled its conditions.[48] He quickly dropped this idea, however, when the moderates within the DNVP rallied later in the month and managed to hold their own against the intransigents. It was then that he completely reversed his position and began to urge that the Nationalists be brought into the government at once.

Contrary to the fears of some observers, this sudden change in his attitude toward the DNVP was not a mere throwback to the Kapp Putsch and his days of fellow-traveling with the right.[49] It was instead a carefully considered move calculated to influence domestic politics in such a way as to give him greater freedom in his conduct of the Republic's foreign relations. His overriding aim as Foreign Minister was a revision of the Versailles Treaty, but in view of Germany's weakness he saw no hope of achieving this in the foreseeable future through an assertion of strength. On the other hand the Dawes Plan negotiations had convinced him that a *rapprochement* with England and France would make it possible gradually to gain concessions that would do away with many of the most objectionable features of the Versailles settlement. He realized, however, that as long as the DNVP remained in the opposition and under the

[48] *Vermächtnis*, ɪ, 559f., letter to Campe, 8.9.1924.
[49] D'Abernon, *An Ambassador*, ɪɪɪ, 119.

control of its right wing he would be handicapped in trying to put this policy into effect. This had been abundantly demonstrated by the May elections, which had shown that the Nationalists would be able to profit handsomely at the expense of the moderate parties whenever governments led by the latter made any conciliatory gestures toward Germany's former enemies. If, on the other hand, the DNVP could be brought into the government he saw that it would have to share the responsibility for his policies and would no longer be able to attack them with the same unbridled vigor. With the DNVP effectively silenced, he expected that he would be able to adopt a bolder and more flexible line in his dealings with London and Paris without having to fear a setback on the domestic scene each time he made a concession.[50]

As long as the right wing had held the upper hand in the DNVP Stresemann had seen no real possibility of bringing the party to accept a share of the responsibility for his policies. But when the moderate group rallied in late September and removed a major obstacle by bringing the Reichstag delegation to drop its insistence on his replacement, he decided that there was hope of breaking the intransigents' domination. The best way to accomplish this was, in his opinion, to bring the DNVP into the government as soon as possible. Once the party was in the government he was confident that the leaders of its right wing would be discredited in the eyes of the electorate, since it would quickly become clear that they could not make good on the extravagant claims they had made while in the opposition. On the other hand, if the Nationalists remained an irresponsible opposition much longer, he was afraid that the intransigents would, like the Social Democrats in the imperial era, continue to reap the advantages of being able to promise the voters everything without having to deliver anything. And if this happened he was aware that the strength of the DNVP, and hence its

[50] *Vermächtnis*, I, 596, speech of 19.10.1924. Also, D'Abernon, *An Ambassador*, III, 14. Also, *Nachlass*, 3114/7136/149212.

capacity to obstruct his foreign policy, would probably increase rather than decrease with the passage of time.[51]

Stresemann attached sufficient importance to the speedy inclusion of the DNVP in the government to jeopardize both his own good relations with Chancellor Marx and the close ties the DVP had formed with the DDP and the Center during the previous four years. Ever since the Nationalists had wrecked the long and tortuous negotiations following the May elections with their excessive demands, the Chancellor as well as the majority of Centrists and Democrats had been decidedly cool toward the idea of accepting the DNVP into the cabinet. Moreover, although the Center had briefly considered doing so, neither it nor the DDP had joined in the DVP's pledge of August 28 to the Nationalists. Even though he was aware of these facts, Stresemann elected to try to push through his project by means of a frontal assault. In late September he began urging that the DNVP be admitted to the government before the opening of the fall session of the Reichstag, which was scheduled for October 21.[52]

Chancellor Marx reluctantly accepted this proposal but sought to offset its impact by demanding that the cabinet be broadened to the left as well by the admission of the SPD, a condition which the DDP also posed. Since his own argument had been based mainly on the necessity of broadening the minority cabinet, Stresemann could find no objections to Marx's project and he made no attempt to block it. When the negotiations quickly foundered on the irreconcilable differences between the SPD and the DNVP, however, he renewed his demand that the latter be admitted alone. After some hesitation, the Center agreed to his demand, but only on the condition that the DDP also do so.

Obviously confident that he could break the resistance of the Democrats, too, Stresemann sought to coerce them by having

[51] *Vermächtnis*, I, 601, speech of 29.11.1924. Also, *ibid.*, 603ff., article for *Hamburger Fremdenblatt*, 25.12.1924. Also, his "Politische Umschau," *Deutsche Stimmen*, 20.10.1924. Also, *Deutscher Geschichtskalender*, XL, Part 2, 205, speech of 23.10.1924.

[52] *Nachlass*, 3111/7125/147148ff., speech of 27.9.1924.

the DVP announce that it could no longer accept a minority cabinet and would withdraw its own support unless the government was at once strengthened by the admission of the DNVP. Contrary to his expectations, the DDP refused to be intimidated and held firm. The DVP was thus forced to make good on its threat and so withdrew its support from the Marx cabinet. As a result, his brusque tactics produced quite a different situation from the one he had sought. On October 20, the eve of the new legislative session, the Chancellor decided it would be futile to face the chamber with only a rump DDP-Center coalition behind him. With the President's approval he therefore dissolved the Reichstag and scheduled new elections for December 7.[53]

Although it came unexpectedly early, the new election campaign was not inopportune from Stresemann's viewpoint. Its timing enabled the DVP to go before the electorate just as the first concrete effects of his foreign policy were being felt by the general public. This was especially evident in the economic sphere, where the flow of foreign credits provided for by the Dawes Plan was already producing signs of improvement. Just as important, though, and even more tangible, was the fact that the evacuation of the Allied troops from the right bank of the Rhine had already begun and was scheduled for completion by the summer of 1925. In hopes of exploiting these dividends from his foreign policy to the profit of the DVP, Stresemann decided to spend the entire campaign speaking on behalf of its candidates throughout the country. Instead of accepting nomination on one of the DVP's election district lists, he relied for his own re-election on the party's national list (*Reichswahlvorschlag*). This arrangement was made possible by the proportional election law of 1920, which awarded the parties one Reichstag seat for each 60,000 votes they obtained in the various electoral districts and then allowed them to apply the unused or surplus votes to the election of a special group of national candidates. As one of the DVP's national nominees he was free

[53] *Schulthess' Europäischer Geschichtskalender*, LXV, 91ff.

from the normal obligations of a candidate and could spend the entire campaign moving about the country.

The main emphasis of the DVP's campaign was once again on foreign relations. Capitalizing on his position as Foreign Minister, Stresemann pledged that the party's special task would be to uphold the traditional German principle of the "primacy of foreign policy." Furthermore, by presenting his own foreign policy as one of Bismarckian *Realpolitik* he sought to parry the Nationalists' uncomfortably accurate charge that in spite of his earlier opposition to the fulfillment policies of the first republican governments, he had in effect become the foremost advocate of fulfillment with his championing of the Dawes Plan. True *Realpolitik*, he argued, did not consist of ignoring realities, as the leaders of the DNVP preferred to do. Instead, he maintained that it lay in a realistic acceptance of the unpleasant facts of Germany's weakness and a readiness to sacrifice material advantages, which were always expendable, in order to preserve that which was not expendable, namely the unity of the Reich. This, he insisted during the campaign, and not a desire to fulfill the Versailles Treaty, had been the explanation for his acceptance of the reparations burden imposed by the Dawes Plan.[54]

On the domestic side the DVP was committed, as it was during the spring campaign, to seek the inclusion of the DNVP in the next government. Stresemann's attitude toward that commitment, however, was naturally quite different than it had been prior to the May elections. At that time he had reluctantly accepted it as a tactical concession necessary to preserve the unity of the party and had seriously doubted whether it could ever be put into effect. During the fall campaign, on the other hand, it occupied a central place in his plans and he gave it his enthusiastic backing in his speeches, explaining his belief that responsibility would have a sobering effect on the Nationalists. But at the same time, he once again emphasized that although the DVP was for the time being in favor of a coalition with the right,

[54] *Nachlass*, 3160/7398/172342, his article for *Die Zeit*, 13.11.1924.

it remained a party of the middle and would be equally willing to work with the left if the situation should change and the SPD should show a willingness for fruitful cooperation. In line with the position he had adopted after the *New York Times* incident in April, the issue of monarchism was virtually ignored in the DVP's campaign.[55]

On the eve of the elections Stresemann was convinced that the DVP would recoup most of the losses it had suffered in May and predicted confidently that it would increase its strength by 10 to 15 seats. This proved to be too optimistic an estimate, for the party gained only 6 seats, emerging with a delegation of 51. On the whole, the elections had little effect on the composition of the Reichstag except to reduce the strength of the Communist and Nazi-Racist delegations, which dropped to 45 and 14 seats. The only significant gains were recorded by the SPD, which obtained 131 seats, while the DDP and the Center made minor advances, emerging with 32 and 69 seats each. Almost as disappointing to Stresemann as the failure of the DVP to recoup its losses was the fact that the Nationalists not only held their own but increased the number of seats they controlled from 106 to 110. He had been hopeful that the elections would deal them a setback and thus strengthen the moderates by discrediting the obstructionist policies of the leadership. He concluded from the results of the balloting, in a letter written to one acquaintance, that the voters of Germany heeded "only their emotions and not political necessities." Moreover, although many observers traced the DVP's failure to regain its former strength to Stresemann's decision to cooperate with the SPD in 1923, he indicated in the same letter his confidence in the correctness of that decision: "We would have had a struggle of the one Germany with the other if the German People's Party had stood under different leadership and we would no longer have understood one another. . . ."[56] He was aware, too, that his conciliatory foreign policy had cost the party the support of many nationalis-

[55] See his "Politische Umschau," *Deutsche Stimmen*, 20.10.1924. Also, *Vermächtnis*, I, 601, speech of 29.11.1924.
[56] *Nachlass*, 3160/7399/172438f., letter to Schowalter, 20.12.1924.

tic voters, but there also he remained certain that he had followed the right course.

✧

While the elections of December 1924 caused no change in
Stresemann's basic position, they did mark a significant juncture
in his career in the Republic's politics. Even before the elections
he was coming to regard most issues in the light of their relationship to his foreign policies, but he had not simply relegated domestic politics to a secondary position. Instead, he had
sought to coordinate the two by exploiting his successes as Foreign Minister at home just as he had used his position as party
leader to support his foreign policy. The failure, however, of the
electorate to respond significantly to his success in bringing the
costly Ruhr-reparations dispute to a peaceful conclusion convinced him that he had been too optimistic. Afterwards, he
remained confident that his foreign policy would eventually have
domestic ramifications. But his actions clearly indicate that he
felt it would take much longer than he had expected to undermine the strong position of the extremist parties. It is also clear
that he had come to the conclusion that this could be accomplished only by a long series of diplomatic achievements so obvious as to convince even the most shortsighted voters of the
correctness of his policy of conciliation. From December 1924
on, the "primacy of foreign policy" was more than a slogan for
him and he focused his attention on his duties as Foreign Minister to an even greater extent than before. As a consequence
he gave less and less of his time and energy to the DVP. He
was confident that the party would eventually be given credit
by the voters for his diplomatic successes, but for the present
he gave up hope of appreciably increasing its strength and even
resigned himself to the possibility of further setbacks at the
polls.[57] In the meantime the DVP was useful mainly as the
political basis of his position as Foreign Minister and as a
domestic buttress for his foreign policy.

[57] See his letter to Dinghofer, 19.12.1924, *Nachlass*, 3160/7398/
172415f.

VI. DIPLOMATIC TRIUMPH AND
DOMESTIC DEFEAT, 1925

FOLLOWING the elections of December 1924, it appeared for a short time that Stresemann would again hold the dual posts of Chancellor and Foreign Minister, for on December 17 President Ebert asked him to try to form a government. He agreed but immediately made it clear that he would accept the chancellorship only if he succeeded in bringing the Nationalists into the cabinet. When the Center promptly stated its opposition to a rightward-oriented coalition he withdrew from consideration later the same day.[1] The result was a lengthy "Christmas crisis" that carried over into January 1925. During the lull provided by the holidays, Stresemann concluded that the situation ruled out the possibility of bringing the DNVP into a normal coalition government. He began to favor instead the looser arrangement of a non-coalition cabinet consisting primarily of expert ministers, some of whom would be drawn from the ranks of the Nationalists.[2] When political activity revived in January the incumbent Chancellor, Marx, sought at the President's request to form a coalition including the DNVP, but he too was unsuccessful. In the wake of Marx's failure, Stresemann prevailed upon the President on January 9 to name as Chancellor Hans Luther, the political independent who had served with distinction as Minister of Finance since he had appointed him in early October 1923.[3]

Luther, who commanded considerable respect among the Nationalists, produced the results Stresemann had desired. His cabinet consisted of one spokesman each from the Center, the Bavarian People's Party, the DVP, and the DNVP, with the remaining posts going to expert ministers associated with those parties. Although he was unable to bring the Democrats to work

[1] *Vermächtnis*, I, 603.
[2] *Nachlass*, 3120/7179/157822, letter to Retzmann, 26.12.1924.
[3] Luther, *Politiker*, p. 315. Also, *Vermächtnis*, II, 11.

with the Nationalists, he managed to prevail upon them to allow Minister of the Army Gessler to remain on as an expert minister. On January 19 Luther presented this cabinet to the Reichstag and received a firm vote of confidence. Officially, his government was not backed by a coalition and the party spokesmen were technically only liaison men between it and the delegations. In most regards, though, it functioned in much the same manner as a coalition.

There was little surprise when Luther announced that he did not intend a change at the Foreign Ministry. As Lord D'Abernon noted in his diary, Stresemann's decisive role in the fall of Marx's government and the formation of Luther's had convinced most observers that he was the "politician behind the throne."[4] Actually, this was less true of the new cabinet than of the old, as D'Abernon also noted. Luther, according to the Ambassador, had "none of the minor graces, but a sturdy presence, not unlike a Thames tug." He was a more willful and assertive personality than the diffident Marx and relied far less on his Foreign Minister for advice.[5] But in spite of the somewhat altered situation within the cabinet, it was clear that Stresemann had come to occupy a special place in the leading circles of the Republic, for it was generally agreed that he would have to remain at his post. To a degree, this could be explained by the political influence he wielded as chairman of the DVP. Already considerable, this influence had been sharply increased during 1924 by the losses suffered by the SPD and the DDP, which ruled out the Weimar Coalition as a workable alternative, making it virtually impossible to form a viable government of either the left, center, or right without the DVP's support.

The key to the unusual position Stresemann had come to occupy, however, was his success in managing the country's foreign affairs. Because of the sweeping effects on the German economy of the Versailles settlement, and subsequently the

[4] D'Abernon, *An Ambassador*, III, 127.
[5] *Ibid.*, 126. See also the cabinet minutes, AR, *Kabinett*, reels 1832ff.

Dawes Plan, the Republic's domestic affairs were dependent to an unusual degree upon its relations with other countries, and especially with the victorious Allies. Since he had made greater progress in dealing with the British and the French than any of his predecessors, Stresemann had thus come to be regarded as virtually indispensable.[6] So secure was his position, in fact, that the incident following the May elections of 1924, when his replacement had been briefly considered, proved to be the last time that the possibility of his exclusion from the cabinet was seriously raised.

While his main importance to the government clearly lay in his skillful management of his post as Foreign Minister, his value to the cabinet did not end there. He also proved successful in the realm of public relations. A part-time journalist himself, he spoke the language of reporters and was popular with them. He recognized the importance of good press relations and since assuming office in 1923 had taken special pains to cultivate the trust and confidence of the Berlin corps of journalists. Particularly effective was his practice of holding frequent and informal news conferences for the representatives of both the domestic and foreign press, including a regularly scheduled tea for foreign journalists each Friday afternoon. Also, he willingly made himself available for interviews with individual reporters.[7] In addition to these attempts to present his point of view to the press, he continued his own direct journalistic activities, though on a reduced scale. In occasional editorials for his *Deutsche Stimmen* and in articles planted in newspapers throughout the country, either anonymously or pseudonymously, he patiently explained his foreign policy as well as the other policies of the government and sought to marshal public support.

Compared with the cynical techniques of modern mass indoctrination, Stresemann's propagandistic endeavors were re-

---

[6] This was noted by D'Abernon, *An Ambassador*, III, 153.

[7] Starkulla, "Organisation und Technik," pp. 95ff. Also, Louis P. Lochner, *Always the Unexpected* (New York, 1956), pp. 128ff.

freshingly naive and old-fashioned. They stood in sharp contrast to those of Alfred Hugenberg of the DNVP, whose hydra-
like press empire was already spreading venom in the local
dailies read by the mass of the German public. Hugenberg
founded his empire on contempt for the intelligence of the public
and sought to indoctrinate the masses by playing upon old fears
and hatreds through the ceaseless repetition of emotionally
charged shibboleths. Stresemann's approach, on the other hand,
was predicated on an optimistic faith in the intelligence of
both the press and the reading public. He honestly believed in
the possibility of persuasion by calm, logical argument and in
his writings and statements to the press rarely appealed to emo-
tion and never indulged in invective. His approach was directed
at the journalistic profession and at the educated, thinking seg-
ment of the reading public, and so ruled out any concerted effort to influence the masses. He was thus at a great disadvantage
in his attempts to counteract the increasingly vitriolic mass
propaganda of Hugenberg and, later, of the Nazis. Still, his
methods were by no means entirely without effect, even where
the extremes of German politics were involved. After his death,
a prominent Nazi journalist, Erich Schneyder of the Essen
Nationalzeitung, confessed that the confidence Stresemann placed
in the Berlin press corps had in his case been thoroughly dis-
arming and had made it impossible for him to attack the Foreign
Minister with the same abandon that usually marked the Nazis'
onslaughts on the leading figures of the Republic.[8]

Because of his success in dealing with the press, Stresemann
had established himself as the unofficial spokesman of the government by the time the Luther cabinet took office. The shift of
chancellors brought no change in this. The rather stiff and
bureaucratic Luther disliked being subjected to the prying questions of reporters and gladly left the bulk of such matters to his
Foreign Minister.[9] Moreover, the Chancellor relied heavily on

[9] Luther, *Politiker*, p. 324.
[8] Louis P. Lochner, "Die aussenpolitische Wirkung der Nachricht,"

him in the cabinet's relations with the Reichstag. Never having served as a deputy himself, Luther was somewhat baffled by the mysteries of the chamber's politics and was full of admiration for Stresemann's ability to keep informed about what was going on there and to exert influence at the right place at the right time, terming him "a master at handling the parliament."[10]

Simultaneously with the installation of the Luther cabinet in January, Stresemann initiated the negotiations that were to lead to the Locarno Pact. The original impetus for this project came from Lord D'Abernon. As an exponent of traditional balance-of-power politics who was concerned about the possibility of a French hegemony on the Continent, the Ambassador was disturbed by his government's apparent readiness to give in to French demands for an Anglo-Belgian-French alliance. The problem of French security had been a diplomatic sore spot ever since the promise to guarantee France's boundaries, made by Britain and the United States in 1919, had been rendered null by America's failure to ratify the Versailles Treaty. By the end of 1924, after the failure of a number of plans, the British seemed ready to agree to a tripartite alliance. Acting apparently on his own, D'Abernon set out to block this development and at the end of December discretely informed the German Foreign Ministry that London might be favorably disposed to a revival of the multilateral Western security pact proposal which the Cuno government had made without success in 1922.

Stresemann welcomed D'Abernon's suggestion. He, too, was disturbed at the prospect of an Anglo-Belgian-French agreement, feeling that it would effectively isolate Germany. Moving swiftly in hopes of seizing the diplomatic initiative, he handed the Ambassador a note for transmission to London on January 20, one day after Luther had taken office and given his approval to the move. In this note, which was intended only for confidential con-

---

Zeitungswissenschaft, 1.7.1934, p. 20. Also, letter, Lochner to author, 23.9.1960.

[10] *Ibid.*, p. 340.

sideration by the British government, he raised the possibility
of a security pact in which the powers interested in the western
boundaries established at Versailles would agree to guarantee
those boundaries. At first this proposal was viewed with skepti-
cism in London, but at length the British indicated that their
reaction was not unfavorable. With this encouragement, Stresemann officially opened formal negotiations by dispatching his
proposal to Paris in a note dated February 9.

In conducting this opening phase of the security pact negotiations Stresemann acted in the strictest secrecy. Within the German government only Chancellor Luther and a few high officials
of the Foreign Ministry knew of the notes sent to London and
Paris. Later, answering criticism of his handling of the matter,
Stresemann maintained that an early announcement would have
given anti-German elements in France a chance to attack the
proposal before the French cabinet could give it fair and objective consideration.[11] This scarcely explains, however, why he refused to inform the German cabinet of his moves. The explanation, which he naturally did not wish to make public, was that
he feared a similar attack on the project from one of the government parties, the DNVP.

From the very beginning, the DNVP had been an important
consideration in his plans for a security pact. His principal aim
in pressing for the Nationalists' entry into the government had
been to saddle them with responsibility and thus make it difficult for them to attack his foreign policy. He was therefore determined to handle the security pact project in such a way as to
keep it from producing an open break that would drive them back
into the opposition, where they could handicap him during the
coming negotiations with the British and French by assailing him
with charges of appeasement. In addition, he hoped to make
diplomatic use of their presence in the government, since his
experience at the London conference of the previous summer
had convinced him that a recalcitrant party at home had definite

[11] *Vermächtnis*, II, 74f., 90.

diplomatic value, especially if its votes were crucial.[12] Finally, it would clearly add to the value of the security pact in the eyes of the rest of the world if the Nationalists could be brought to accept it, since they were regarded abroad as the major party of revenge in Germany and hence the greatest potential threat to the peace.

Knowing that it would be difficult to bring the Nationalists to agree to the dispatch of the notes to London and Paris, Stresemann's plan was to avoid informing them until he had received a reply from the French. If the answer was favorable, he would be able to present the DNVP with a *fait accompli* which the rest of the cabinet would in all probability accept. If the reply was not favorable, the negotiations would in any case be terminated. This plan, however, was upset by the French government, which showed no hurry to answer his note. By March, rumors of the German proposal had reached the press in both Britain and France and Stresemann was forced to inform the parties of his action. The Nationalist spokesman in the cabinet, Martin Schiele, who was associated with the moderate group within the party, proved to be quite cooperative. He had misgivings about the pact proposal but his main concern was not to lose his party's newly gained voice in the government. In mid-March he indicated to Stresemann and Luther that it would probably be possible to hold the DNVP behind the government's policy for the time being if a Reichstag debate on the security pact plan could be avoided. If a debate took place, he warned that the Nationalists would come under attack from the more radical Nazi-Racist group and would find it difficult, if not impossible, to stand with the government.[13]

Since he still had no reply from Paris, Stresemann accepted Schiele's suggestion. Employing all his skill at parliamentary maneuver, he contacted the parties separately and accompanied

---

[12] *Deutsche Volkspartei Papers*, Vol. 105o, p. 42, speech to the Central Committee, 22.11.1925.

[13] *Nachlass*, 3114/7135/149013ff., minutes of meeting of Stresemann, Luther, and Schiele, 17.3.1925.

his requests for support and for a postponement of debate with arguments tailored to suit the outlook of each party. He based his approach to the Social Democrats on the warning that a debate would endanger the position of the left-of-center Herriot government in France by forcing the German government to emphasize the diplomatic gains it had made at the expense of France during the past year.[14] In speaking to the Nationalists, on the other hand, he stressed the advantages of the security pact for Germany. The most important of these, he maintained, was the fact that the pact would bring the Anglo-French Entente to an end and force Britain to take Germany's side in the event of a repetition of the French march into the Ruhr. Moreover, he confidently predicted that a relaxation of tensions in the west would do away with the Western powers' apprehensions about Germany and thus open the way for "a development in the east which will bring us new boundaries there."[15]

In addition to these long-range advantages of a pact, he assured the Nationalists that there would also be more immediate returns. In particular, he indicated that he expected it to produce a quick solution of the troublesome Rhineland problem. The situation there had become acute in January when the Allies had refused to evacuate the Cologne zone as scheduled under the Versailles Treaty after an arms inspection had, in their opinion, shown that Germany had not complied with its disarmament obligations. This development had caused considerable apprehension in Germany and raised fears of a permanent occupation of the Rhineland. Stresemann predicted to the Nationalists, however, that the Allies would agree to evacuate the Cologne zone in return for German acceptance of the obligations of a security pact. He also indicated that he expected the pact to shorten the occupation of the two remaining zones of the Rhineland, which were not scheduled for evacuation until 1930 and

[14] *Ibid.*, 149016.
[15] *Nachlass*, 3166/7312/158680, minutes of meeting of Stresemann, Luther, and a group of DNVP deputies, 2.4.1925.

1935. Finally, he sought to dispel the Nationalists' concern about Germany's entrance into the League of Nations, which had been pending for some time and which would become unavoidable with the adoption of the security pact. Germany would agree to enter, he promised them, only if its obligation to participate in League sanctions was limited to take into account its state of disarmament and its exposed geographical position.[16]

Although many Nationalist deputies objected to the pact on the grounds that it involved recognition of French possession of Alsace-Lorraine, the party's leaders did not flatly reject Stresemann's arguments. They protested, however, that he was not asking a high enough price for German acceptance of the boundary settlement of 1919. Moreover, they objected to the fact that in the notes to London and Paris he had not mentioned the concessions he expected. In a letter addressed to Stresemann on March 21 the DNVP delegation announced that if he wished its support he would have to inform the Allies that Germany expected a number of concessions in return for acceptance of the pact. The most important of these were a prompt evacuation of the entire Rhineland, Allied recognition of Germany's intention to seek a territorial revision in the east, and Allied acceptance of Germany's repudiation of the war-guilt clause of the Versailles Treaty.[17]

The Nationalists' demands were clearly the product of either a lack of diplomatic talent or a desire to wreck the security pact by deliberately making it unacceptable to the Allies. In the hope that the former might be the case, Stresemann patiently informed their spokesmen that he was confident he could gain concessions from the Allies once the negotiations had gone far enough to create an atmosphere of mutual trust. But he pointed out that the project would have no chance at all if he attached a string of conditions to it from the outset. Moreover, he warned them that

---

[16] *Ibid.*, 158677ff. Also, *Nachlass*, 3114/7135/149013ff., meeting of Stresemann, Luther, and Schiele, 17.3.1925.

[17] *Nachlass*, 3166/7311/158590ff.

some of his expectations for the future, and especially those regarding revision in the east, could not be discussed publicly without producing a storm of hostility in France.[18] His arguments, however, had little effect on the Nationalist leaders and by April a stalemate had been reached. But since the French had still not replied to his note the whole matter was, for the time being, at a standstill and the DNVP's recalcitrant attitude did not produce a crisis.

In the midst of this opening phase of the security pact negotiations an era in the history of the Republic came to an end with the death on February 28, 1925, of President Ebert. Stresemann was genuinely saddened by this news. At the beginning of Ebert's term, he, like many other middle-class Germans, had been uncomfortable about the elevation of a former harness-maker's apprentice to the country's highest political office. But in the course of his close association with the President, first as Chancellor and then as Foreign Minister, his reservations had been dispelled and he had come to admire the unassuming Social Democrat sincerely. In his opinion, Ebert's steadfast refusal to use the presidency for partisan purposes and his establishment of the office as a symbol of national unity was especially praiseworthy.[19] As a man who knew something of such problems himself, Stresemann also admired the manner in which Ebert surmounted the handicap of his humble origins and characterized him to one correspondent as "a man of inborn tact."[20]

If Ebert had lived, his term as President would have come to an end on June 30 and even before his final illness he had indicated that he would probably not seek re-election. It had been Stresemann's hope that if the President retired he would resume

[18] *Nachlass*, 3166/7312/158677ff., minutes of meeting of Stresemann, Luther, and a group of DNVP deputies, 2.4.1925. See also his earlier warnings to Schiele at meeting of 17.3.1925, *Nachlass*, 3114/7135/149014f.

[19] See his "Dem Reichspräsidenten zum Gedächtnis," *Vermächtnis*, II, 37ff.

[20] *Nachlass*, 3161/7400/172776, letter to Heyd, 27.5.1925.

his leading position within the SPD. In June 1925, he explained his views in a letter to Ambassador Houghton, who had left Berlin to take over the American Embassy in London: ". . . even if he had not run again as President, [he] would have had the great task of being the leader . . . of a Social Democracy which would make its peace with the state and assume in our country the role that the British Labour Party plays in England."[21] Ebert's death, he felt, had deprived the country of a devoted and formidable advocate of domestic reconciliation: "The old and the new Germany must not permanently stand opposed to each other. . . . There must be a fusion between the old and the new. And the deceased would certainly have been one of those who would have devoted himself fully to this task."[22]

During the presidential campaign that followed Ebert's death, Stresemann again intervened decisively in the politics of the Republic. Once more he was motivated primarily by considerations of foreign policy, but on this occasion his efforts produced results very different from what he had intended. In fact, the whole episode can only be described as a complete failure from his point of view, since he ended by contributing to the very sort of outcome he had sought to avert.

Because of the approaching end of Ebert's term, the preparations for the campaign had actually begun before the President's death. The first step came in early February, when Friedrich von Loebell, chairman of the conservative, quasi-political *Reichsbürgerrat*, proposed a meeting of all non-socialist groups to consider a unity candidate. Stresemann agreed to this proposal but in deference to Ebert, who was still regarded as a possible SPD candidate, he refused to take part himself.[23] The first meeting of the non-socialist groups took place on February 12 and resulted in the election of a nominating committee presided over by Loebell. Included on this committee were representatives

---

[21] *Nachlass*, 3114/7133/148766, letter of 4.6.1925.
[22] *Vermächtnis*, II, 40.
[23] Kessler, *Tagebücher*, p. 435.

of the DVP, DNVP, BVP, the new Economics Party, the *Land-bund*, banking and industry, and a number of small political groups and splinter parties. Not represented were the Center, whose spokesman at the meeting of February 12 had refused membership in the committee, and the DDP, which had declined even to send a representative to the meeting. During February the nominating committee, which soon became known as the Loebell committee, met frequently. By the end of the month it had narrowed the field of candidates to three: General von Seeckt, Minister of the Army Gessler, and Karl Jarres, the DVP mayor of Duisburg, who had won national acclaim for his resistance to the French during the Ruhr struggle of 1923.

The possibility that Seeckt might become President was extremely disturbing to Stresemann. This was apparently not due to any fear of a military dictatorship, for in spite of the incident during his chancellorship when Seeckt had all but demanded his resignation, there is no evidence to indicate that Stresemann's faith in the General's loyalty to the constitution had been shaken. The explanation for his reaction lay in his fear that the election of such an obvious symbol of the military would be a severe blow to his foreign policy. In view of the latent distrust of the British and the French, he felt that the election, or even the nomination, of the General would inevitably arouse suspicions and thus complicate, if not wreck, his security pact project. He therefore made known his opposition to Seeckt.[24] Yet there was no need to exert himself greatly, for the General had little real support outside the Army and his candidacy quickly collapsed.

The removal of Seeckt left only Gessler and Jarres in contention. By the end of the first week of March it seemed that the nomination would go to Jarres, since a majority of the Loebell committee had united behind him. The whole situation was abruptly altered, however, by the two unrepresented non-so-

[24] *Nachlass*, 3166/7311/158505f., letter to Prince von Bülow, 17.3. 1925.

193

cialist parties, the Center and the DDP. Shortly after the majority of the Loebell committee had expressed its preference for Jarres, these two parties indicated their willingness to join with the committee if it would nominate Gessler, who enjoyed the advantages of being both a Catholic and a Democrat. Since Gessler was also acceptable to the DVP and the DNVP it seemed that the long-sought unity candidate had at last been found.

In spite of this unusual unanimity among the parties Gessler's candidacy was never realized. The responsibility for this lay solely with Stresemann. It has been suggested that this action on his part can be explained by the fact that his personal relations with Gessler were on terms that could at best be described as polite mutual dislike.[25] Although this may have played a contributing role in his decision, there is no reason to doubt the sincerity of the objection he used to block the nomination. His objection, as he frankly informed Gessler at the time, was that according to reports from the Paris Embassy, the election of the Minister of the Army would have much the same effect as the election of Seeckt, since the French were convinced that the Minister was simply a tool of the Army. Even though Stresemann agreed that this was an inaccurate assumption on the part of the French, he felt that it would definitely be a foreign policy handicap and therefore served notice on Gessler that he had decided to make no secret of his objection to his nomination.[26]

Stresemann's objection quickly had the desired effect on the Center and the bulk of that party turned against Gessler's candidacy. The DVP, on the other hand, proved more difficult and on the morning of March 12 the Reichstag delegation openly defied him by voting to back Gessler. Unwilling to accept such a defeat, he promptly went over the head of the delegation and summoned a seldom-used central organ of the party, the Reich Committee. Meeting on the afternoon of the 12th, it upheld his

---

[25] Theodor Heuss, in his introduction to Gessler, *Reichswehrpolitik*, p. 9.

[26] *Vermächtnis*, II, 44, letter of 11.3.1925.

position, voting to reject Gessler and back Jarres. Finally, after what Stresemann described in his diary as a *Grosskampftag*, the delegation gave in during the evening and agreed to drop Gessler rather than set off a bitter intraparty struggle.[27]

Since the Center and the DDP were unwilling to accept Jarres, the united non-socialist front collapsed as a result of Stresemann's intervention. Only the DVP and the DNVP managed to agree on a joint nomination and entered the campaign as the *Reichsblock*, with Jarres as their candidate. When the balloting took place on March 29, Jarres received more votes than any of the other major candidates—Otto Braun of the SPD, Willy Hellpach of the DDP, former Chancellor Marx of the Center, and the Communist Ernst Thälmann. However, he failed to obtain the absolute majority specified by the constitution and a second election had to be scheduled for April 26. Since only a plurality was required on the second ballot, the SPD and the DDP realized that Jarres would win if they presented separate candidates again and therefore decided to back the Center's nominee, Marx. Even in the face of this realignment, Stresemann and the rest of the DVP remained confident that Jarres could be elected. The Nationalists, on the other hand, insisted that a stronger candidate must be found and at the beginning of April proposed Hindenburg to the Loebell committee, which had been reconstituted after the first election.

This move alarmed Stresemann. Since the period following the revolution—when he had enthusiastically supported Hindenburg's candidacy for the presidency—his thinking had undergone a complete reversal. A large factor in this was undoubtedly his memory of the Field Marshal's sympathetic attitude toward the rebellious Bavarian authorities during the dark days of the autumn of 1923. But more immediately, he was opposed to the Nationalists' proposal on the grounds that Hindenburg, the very personification of German militarism to the outside world, would

[27] *Ibid.*, 45.

be an even greater foreign policy liability than Seeckt or Gessler.[28] Moreover, he was probably also concerned about the possibility that the aged war hero might take issue with his policy of conciliation toward Germany's former enemies. He therefore brought the DVP to reaffirm its support of Jarres. Knowing that Hindenburg had stipulated that he would run only as the nominee of the united *Reichsblock* parties, Stresemann also considered sending a confidential emissary to inform the Field Marshal of his objections. He dropped this plan on April 7, however, when word reached Berlin from Hanover, where Hindenburg was living, that the latter had heard of the DVP's attitude from the local DVP officials and had prepared a statement ruling out his candidacy which he intended to release the next day.[29]

Stresemann was later to regret not having sent his emissary, for the Nationalists were not easily discouraged. On the afternoon of the 7th Admiral Tirpitz called upon Hindenburg on their behalf. In the course of a long conversation he succeeded in prevailing upon his old colleague to hold off the publication of his statement. In the wake of this news the Bavarian People's Party and a number of smaller rightist parties and groups promptly indicated their intention of joining the Nationalists in backing the Field Marshal.

In spite of these unexpected developments, the DVP spokesmen in the reconstituted Loebell committee, Admiral Willi Brüninghaus, Julius Curtius, and Adolf Kempkes, held firm in their support of Jarres when the committee convened to reach its decision on April 8. Jarres, however, had grown disgusted at the behind-the-scenes maneuvering around Hindenburg, and in a telegram which arrived during the meeting informed the committee that he was withdrawing from the race. Left without their

[28] Germany, Auswärtiges Amt, Büro des Staatssekretärs, *Innere Politik*, Vol. 7, microfilm, National Archives of the United States, reel 2281, frame 136816, telegram, Stresemann to German Embassy, Washington, 8.4.1925.

[29] *Nachlass*, 3161/7400/172676f., letter to *Saale-Zeitung*, 21.4.1925. See also Walter Görlitz, *Hindenburg* (Bonn, 1953), pp. 249ff.

candidate, the DVP representatives agreed to drop their opposition to Hindenburg's nomination, but only if the Field Marshal still agreed to run after being informed that the DVP had doubts about his candidacy—a move which they hoped might discourage him in view of his earlier insistence on the united backing of the *Reichsblock* parties. Loebell immediately informed Hindenburg of the situation by telephone. After hearing of the DVP's attitude, Hindenburg requested more time before he made his decision. When Loebell insisted that it was impossible to delay his decision any longer, the supposedly iron-willed soldier asked in effect to be told what to do. Loebell's advice was to take the nomination. This sufficed for Hindenburg and he gave Loebell permission to announce at once that he was accepting.[30]

This sudden rush of events passed Stresemann by. He learned of Jarres' decision to withdraw only at the last minute and sought in vain to block the move in a telephone conversation with the disgusted candidate.[31] On the other hand, he was not informed at all of the stand taken by the DVP spokesmen on the Loebell committee until after the meeting of the 8th. Their clumsy handling of the situation naturally upset him and he regretted not having accepted a place on the committee himself.[32]

But while he was displeased with the actions of the DVP spokesmen on the Loebell committee, Stresemann made no effort to reverse their acceptance of Hindenburg's nomination on behalf of the party. As long as the nomination was being discussed confidentially in political circles Stresemann had not hesitated to make known his apprehensions about the effect Hindenburg's election might have on his foreign policy. He was, however, unwilling to make his objections public or to endorse Marx once the nomination had been made. As he explained it at the time, he felt that the effect of such a move on his part would be just the

---

[30] *Deutsche Volkspartei Papers*, Vol. 111, typed account of the meeting, apparently by Curtius.
[31] *Nachlass*, 3166/7312/158731ff., Jarres to Stresemann, 15.4.1925.
[32] Kessler, *Tagebücher*, p. 436.

opposite from what he desired; it would be widely interpreted as an attempt to subordinate Germany's internal affairs to the likes and dislikes of its former enemies—a development that would only stir up nationalistic resentment and thus aid the cause of Hindenburg.[33] A more likely explanation might be that he was unwilling to add still another crisis to the political situation by triggering the collapse of the Luther cabinet, which would almost certainly have happened if he had defied the DNVP and rejected Hindenburg. In addition, he may well have been concerned about the fact that his own position as Foreign Minister would be jeopardized if Hindenburg won despite his opposition.

Whatever his motivations, Stresemann approached the second presidential campaign in the paradoxical position of being opposed to the candidate endorsed by his own party. At first he sought to cope with this unusual situation by avoiding any public statements on the election. This conspicuous silence on his part only attracted the attention of the press and the resulting speculation about his attitude became in itself a perplexing problem.[34]

In the week following Hindenburg's nomination Stresemann's apprehensions were greatly increased by the reports received at the Foreign Ministry on the reaction abroad to the Field Marshal's candidacy. Particularly disturbing were the reports from Paris and Washington, where the response was described as especially unfavorable.[35] With the security pact negotiations still pending, a wave of anti-German sentiment in France could easily upset all of his diplomatic plans. Similarly, a strong reaction in the United States could jeopardize the American financial credit that had been flowing into Germany since the adoption of the Dawes Plan.

By April 15 Stresemann had grown sufficiently concerned to consider seriously the possibility of ruling out Hindenburg's election by bringing about the withdrawal of both major nominees

[33] *Ibid.*
[34] *Nachlass*, 3166/7312/158780, article from *Germania*, 17.4.1925.
[35] *Nachlass*, 3113/7129/147779ff., diary for 15.4.1925.

in favor of an uncontroversial unity candidate. Such a move, he thought, might be possible if it were justified not in terms of foreign policy but on the grounds that the Marx-Hindenburg race was dividing Germany between left and right. In an effort to find a compromise candidate he sounded out Chancellor Luther and former Foreign Minister Walter Simons, who as head of the *Reichsgericht*, or high court, had been called in to serve as interim-President after Ebert's death. Both, he discovered, were receptive to the idea of accepting the nomination, although Luther protested that the presidency would not provide him with enough activity. His plan, however, aroused no enthusiasm in other quarters and he decided to drop it.[36]

With no further hope of blocking Hindenburg's candidacy, Stresemann decided to try at least to allay the suspicions of the Western powers. In the second week of the campaign he broke his silence and defended the DVP's support of the Field Marshal. In an article in *Die Zeit* on April 19 he rejected the argument of those who maintained that Hindenburg was the candidate of militarism and reaction and confidently predicted that his election would affect neither the country's republican form of government nor his own foreign policy.[37] But even though he had finally accepted Hindenburg's candidacy, he displayed no enthusiasm for it and offset the effect of this article with another statement in *Die Zeit* four days later in which he defended Marx against charges that he had proved ineffectual during his term as Chancellor.[38]

The explanation for this reserve on his part was, as some of the press surmised, that he was still opposed to Hindenburg.[39] The confidence he had expressed about the Field Marshal in his article of the 19th did not reflect his own views and was designed only for its effect abroad. On the day the article appeared, he noted with concern in his diary that contrary to what he had

[36] *Ibid.*
[37] *Nachlass,* 3161/7400/172660.   [38] *Nachlass,* 3166/7312/158802.
[39] *Nachlass,* 3161/7400/172663, article from *Vorwärts,* 20.4.1925.

written, Hindenburg had thus far failed to adopt what he considered a clear position on either the form of government or foreign policy.[40] On the same day, he confided to Count Harry Kessler that he expected all he had accomplished in his two years as Foreign Minister to be destroyed if Hindenburg was elected. The consequences of such a development, he predicted, would be no less than catastrophic. His only consolation in the whole situation, he told Kessler, was that "Hindenburg won't be elected in any case."[41]

Hindenburg was, of course, elected. Stresemann's reaction is not recorded but the results of the balloting of April 26 must have disturbed him greatly. However, by May 12, the day of Hindenburg's inauguration, his tendency to seek the optimistic side of all situations had asserted itself. As his diary entry reveals, he came away from his first official encounter with the new President with an impression that was mainly positive: "Hindenburg makes a powerful personal impression, a mighty figure who towers above the people by a head's length, a great statue, his face often motionless, as if carved. For the time being I do not have the feeling that Hindenburg will be under the influence of any political camarilla, at least not consciously." His consoling verdict was that the Field Marshal "belongs more to the period of Wilhelm I than of Wilhelm II and will certainly endeavor to be a constitutional President. . . ."[42]

Before the election, Stresemann had told Count Kessler that he could not imagine making a report on foreign policy to Hindenburg.[43] On May 19 he had his first opportunity to do so. Afterwards, he admitted in his diary that he had gone into the meeting very worried about what the new chief executive's attitudes would be. Furthermore, he noted that he had been initially put off by discovering a copy of the reactionary *Kreuzzeitung* prominently spread out before the President. The results of the conference, however, left him considerably relieved. He had found,

---

[40] *Vermächtnis*, II, 50.   [41] Kessler, *Tagebücher*, pp. 435f., 439.
[42] *Vermächtnis*, II, 59.   [43] Kessler, *Tagebücher*, p. 436.

he wrote, that Hindenburg was in agreement with most of his policies and was pleasantly surprised to learn how actively the Foreign Ministry was pursuing them. To his relief, the President had raised no objections to his plans for a security pact, although he did have reservations about Germany's entry into the League. In general, he concluded that Hindenburg was a very conservative person, but he felt that he was honestly trying to be loyal and objective. "The main thing," Stresemann observed in what was to be a fateful prophecy, "is not to let irresponsible people gain influence over him."[44]

His doubts about the new President were revived by their second conference, which took place on June 9. At that time he decided that irresponsible influences were in fact in operation, since Hindenburg seemed to be getting only those press reports that were unfavorable to the Foreign Ministry. This meeting left him far less confident than their first conference and he concluded that in the realm of foreign policy the President was "trapped within his own preconceptions." In addition, Stresemann was shocked to hear Hindenburg object to his candidate for an important diplomatic post on the grounds that he was not a man who could "pound on the table."[45]

In spite of his own doubts and misgivings, Stresemann adopted, for public consumption, the viewpoint that Hindenburg's election had made an important contribution to the consolidation of the Weimar state by rallying to it many Germans whose loyalties had previously been tied to the old regime.[46] During his own lifetime this proved, within limits, to be the case. His fears failed to materialize and the aged war hero scrupulously refrained from any interference with either the affairs of the cabinet or his foreign policy. But in view of the role that Hindenburg later played in the eventual destruction of the Republic, Stresemann's failure to act on his convictions and make public his opposition to the

[44] *Nachlass*, 3113/7129/147822f.
[45] See his diary, *Nachlass*, 3113/7129/147840f.
[46] *Nachlass*, 3114/7133/148765ff., letter to Houghton, 4.6.1925.

Field Marshal stands as one of the most unfortunate incidents of his career. In falling back on the facile assumption that Hindenburg would lose in any case, he succeeded in keeping the DNVP in the government and so avoided adding a cabinet crisis to the presidential crisis. In addition, he safeguarded his own position as Foreign Minister. These short-term gains pale, however, when compared to the long-term consequences of Hindenburg's election. It may be questioned whether Stresemann's opposition would have been sufficient to tip the balance against Hindenburg, even if he had succeeded in carrying the DVP with him (which was by no means certain). But in view of the risks at stake, it is difficult to avoid the conclusion that the effort would have been worthwhile. In any event, it was at the time of the second campaign, and not, as some have argued, the first, that Stresemann showed bad judgement with regard to the presidential election.[47] His opposition to Gessler in the first campaign was the result of an honest, and not unfounded, assessment of the national interest; he had no way of knowing that it would produce a stalemate and so open the way for Hindenburg.

While Hindenburg's election produced a generally negative reaction abroad, Stresemann's fear that it would upset his plans for a security pact was not realized. Throughout the presidential campaign, the project had been at a standstill because of the continuing failure of France to reply to the German note of February 9. In part this delay was due to a French government crisis set off by the fall of the Herriot cabinet on a domestic issue in early April. The crisis lasted only a week, however, and it was clear that the new government, headed by Paul Painlevé, with Aristide Briand as Foreign Minister, was waiting to see whether Hindenburg's election would bring any sharp change in German foreign policy. By June, the French were apparently satisfied that this would not be the case and on the 16th of that

[47] Cf. Theodor Heuss's introduction to Gessler's *Reichswehrpolitik*, p. 9.

month they set negotiations in motion with a reply to the German note. Their response was, on the whole, positive but went further than Stresemann was prepared to go. Particularly unacceptable from his point of view was their suggestion that Germany sign with its eastern neighbors treaties which would provide for compulsory arbitration of all disputes and which would be guaranteed by the Western powers. In effect, this amounted to a proposal to extend the security pact to the east, a move which Stresemann was determined to avoid. But since the British had made no secret of their unwillingness to accept binding commitments in the east, he remained confident that the French would have to drop this proposal and thus saw no insurmountable diplomatic obstacles to the realization of his plans.[48]

There were, however, obstacles on the domestic scene. On the far right, the Nazis and the radical Pan-German League had launched a vitriolic propaganda campaign against the security pact plan during the spring, labeling it "a third Versailles" and calling for Stresemann's indictment for treason. In contrast to his stand on the Dawes Plan, General von Seeckt was also opposed to the project. As an advocate of an eastward orientation and strong ties with Russia, Seeckt was extremely cool to the idea of a pact with the Western powers. Moreover, he feared that the agreement would handicap his illegal attempts to rearm the German Army.[49] His own prescription for foreign policy, the General informed the startled cabinet on one occasion, was much simpler: Germany should acquire power again and as soon as it had that power it should conquer back everything it had lost.[50]

From Stresemann's point of view the opposition of Seeckt and the radical right, though annoying, was less of a cause for concern than the continuing refusal of the Nationalists to endorse the pact proposal. As he had anticipated, the DNVP's participa-

[48] *Vermächtnis*, II, 103ff.   [49] Rabenau, *Seeckt*, p. 421.
[50] *Nachlass*, 3113/7129/147890, diary for 26.6.1925.

tion in the government had kept all except its radical fringe from attacking his policy publicly. By June, however, it had become clear that the intransigent group, headed by the new chairman of the Reichstag delegation, Count Westarp, were again firmly in control and were determined to block the pact. This was revealed when by error a DVP deputy received a confidential DNVP policy statement which announced that the leadership had decided the best way to defeat the pact was to stay in the cabinet and use the party's voice there to sabotage the project. By leaving the government, it was argued, the DNVP would only be serving Stresemann's purposes, since its place would be taken by the DDP and the SPD, a development that would virtually assure adoption of the pact.[51]

Soon after the arrival of the French note of June 16 the Nationalists revealed the line of attack they intended to use. Seizing upon the fact that the original German notes proposing the pact had been dispatched to London and Paris without the knowledge of the DNVP ministers, they maintained that the project was an independent undertaking on the part of the Foreign Ministry and that the cabinet and the government parties were in no way bound by the terms of the notes. Hence, they insisted, the whole project would have to be reviewed in detail, and possibly revised, by the cabinet—a procedure that would give them an opportunity to insist upon the inclusion of demands specifically designed to provoke an Allied rejection of the pact.[52]

Stresemann was strongly opposed to the Nationalists' argument, realizing that if he gave in it would probably mean the end of the security pact. The only hope he saw of bringing the DNVP behind the project was to confront it with the alternatives of acceptance of the proposal as it stood or rejection and withdrawal from the government. At a meeting of the Reichstag's Foreign Affairs Committee on July 1 he sought to counter

[51] *Nachlass*, 3161/7401/172814f.
[52] *Vermächtnis*, II, 109ff. Also, Stresemann's memorandum of 5.7.1925, *Nachlass*, 3114/7132/148518ff.

the Nationalist argument by insisting that the pact proposal was in fact a policy of the government and not simply of the Foreign Ministry. This was the case, he maintained, since the dispatch of the notes had been approved by the Chancellor, who under the constitution had sole responsibility for determining the basic lines of government policy. In executing policy within those lines, the ministers functioned independently and were obligated to report only to the Chancellor, as he had done in this case.[53]

To his surprise and indignation, he was not supported in this contention by Chancellor Luther, who remained conspicuously silent during the Committee meeting. Although Stresemann's constitutional argument was unassailable, it had long been common practice in the Republic's cabinets for the ministers to consult with the representatives of the various participating parties before taking important steps. Apparently, the Chancellor had misgivings about the fact that the Nationalists had not been informed about the notes to London and Paris. Also, as a politician without a party, Luther was evidently reluctant to offend the powerful DNVP, especially since its favorable attitude toward him had been a factor in his selection as Chancellor. He thus elected to give ground to the Nationalists in spite of the dangers involved for the security pact. On the evening of July 1 he asked Stresemann to his office and read him portions of a statement he was preparing. Its most important point was that while he remembered discussing the matter with Stresemann as early as January 19 he was unable to recall having seen the actual text of the pact proposal before February 21 and so could not assume responsibility for what had happened before that date.[54] Since the proposal had been dispatched to both London and Paris before February 21, this amounted to a refusal

[53] *Nachlass*, 3143/7315/159336.
[54] *Ibid.*, 159347ff., the statement was prepared in the form of a letter to Stresemann. See also the latter's memorandum of 5.7.1925, *Nachlass*, 3114/7132/148523ff. In his recent memoirs, Luther admits being fully informed by Stresemann from January 19 on, see his *Politiker*, pp. 356ff.

on his part to accept Stresemann's argument that the project had been a policy of the government and not simply an independent undertaking of the Foreign Ministry.

Taken aback by Luther's sudden lapse of memory, Stresemann at once offered to resign and let the Chancellor take over the Foreign Ministry. At first Luther seemed inclined to accept this offer and hinted that the London Embassy would be available for Stresemann. It apparently occurred to him, however, that the Foreign Minister's exit from the government would probably bring with it a withdrawal of the DVP's backing and he quickly reversed himself, stating that a resignation was out of the question. Stresemann then indicated that he would prepare a statement of his own on the origins of the pact proposal to offset the Chancellor's. Using Luther's telephone, he immediately summoned to his residence the Secretary of State in the Foreign Ministry, Carl von Schubert, and the Ministry's legal expert, Friedrich Gaus, both of whom had worked on the pact project from its inception. When Schubert and Gaus arrived at his residence later in the evening, neither they nor he could remember precisely when Luther had first seen the exact text of the pact proposal. They agreed with him, though, that the Chancellor had been well informed of its nature prior to its dispatch. Moreover, both offered to record this in statements setting forth their recollection of the events.[55]

On the morning of the next day, July 2, Stresemann awoke in an angry mood and concluded that it was pointless to try to counter the Chancellor's retreat by refuting his version of the events of January and February. Instead, he decided upon a direct frontal assault. Telephoning from his bed, he informed Luther's State Secretary, Franz Kempner, that if the Chancellor released his statement he would refute it from the floor of the Reichstag. He warned, though, that if it came to such

---

[55] His memorandum of 5.7.1925, *Nachlass*, 3114/7132/148527ff. The memoranda of Gaus and Schubert, dated 2.7.1925, are in *Nachlass*, 3168/7316/159363ff.

an open break he would be speaking only as a deputy and no longer as a minister.[56]

This move had the desired effect. Being a practical man, Luther chose to risk a possible clash with the Nationalists rather than face the apparently certain loss of the backing of Stresemann and the DVP. Later on the 2nd, State Secretary Kempner appeared at the Foreign Ministry on a peace-making mission. The Chancellor, he announced, had decided not to release his statement. Instead, he indicated that Luther would be content to exchange confidential memoranda on the matter. Stresemann consented to this but warned that he would not accept a memorandum in which doubt was cast on Luther's responsibility for the dispatch of the notes to London and Paris.[57] The next day the Chancellor's memorandum arrived—minus the offending passage about his responsibility.[58] This development naturally gratified Stresemann. But he was slow to forgive Luther, whom he himself had picked as Chancellor, for what he considered a breach of loyalty. During the next months the two were barely on speaking terms and communicated almost exclusively through the intermediacy of Kempner.[59]

Luther's acceptance of Stresemann's position led the Nationalists to beat a tactical retreat. With the Chancellor supporting the Foreign Minister, they obviously realized that if they pressed their argument on the responsibility for the pact proposal the result could only be their own withdrawal from the cabinet. For the time being, they were determined to avoid this, for the Reichstag was scheduled to enact new tariff legislation during the summer and they were anxious to exploit their position in the government to press for high protectionist duties, particularly on agricultural products.

Stresemann learned of the Nationalists' position from his

[56] *Nachlass*, 3114/7132/148531, his memorandum of 5.7.1925.
[57] *Ibid.*, 148532.
[58] *Nachlass*, 3114/7132/148513ff.
[59] Hans Luther, "Erinnerungen an Gustav Stresemann," *Schweizer Monatshefte*, xxxiv (1954), 432. Also Luther, *Politiker*, pp. 363f.

sources in the Reichstag. He decided to take advantage of the situation and try to maneuver the DNVP into accepting his policy.[60] He planned to accomplish this by confronting the DNVP Reichstag delegation with the choice of approving his reply to the French note of June 16 or rejecting it and withdrawing from the government. In this undertaking he had the support of his own party. Throughout the spring, the DVP delegation had loyally backed the security pact project. Moreover, in June the delegation had realized that their party would again be the target of charges of fulfillment from the DNVP if the Nationalists succeeded in placing sole responsibility for the pact proposal on Stresemann. In an effort to block the Nationalists' move, the DVP delegation therefore demanded a full-scale foreign policy debate that would force the DNVP to support the government's actions or leave the cabinet. Since this demand coincided closely with Stresemann's plans, he gave his full backing to it. At first there was strong opposition from Luther, who was anxious to avoid the danger of a break with the DNVP. But when Stresemann and the DVP delegation held firm, the Chancellor gave in, consenting to a debate on the answer to the French note and agreeing to stake the cabinet's survival on a confidence measure.[61]

The note which Stresemann dispatched to Paris on July 20 was the product of a delicate balancing of diplomatic and domestic considerations. On the one hand, he was anxious not to endanger the progress he had already made by provoking a French rejection. On the other, he had to risk offending the French in order to make the reply as palatable as possible for the DNVP. The final note was thus a strongly worded document which left no doubt that Germany expected concessions from the Allies in return for the recognition of the boundary settlement of 1919. These, it made clear, would have to include a revision of the

---

[60] *Nachlass*, 3113/7129/147903, diary for 3.7.1925. The sources are not identified.

[61] *Nachlass*, 3114/7132/148524, 148533f., his memorandum of 5.7. 1925.

Rhineland situation and a reduction of Germany's obligations as a member of the League in line with its state of disarmament and its geographical position.[62]

The note struck the right balance. The French accepted it and so did the Nationalists. Although Count Westarp roundly attacked the French note of June 16 in the foreign policy debate which took place on July 22, he indicated that his party found nothing objectionable in the Foreign Ministry's reply. On the next day the DNVP delegation voted for the government's confidence measure, which was carried by a wide margin, with the SPD and the DDP joining the government parties in the affirmative.

While this was an important victory for Stresemann, he had no illusions about the Nationalists' motives. Shortly before the foreign policy debate, Rudolf Breitscheid of the SPD had approached him with information gained in conversations with leading Nationalists. The DNVP delegation, Breitscheid reported, intended to vote for the confidence measure rather than risk losing its place in the government. He warned, though, that the Nationalists were determined to keep the pact negotiations from reaching the conference stage and were hopeful of bringing about the Foreign Minister's fall, if necessary by reviving their argument about the responsibility for the original German notes to London and Paris. In this connection, Breitscheid reported, they had already approached the SPD delegation, though without success, with the offer of a voice in the selection of Stresemann's successor in return for help in felling him.[63] The actions of the Nationalists quickly substantiated Breitscheid's information. In his speech in the foreign policy debate, Westarp carefully referred to the pact proposal as "the Foreign Ministry's memorandum" and in the cabinet meetings Schiele performed what Stresemann described as "nothing short of mental gym-

[62] *Vermächtnis*, II, 155.
[63] *Nachlass*, 3113/7129/147913f., diary for 17.7.1925.

209

nastics" to avoid conceding the DNVP's responsibility for the project.[64]

In spite of these rather discouraging signs Stresemann remained hopeful that it would be possible, as at the time of the Dawes legislation, to bring at least part of the Nationalists behind the security pact. He therefore set out to try to break down their resistance. Having exhausted his store of arguments on the party's leaders, he sought to influence the attitude of its rank and file. Since it was, as he had explained to the Nationalist leaders on several occasions, "difficult to say in public why our action was good" without offending the French, he had to resort to indirect methods.[65] Thus, in August and September he published two long articles on the pact, one under a pseudonym in his magazine *Deutsche Stimmen*,[66] and the other anonymously in the newspaper *Hamburger Fremdenblatt*, which he frequently used for such purposes.[67] In addition, he sent a long letter on the subject to the Crown Prince, who commanded considerable respect in Nationalist circles.[68]

In all of these discussions of the security pact he emphasized the advantages it offered Germany. As he had done in his confidential talks with the DNVP leaders, he confidently predicted that it would destroy the Anglo-French Entente and open the way for sweeping territorial revisions in the east. He also held out the prospect of a recovery of Germany's overseas colonies and a completion of the Austro-German *Anschluss* vetoed in 1919 by the Allies. In addition, he sought to overcome the Nationalists' strong emotional objection to the fact that the agree-

[64] *Verhandlungen* (Reichstag), CCCLXXXVII, 3399, Westarp's remarks. Also, *Nachlass*, 3113/7129/147917, diary for 19.7.1925.

[65] *Nachlass*, 3114/7135/149014f.

[66] "Sicherheitspakt, Völkerbund und Ostfragen," by "Dr. Hans Schumann," 20.8.1925. Manuscript in *Nachlass*, 3168/7316/159579ff.

[67] Dated 14.9.1925, reprinted in *Vermächtnis*, II, 170ff.

[68] *Nachlass*, 3168/7318/159871ff., letter of 7.9.1925. For a discussion of its political significance, see Harald Schinkel, *Entstehung und Zerfall der Regierung Luther* (printed dissertation, Berlin, 1959), pp. 138ff. Cf. Thimme, "Gustav Stresemann, Legende und Wirklichkeit," pp. 331ff.

ment would require Germany to recognize French possession of Alsace-Lorraine and accept membership in the League of Nations. A close reading of the drafts of the pact, he pointed out, would reveal that Germany was not renouncing Alsace-Lorraine but only the possibility of regaining the provinces by force. Peaceful revision, perhaps through an eventual plebiscite, thus remained a possibility under the agreement. In answer to those who argued that Germany would be subjecting itself to the will of its enemies by entering the League, he emphasized that the government's position was that entrance was only possible if Germany received a permanent seat on the Council, which brought with it the power of veto. Instead of reducing the country's stature, he argued, League membership would greatly strengthen Germany's diplomatic position by giving it a new weapon with which to defend its own interests as well as those of the German minorities in surrounding countries.

These propaganda efforts were apparently not without effect. As might have been expected, the radical right wing of the DNVP remained unmoved and during August the newspapers controlled by the reactionary Alfred Hugenberg dropped their neutral pose and began to criticize the pact openly.[69] On the other hand, the position of the moderate elements, led by Schiele, seemed to be strengthened. When the Allies issued a proposal in mid-September for a conference at Locarno the following month, the attempts of the DNVP right wing to torpedo the meeting by loading the German delegation with demands that France was certain to reject were successfully resisted by Schiele. Instead, he presented a set of conditions which, while going somewhat further than the Foreign Ministry's, were not completely unacceptable.[70]

At the Locarno conference of October 1925, Stresemann met with considerable success. The final version of the security pact

[69] *Nachlass*, 3113/7129/147937, 147959, diary for 2.8.1925 and 16.9. 1925.
[70] *Ibid.*, 147967f., diary for 23.9.1925.

was basically what he had envisioned; Belgium, France, and Germany agreed to refrain from any forceful revision of their mutual boundaries, and Britain and Italy acted as guarantors. Just as he had expected, the British vetoed the French attempt to extend the territorial guarantees to the east. In place of such an eastern settlement the French had to content themselves with non-compulsory, and hence virtually meaningless, arbitration treaties between Germany on the one side and Poland and Czechoslovakia on the other.

While Stresemann's views prevailed for the most part in the final drafting of the security pact, he encountered more difficulty than he had expected with regard to concessions from the Allies. Both the British and the French eventually gave in to his insistence that Germany's obligation to participate in League sanctions be reduced in view of its state of disarmament. He was less successful, however, with his other requests, the most important of which involved a prompt evacuation of the Allied troops from the Cologne zone, a lessening of the rigors of the occupation in the two remaining zones, and a reduction of the authority of the Allied Military Control Commission, which was in charge of checking on Germany's adherence to the disarmament clauses of the Versailles Treaty. The main obstacle was French Foreign Minister Briand, who adroitly countered Stresemann's insistence that he had to have concessions to placate the recalcitrant DNVP by summoning up the spectre of Poincaré and pointing out that he, too, had an intransigent right to contend with.[71] After lengthy negotiations, Briand finally indicated that he saw no reason why most of the German requests could not be met. But because of domestic political considerations he insisted that this would have to come as a voluntary act on the part of France and not as a concession attached to the security pact. While he was unable to make any promises, Briand assured Stresemann that he

---

[71] *Nachlass*, 3113/7131/148483, Stresemann's speech in Berlin, 14.12. 1925.

would seek to bring the French government to agree to the German requests upon his return to Paris.[72]

Before the German delegation had left for Locarno the Nationalists had insisted that the meeting be conducted on an informal non-binding basis. However, Stresemann and Luther, who had accompanied him, regarded the results of the conference as so successful that they agreed to initial the draft treaties, thus ruling out any changes and committing themselves to seek a prompt ratification. While Stresemann was aware that it would be difficult to secure the Nationalists' approval of the agreement, he was cautiously optimistic when he returned to Berlin on October 18. The deadline set at Locarno for the final signing of the security pact was a month and a half off and he was hopeful that in the interval concessions would be forthcoming from France that would overcome the objections of the DNVP. On the day after his return, at the first cabinet meeting following the conference, his optimism was reinforced by the attitude of Schiele. After hearing the reports of the Chancellor and the Foreign Minister, the Nationalist spokesman announced that his own reaction was to give "a loud yes" to the Locarno settlement but that his party would have to await the actions of the French before making a final decision.[73]

The intransigents within the DNVP were unwilling to wait. When the party's Executive Committee met on October 23 with the chairmen of its powerful provincial organizations to consider the situation, sentiment was overwhelmingly against the pact. In a last-minute attempt to shift the tide Schiele appealed to Luther to issue an official communiqué stating the government's view that the security agreement did not rule out a peaceful reacquisition of Alsace-Lorraine. Since one of the principal objections of the DNVP's provincial leaders was that some of the wording of the pact might possibly be construed as an un-

---

[72] *Nachlass*, 3169/7319/160164f., Stresemann's remarks to cabinet, 19.10.1925.
[73] See the cabinet minutes, *ibid.*, 160160ff.

conditional acceptance of the territorial *status quo*, Schiele hoped that such an announcement would overcome their opposition.[74]

Luther readily agreed to Schiele's proposal, but Stresemann, who had gone to Karlsruhe to make a speech on behalf of the pact, rejected it flatly. Reached by telephone at the hall where he was speaking, he protested that it would involve an unacceptable foreign policy risk, since such a conspicuous action on the part of the German government would undoubtedly arouse hostility in France and thus endanger the whole Locarno agreement.[75] He then promptly broke off his trip and set out for Berlin in hopes of rescuing the situation. When he arrived in the capital, however, the decision had already been reached. On the evening of the 23rd the Nationalist leaders had voted to withdraw their ministers from the cabinet and instruct their Reichstag delegation to oppose ratification of the security pact and the appended treaties. On the 25th the DNVP delegation accepted this decision and the next day an embarrassed Schiele left the cabinet, explaining that he and those who shared his views within the DNVP had been "overwhelmed by a tidal wave."[76]

Stresemann was disgusted at what he termed the "inconceivable stupidity" of the Nationalists.[77] Even if they were determined to vote against the security pact he was unable to understand why they had not at least held off the announcement of their decision until after the French concessions had been granted. As it was, he was afraid that with the problem of bringing the Nationalists into line apparently removed, Paris would feel there was no need to be generous with its concessions.[78] However, his concern proved groundless. Early in November Briand notified him that the Cologne zone would be evacuated by February 1926, at the latest and that a number of changes would promptly be effected to make the occupation of the remaining two zones less

[74] *Nachlass*, 3113/7129/148002ff., diary for 27.10.1925. Also, *Ibid.*, 147999f., memorandum by Kempner, 23.10.1925.

[75] *Ibid.*   [76] *Nachlass*, 3113/7129/148004, diary for 27.10.1925.

[77] *Ibid.*, 148008, diary for 28.10.1925.

[78] *Ibid.*, 148009, diary for 29.10.1925.

burdensome. In addition, the French government consented to reduce the size and the activities of the Allied Military Control Commission.[79]

For a short time it appeared that there might be a repetition of the collapse of Nationalist unity that had made possible the passage of the Dawes legislation the previous summer. Realizing that rejection of the security pact would probably have an adverse effect on Germany's economic relations with the Western powers, a group of prominent businessmen associated with the DNVP protested in early November against the decision to oppose the Locarno settlement. So, too, did a number of spokesmen of the agricultural wing of the party.[80] Moreover, although he remained skeptical about the value of the security pact, General von Seeckt had dropped his outspoken opposition to the agreement after satisfying himself that it did not tie Germany's hands in the east.[81]

These developments, however, had no visible effect on the DNVP deputies. They would have had more effect, Stresemann felt, if a two-thirds margin had again been necessary in the Reichstag, making passage impossible without the votes of at least part of the DNVP. But despite encouragement from both Luther and Stresemann, the Ministry of Justice had been able to find nothing in the Locarno treaties that would impinge upon the constitution and thus necessitate a two-thirds vote.[82] As a result, even those Nationalists who favored the pact decided to hold to the party line and hope the SPD would provide the votes needed for a majority.

The fate of the pact was thus in the hands of the Social Democrats. They were known to be favorably disposed to the agree-

---

[79] *Vermächtnis*, II, 227ff., 269ff. Also, Hans W. Gatzke, *Stresemann and the Rearmament of Germany* (Baltimore, 1954), pp. 41ff.

[80] *Schulthess' Europäischer Geschichtskalender*, LXVI, 161. Also, *Nachlass*, 3113/7129/148048, memorandum, dated December 1925.

[81] Rabenau, *Seeckt*, p. 422.

[82] *Nachlass*, 3113/7129/148048, memorandum, dated December 1925. Also, Luther, *Politiker*, pp. 395f.

ment, but the situation was complicated by the fact that they were also strongly opposed to many of the domestic policies of the Luther government. This was especially true of the new tariff schedule adopted during the summer, which placed high duties on agricultural products and thus had the effect of keeping the price of food high for urban workers.[83] In view of this, Stresemann was concerned about the possibility that the SPD might exploit the rump cabinet's position by demanding immediate admission to the government and sweeping domestic concessions in return for its support for the Locarno treaties. Because of the attitudes of the non-socialist parties on the domestic issues at stake, he felt that this could easily set off a crippling government crisis and possibly even necessitate new elections, thus delaying and perhaps endangering final action on the security pact.[84] He had, however, underestimated the Social Democrats' ability to rise above partisan politics when the national interest was at stake. Without making any demands in return, the SPD gave its votes to the government when the Locarno agreement came up for ratification on November 27, thus providing the margin necessary for passage.

To Stresemann's relief, the defection of the DNVP had no effect on Hindenburg's stand. Both he and Luther had been worried about the possibility that the Nationalists' opposition might lead the President to reject the pact also, thus adding a constitutional crisis to the cabinet crisis. Although Hindenburg was still not completely happy about all aspects of the agreement, particularly the fact that it committed Germany to join the League, he upheld the rump cabinet's position. Characteristically, he viewed the DNVP's bolt in military terms, concluding that the Nationalists had been guilty of a breach of discipline and complaining to Stresemann: "I'm sorry about the *Deutschnationale*. They will do themselves a lot of harm."[85]

---

[83] *Nachlass*, 3113/7129/147890, diary for 26.6.1925.
[84] *Ibid.*, 148009, diary for 29.10.1925. Also, *Ibid.*, 148048, memorandum, dated December 1925.
[85] *Ibid.*, 148003, diary for 27.10.1925.

In Stresemann's opinion most of the credit for Hindenburg's support belonged to Luther. The Chancellor, he observed, had "performed the great service of keeping the old gentleman in line."[86] This important contribution on Luther's part did away with the last of Stresemann's resentment at his lapse of memory during July. Their relations had already been greatly improved in October by Luther's decision to accompany him to Locarno. By taking this step, the Chancellor in effect tied the fate of his government to the security pact and ruled out another attempt on the part of the Nationalists to wreck the project by presenting it as an independent undertaking of the Foreign Ministry. While Stresemann's diary indicates that he suspected that Luther's decision to go to Locarno was dictated at least in part by vanity and a desire not to be left out of such an important event, he was nevertheless grateful for the Chancellor's backing.[87]

When the final vote was taken on the Locarno agreement, Count Westarp of the DNVP, not content with opposing ratification, announced that his party would refuse to recognize the validity of the treaties. They infringed, he insisted, on Germany's sovereignty and so amounted to a revision of the constitution that would require a two-thirds margin for adoption. This extreme stand threatened to set off a revolt of the left-wing Nationalists. Even before the final vote on ratification there had been signs of dissatisfaction in this group and several of its members had revealed to Stresemann that they were thinking of refounding the old Free Conservative Party, an idea which he had readily endorsed.[88] Nothing came of this project until December when, after the vote on the treaties, Stresemann was approached by spokesmen of the DNVP's agricultural group, who sought his reaction to their formation of a new party. Disgusted with the unyielding attitude of the Nationalist leadership, he sought to encourage the would-be rebels by offering to press for

[86] *Ibid.*, 148048, memorandum, dated December 1925.
[87] *Ibid.*, 147967f., diary for 23.9.1925.
[88] *Vermächtnis*, II, 210, 246, 248.

their admission to the government if they succeeded in breaking away an appreciable part of the DNVP.[89] To his disappointment, however, the revolt did not take place. Still, he remained hopeful that the moderate Nationalists would eventually bring their party to accept at least the binding nature, if not the correctness, of the Locarno agreements. In order to provide them with an incentive, he resolved to oppose the DNVP's re-entry into the government until it had recognized the validity of the treaties.[90]

❖

Although opinions differ widely as to its meaning, Locarno stands without question as Stresemann's greatest diplomatic triumph. In terms of domestic politics, however, it must be regarded, along with the election of Hindenburg, as a defeat, since it marked the failure of more than a year's efforts to bring the DNVP to accept his foreign policy. His efforts had not been altogether unsuccessful, for the Nationalists' presence in the government until October had enabled him to conduct the security pact negotiations relatively free from their criticism at home. But the fact remained that his faith in the moderating effects of responsibility had not been borne out. The right wing of the DNVP had regained the upper hand and had succeeded in taking the party's Reichstag delegation into the opposition at a highly inopportune moment from his point of view. Moreover, after the Nationalists left the government, their leaders joined the Nazis and other extremist groups in hurling charges of appeasement and fulfillment at Stresemann and the DVP. This smear campaign was even more vitriolic and emotional than the one conducted at the time of the Dawes Plan. It deprived him of full recognition for his diplomatic achievement by blinding much of the German public to the gains he had made. In addition, the campaign succeeded in branding him as a traitor in the eyes of many. During November and December there were a

[89] *Ibid.*, 380.
[90] *Ibid.*, 248.

number of threats on his life and shortly after the Reichstag had ratified the treaties, two demented persons were arrested in Berlin on charges of plotting his assassination.[91] From his point of view, the one mitigating feature of this disappointing domestic aftermath of Locarno was that there was no need to face new elections. Under the circumstances a recourse to the polls would probably have dealt his party a setback, thus undermining his diplomatic success by casting doubt on the firmness of Germany's commitment to the agreements reached at Locarno.

[91] *Ibid.*, 319ff.

VII. THE FOREIGN MINISTER'S
POLITICS, 1926-1929

ON DECEMBER 4, 1925, Stresemann and Luther returned to Berlin from London, where the final signing of the Locarno Pact had taken place on the 1st. The following day the Chancellor announced the dissolution of his rump cabinet and submitted his resignation to President Hindenburg. At Hindenburg's request, Erich Koch-Weser of the DDP undertook the task of setting up a new government and sought to form another Great Coalition. His attempt soon met defeat, for the SPD was still unwilling to enter the government until the eight-hour workday was reinstated, a concession which the DVP, with Stresemann's concurrence, refused to make. The result was the Republic's second lengthy "Christmas crisis." It was finally resolved in late January 1926, when Luther returned to office at the head of a minority cabinet based on a DDP-Center-BVP-DVP coalition and tolerated by the SPD.

Once again the change of cabinets left Stresemann at the Foreign Ministry. He was thus able to proceed with the preparations for what were to be his two principal diplomatic achievements of 1926: Germany's entrance into the League of Nations and the conclusion of the Treaty of Berlin with the Soviet Union. The entry into the League, which had been approved by the Reichstag at the time of the ratification of the Locarno agreements, was originally scheduled for March. But to the disappointment of Stresemann and Luther, who had gone to Geneva to take part in the ceremonies, it had to be postponed at the last minute when a deadlock developed after several other countries demanded that they as well as Germany be given permanent seats on the League Council. After months of behind-the-scenes bargaining a solution was finally found in September by increasing the number of permanent seats on the Council and the German delegation, led by Stresemann, could take its place in the international body. The Treaty of Berlin, which was initialed on

220

April 24, was the product of lengthy negotiations with the Soviet Union. It was designed mainly to dispel Russian uneasiness about Germany's close cooperation with the Western powers in entering into the Locarno agreements and agreeing to join the League. Its provisions reaffirmed the pledge of friendship made in the Rapallo Treaty of 1922 and committed both signatories to remain neutral in the event of an attack upon the other by a third power. In contrast to most of Stresemann's diplomatic undertakings, the treaty occasioned no controversy and was accepted by all the parties when it was presented to the Reichstag for ratification on June 10.

The Luther cabinet did not survive to see either the ratification of the Russo-German treaty or the completion of Germany's admission to the League. It was felled on May 12 by a no-confidence measure occasioned by a presidential decree which ordered German diplomatic missions in foreign ports to fly the country's maritime flag as well as the regular flag of the Republic. The controversial aspect of this seemingly inoffensive decree lay in the fact that the maritime flag consisted, by the terms of the Weimar constitution, of the old imperial colors, black-white-red, with the republican black-red-gold relegated to a small inset in one corner. Although the SPD, the DDP, and the Center had approved the adoption of this flag, their republican sensibilities were offended by the idea of flying it from buildings as well as from ships. Since the decree had been issued over the signature of Hindenburg, some of their number began to talk of a devious monarchist plot. When the cabinet, which had approved the measure, held stubbornly to its decision, they united to bring down the Luther government.

After Minister of the Army Gessler had failed to find a solution to the resulting crisis, the nomination for the Chancellorship went to Konrad Adenauer of the Center, who had gained national prominence as the mayor of Cologne. Adenauer's candidacy, however, was to be short-lived. From the outset, he stipulated that he was interested only in a Great Coalition and

221

when Scholz informed him that the DVP was not willing to work with the SPD he quickly withdrew his name from consideration. Stresemann took no direct part in these negotiations, but both Adenauer and Gessler, who acted as an intermediary on behalf of the President, suspected that he had used his influence to turn the DVP delegation against the Centrist politician in order to block his candidacy.[1] There is, moreover, circumstantial evidence that can be introduced to support such a conjecture. For instance, there is little doubt that Stresemann disliked Adenauer personally, probably because of their disagreements in November 1923. Also, he undoubtedly knew that Adenauer was an advocate of an uncompromising Western orientation in foreign policy and may have been concerned about the effect the latter's elevation to the chancellorship would have on the newly signed Russo-German treaty and on his own position at the Foreign Ministry.[2]

But in spite of the indications that Stresemann was not pleased at Adenauer's candidacy, it seems unlikely that his opposition was decisive in its collapse. To the contrary, it appears that Adenauer's own demands condemned him to failure. By insisting upon the immediate formation of a Great Coalition he was in effect attempting the impossible, since the SPD and the DVP were farther apart in May 1926, than at any time since the first Great Coalition collapsed in 1923. They were at odds on a number of fiscal and social issues, including the old workday controversy, and also on the still unsettled flag question. But even more important was a new and explosive issue that had developed during the spring of 1926 when the SPD joined with the Communists in sponsoring a plebiscite aimed at expropriating the former German ruling houses, totally and without indemnification. This project aroused the indignation of the entire

---

[1] See Adenauer's memorandum, based on notes taken at the time, in Weymar, *Adenauer*, pp. 129ff.

[2] See Fritz Stern, "Adenauer and a Crisis in Weimar Democracy," *Political Science Quarterly*, LXXIII (1958).

DVP, which saw it not only as a vindictive assault on the survivors of the princely families but also as a challenge to the inviolability of private property. At the time of the May crisis it was already evident that the plebiscite, which was to take place later in the spring, would be defeated, thus throwing the issue back to the Reichstag. The DVP delegation was convinced, as Scholz made clear to Adenauer at the time, that it would be pointless even to attempt a Great Coalition since it would be almost certain to collapse when the expropriation issue came before the chamber. Therefore, there was no necessity for Stresemann to exert himself, whatever his feelings about Adenauer's candidacy may have been.[3]

A solution to the crisis was finally found on May 16. At that time ex-Chancellor Marx returned to office at the head of almost exactly the same cabinet that had fallen four days earlier. Since the Center had been reluctant to accept another minority government, the way was cleared for the new cabinet only when the DVP agreed that the question of the SPD's entry should be reopened in the near future, presumably after the settlement of the expropriation issue. Stresemann readily gave his consent to this agreement. Because he had ruled out the alternative of a cabinet of the right on foreign policy grounds for as long as the DNVP persisted in its refusal to recognize the validity of the Locarno agreements, the Great Coalition offered the only possibility of a majority government as far as he was concerned. In view of the Center's attitude, he apparently concluded that the time had come to make good on his repeated pledges

---

[3] Scholz presented the DVP's views to Adenauer in their talk on May 15: Weymar, *Adenauer*, p. 135. Stresemann's private secretary, Bernhard, later asserted in the *Vermächtnis* (II, 392), that Adenauer's candidacy "failed because of the opposition of the German People's Party, which acted in closest agreement with Stresemann." Doubt is cast on Bernhard's account, however, by the fact that still later he gave an entirely different version of the affair, maintaining that Stresemann had blocked Adenauer personally by refusing to serve as his Foreign Minister: see Bernhard's "Seeckt und Stresemann," *Deutsche Rundschau*, LXXIX (1953), 466f.

that the DVP was willing to work with the left as well as the right.[4]

Not all of the DVP was pleased at this prospect. Among those who were not was Karl Jarres, the unsuccessful presidential candidate of the previous year, who preferred another attempt at closer cooperation with the Nationalists. Early in July he set out, without consulting Stresemann, to work toward such a development. Acting in his capacity as the DVP's spokesman in the Prussian Staatsrat, or upper chamber, he joined with Baron Wilhelm von Gayl, the DNVP spokesman, in issuing an appeal to the deputies of the two parties in the Reichstag and the Prussian Landtag to join together and form united DVP-DNVP delegations. A similar procedure had been followed in the Staatsrat since 1920 and he and Gayl argued that there was no reason why it should not be extended to the other chambers.[5]

When he learned of Jarres' action, Stresemann was furious. He recognized that a fusion of the DVP's delegations with those of the DNVP would effectively end the party's independence and clear the way for its absorption into the larger party. This was totally unacceptable from his point of view. While he was ready to cooperate with the DNVP under certain conditions, he still felt that on many issues, particularly those of foreign policy, the gap between it and the DVP could not be bridged. He quickly made his viewpoint known in the party press and in letters to Jarres and the other leaders of the party.[6] Although Jarres had easily gained the backing of most of the DVP members of the Staatsrat for his plan, he was evidently unwilling to risk an open struggle with the head of the party. In the face of Stresemann's vigorous opposition he made no attempt to pursue the project further.

[4] *Berliner Tageblatt*, 17.5.1926 (No. 229), p. 1. Also, *Nachlass*, 3161/7402/173064, his speech of 29.5.1926.

[5] *Nachlass*, 3161/7402/173077, article in *Nationalliberale Correspondenz*, 6.7.1926.

[6] *Nachlass*, 3161/7402/173090ff. Also, *Ibid.*, 173105ff., letter to Jarres, 30.7.1926.

The Jarres-Gayl episode was of little intrinsic importance. It was, however, not without significance since it revealed that Stresemann's belief that the DVP should be a middle party, ready to work with either the left or the right, was still not shared by all of his colleagues. This fact had been obscured during the period from the fall of 1924 to the end of 1925, when the entire party had been united in supporting the rightward course which he had charted at that time for foreign policy reasons. But with the revival of the possibility of a Great Coalition in the middle of 1926 it became increasingly evident that the party crisis of 1924 had not eliminated the problem of the DVP right wing.

In large measure, Stresemann was himself responsible for this. Following the National Liberal Union revolt of 1924 he had made no concerted effort to rid the party of those who were stubbornly opposed to all cooperation with the SPD or to recruit for it persons who shared his own views. In particular, he left unchallenged the real source of the opposition's strength: the dozen or so of the party's 35 electoral district organizations where those elements that had rejected the course he had set predominated. His failure to open an attack on the oppositional group was undoubtedly due in part to his recognition of the difficulties involved in carrying off such an operation within the DVP. The party had inherited the organizational traditions of the National Liberal Party, which had remained essentially a loosely knit club until its dissolution, and any attempt at a purge from above would have occasioned much resentment, even in the circles that usually backed him loyally. More important than this problem, however, was the fact that Stresemann was simply no longer deeply involved in the internal affairs of the party, having shifted the focus of his attention increasingly to foreign affairs since 1924.

Unopposed from above, the survivors of the National Liberal Union episode had experienced no difficulty in maintaining their Reichstag seats after the collapse of their revolt. By 1926 they made up, together with those right wingers who had remained aloof from the revolt, a potential opposition group which, while weaker than that of 1923 and 1924, nevertheless controlled more than a quarter of the party's smaller Reichstag delegation. But in spite of the dangers inherent in this situation, Stresemann showed no signs of concern. The unanimity with which the right wing had supported him while the DVP was cooperating with the Nationalists had lulled him into concluding that it had recognized the correctness of his views on the party's role in the Republic's politics.[7] Since he had no difficulty in quashing it, the Jarres-Gayl project did nothing to alter this complacency.

The opposition group in the DVP Reichstag delegation took no active part in the Jarres-Gayl episode and it was not until December 1926, that it reasserted itself openly. At that time the question of the Great Coalition arose again. Since the May crisis the Social Democrats had cooperated closely with the Marx cabinet in an effort to speed their re-entry into the government. By the beginning of December the prospects for a Great Coalition seemed extremely good, for a major obstacle had been removed during the fall when a compromise property settlement between the Prussian *Land* and the Hohenzollern family eliminated the controversial expropriation question as a national issue. The whole project of widening the government to the left was, however, unexpectedly brought into question on December 5. Behind this development was Scholz, one of those in the DVP who had not given up hope of renewing the party's cooperation with the DNVP in a rightward-oriented government. With Stresemann away at a session of the League in Geneva, the delegation chairman seized the initiative with a speech in which he intimated that a cabinet of the right, and not a Great Coalition, should be the goal of the DVP. Angrily, the Social Democrats protested that Scholz's speech amounted to a repudiation of the DVP's pledge of the previous May. They immediately announced

[7] *Nachlass*, 3113/7129/147826, diary for 25.5.1925. *Ibid.*, 147918, diary for 19.7.1925. *Ibid.*, 148007, diary for 28.10.1925.

that they would withdraw their support from the government unless they were admitted.[8]

The news of Scholz's action and the incipient crisis in Berlin disturbed Stresemann greatly. He was in the midst of delicate negotiations with the British and French regarding the withdrawal of the Allied Military Control Commission from Germany and was concerned lest a government crisis weaken his position and give the Allies an excuse to postpone the whole affair indefinitely. Since the alternative of a cabinet of the right was in his opinion still out of the question because of the Nationalists' continuing refusal to recognize the validity of the Locarno agreements, he concluded that there was no choice except to give in to the SPD's ultimatum.[9]

When Stresemann returned to Berlin from Geneva on December 14, he found the long-dormant right wing of the DVP delegation strongly opposed to his proposal for a Great Coalition. He did manage to get a majority of the party's deputies to agree to at least an attempt at cooperation with the Social Democrats. But it seemed certain that the old right-left conflict would break out again when it came to working out a governmental program with the SPD.[10] The issue was never called, however. On the 15th the SPD demanded the resignation of the entire Marx cabinet and called for its replacement by a new cabinet, presumably headed by a Social Democrat, a move that none of the government parties was willing to accept. In addition, on December 16 Philipp Scheidemann of the SPD startled the cabinet and the Reichstag with a scathing speech in which he charged that Germany was violating the disarmament clauses of the Versailles Treaty and supported his argument with detailed accounts of the Army's clandestine dealings with the Soviet Union and the Red Army.

Stresemann regarded Scheidemann's speech as inexcusable. He had long known the essential facts of Germany's rearma-

---

[8] *Nachlass*, 3167/7337/163462ff., Stresemann's memorandum.
[9] *Ibid.*   [10] *Ibid.*

ment but, unlike the indignant Social Democratic leader, he did not feel Germany was morally bound to adhere to the letter of the disarmament clauses of the Versailles Treaty. Also, from the point of view of foreign policy he considered Scheidemann's disclosures extremely ill-considered and ill-timed in view of the announcement only a few days earlier of the Allies' agreement to withdraw the Military Control Commission from Germany.[11] In addition, Stresemann felt that the speech might set what he considered a dangerous precedent on the domestic scene. In the years since the revolution he had broken with many of his old prejudices and attitudes, but he had never completely lost the awe for the Army that had won him the reputation of "Ludendorff's young man" during the war. He regarded it as an unimpeachably patriotic and politically disinterested institution "created not for the parties but for the Fatherland," and felt that "the parties should keep their hands off."[12] His opinion, in other words, was that the Army should be free from all political interference. Hence the sort of parliamentary control Scheidemann and the SPD wanted to impose upon it was totally unacceptable to him.

Scheidemann's speech effectively eliminated the last hopes for a Great Coalition, since it also offended Chancellor Marx and the rest of the cabinet. The Chancellor at first considered protesting by leading the cabinet out of the chamber. He reconsidered, though, when Stresemann pointed out that such a dramatic move would only increase the impact of Scheidemann's speech. Instead, at Stresemann's suggestion Marx contented himself with a few remarks designed to belittle the Social Democrat's disclosures. In addition, he made it clear that he was no longer interested in widening his cabinet by including the SPD in it. The next day, the 17th, the Social Democrats answered the Chancellor by joining the DNVP in felling his cabinet with a no-confidence measure.[13]

[11] Gatzke, *Stresemann and the Rearmament of Germany, passim.*
[12] *Nachlass*, 3162/7404/173413, his speech to DVP, 18.1.1927.
[13] *Nachlass*, 3167/7337/163465ff., Stresemann's memorandum.

This rapid and unexpected sequence of events forestalled the incipient right-left conflict within the DVP. With the Great Coalition no longer a possibility, the tension within the delegation relaxed at once. Stresemann, who was just as annoyed with the SPD as was the right wing of the DVP, chose once again to overlook the fact that part of his party was fundamentally opposed to his policy of keeping the way open for cooperation with the left as well as the right. He thus postponed the inevitable showdown with the resurgent right wing until a time that was to prove much less favorable from his point of view and much more hazardous for the political stability of the Republic.

Because of the nearness of the holiday season, the fall of the Marx cabinet produced the Republic's third consecutive "Christmas crisis." In January 1927, President Hindenburg assigned the task of forming a new government to Julius Curtius, the DVP Minister of Economics. Curtius, a lawyer from Baden, had been one of the most outspoken leaders of the opposition group in the Reichstag delegation during the fall of 1923. Since that time, he had moved steadily closer to Stresemann and had been approved by the latter as the party's second minister in the Luther cabinet which was formed in January 1926. After his nomination for the chancellorship, Curtius promptly expressed the intention of forming a cabinet extending from the Center to the DNVP. But after only four days his candidacy came to an end when the Center indicated its unwillingness to cooperate with the Nationalists. The President then called again upon Marx. At first Marx tried to form another minority cabinet of the middle but he had to abandon the attempt because of the SPD's refusal to renew its toleration. Then, in spite of the fact that his own party had just rejected Curtius' proposal of a similar arrangement, he set out to bring the DNVP into the government. In this undertaking he received the full support of Stresemann, who was anxious to end the month-old crisis. Finally, in late January the principal obstacle was removed when, after a lengthy conference with Stresemann, the Nationalist leaders grudgingly gave in and agreed to recognize the binding nature and validity of the Locarno agreements. At the beginning of February 1927, Marx was thus able to take office at the head of just the sort of cabinet Curtius had sought. With the backing of a coalition consisting of the Center, the BVP, the DVP, and the DNVP, it was the Republic's first majority government since the fall of 1925.

Curtius, who remained as Minister of Economics in the new cabinet, later complained in his memoirs about the fact that he had received less support from Stresemann in his bid for the chancellorship than Marx. His conclusion was that, as Foreign Minister, Stresemann feared he would be a more forceful Chancellor than Marx and would thus want a larger voice in the formation and execution of foreign policy.[14] Another possible explanation, however, could be that Stresemann was not pleased at the prospect of sharing the limelight within the DVP with a Chancellor or another ex-Chancellor. According to Hans von Raumer, a DVP deputy from 1920 until 1930, he was constantly apprehensive about possible rivals.[15] On at least two earlier occasions he had shown himself extremely sensitive to challenges to his position of pre-eminence within the party. The first of these occurred in 1922, when Admiral Reinhard Scheer, a hero of the war, joined the DVP and opened an obvious bid for recognition with a series of speeches in various parts of the country. For a time Stresemann tolerated the Admiral's actions. But his patience quickly faded when Scheer aligned himself with the extreme left wing of the DVP and began criticizing him for not making more progress toward cooperation with the SPD. Reacting angrily, he brought the Admiral's bid for power to an abrupt end by securing a motion of censure against him from the Reichstag delegation.[16] The second incident occurred in 1923

---

[14] See Curtius, *Sechs Jahre Minister der Deutschen Republik* (Heidelberg, 1948), p. 50.
[15] Letter to the author, 17.6.1958.
[16] See *Nachlass*, 3110/7009/143359ff. Also, *Nachlass*, 3110/7013/

after the end of his own chancellorship, when President Ebert called upon Siegfried von Kardorff of the DVP to form a government. Kardorff accepted but had to withdraw at once, in large part because, to his surprise, Stresemann refused to remain on as his Foreign Minister—although Stresemann then promptly agreed to do just that under the Centrist Marx.[17] These two incidents, when added to Curtius' experience, would seem to substantiate Raumer's observation and to indicate that Stresemann preferred to remain as the DVP's one nationally prominent figure, even at the cost of sacrificing important increases in the party's strength and influence.

In the new Marx cabinet Stresemann was once again reappointed Foreign Minister. For the second time he thus took his place in a cabinet that included representatives of the DNVP. At the outset the prospects seemed greatly improved over those of 1925. In his discussion with the Nationalist leaders in late January he had finally succeeded in bringing them to drop their bitter opposition to Locarno. Furthermore, after hearing him set forth his policies at that time, Westarp had been moved to concede that he objected only to Stresemann's methods, not to his basic goals of strengthening Germany and freeing it from the bonds of the Versailles Treaty.[18] Stresemann was, however, to have no opportunity to test the degree of the Nationalists' reconciliation to his foreign policy, since 1927 proved to be an uneventful year on the international scene.

143770. Scheer remained in the party for a time, but was completely without influence: see *Nachlass*, 3097/7019/144656ff.

[17] See *Deutsche Volkspartei Papers*, Vol. 104h, for a memorandum by Kardorff on this incident. Also, *Nachlass*, 3099/7120/146354ff., his letter to Stresemann, 23.12.1923. Afterwards Stresemann explained to Kardorff that he had felt the DNVP should have the next chance at forming a cabinet and, in addition, had not wanted to give the impression that he was "clinging to office" himself: *Nachlass*, 3159/7395/171650ff., letter of 25.1.1924. Neither of these explanations is convincing, however, in view of his concern about the Nationalists' inclination toward a dictatorship and his ready acceptance of the Foreign Ministry under Marx.

[18] *Nachlass*, 3167/7338/163632.

His next diplomatic goal was an early withdrawal of Allied troops from the two remaining occupied zones of the Rhineland, which were not scheduled for evacuation until 1930 and 1935. On the occasion of his much-publicized breakfast with Briand at Thoiry in September 1926, the prospects had seemed good for a quick realization of this goal. At that time the French Foreign Minister had put forward a bold plan calling for the prompt evacuation of the rest of the Rhineland and the immediate restoration of the Saar to Germany. In return Germany was to extend financial aid to the faltering French franc in the form of accelerated reparations payments. But after a brief period of optimism it quickly became obvious that Briand had overreached himself. When he returned to France he came under heavy attack, both from the rightist opposition and from the rest of the cabinet, which was headed by the unyielding Poincaré. In addition, the financial measures introduced by Poincaré soon succeeded in checking the French inflation, thus removing the *raison d'être* for the Thoiry program. As a result, much to Stresemann's disappointment, Briand failed to follow through with his plan. Moreover, during 1927 the Frenchman repeatedly put off the question of the occupation with the argument that nothing could be done until after the Assembly elections of 1928, which he confidently predicted would weaken the position of Poincaré.[19]

While it yielded little in the way of progress on the diplomatic front, the Marx cabinet provided the Republic with a year of political calm at home. In spite of its stormy course, the DNVP's experience as a government party in 1925 had apparently convinced many Nationalists of the value of being on the side of the majority and having a hand in the shaping of legislation. In the Marx cabinet their representatives, led by Oskar Hergt, made a genuine effort to cooperate and to keep the more reactionary elements in the party under control. As a result, the cabinet proved to be one of the more stable in the Republic's

[19] *Vermächtnis*, III, 15ff., 198.

short and turbulent history. In addition, despite its conservative orientation it was responsible for two of the Republic's most important items of social legislation: a comprehensive system of unemployment insurance and a measure that settled the troublesome workday issue by requiring extra pay for work in excess of eight hours. The Nationalists' moderation on domestic issues was gratifying to Stresemann but the decisive question—the extent of their acceptance of his foreign policy—remained unanswered because of the lull in diplomatic activity.[20]

Taking advantage of the political calm of 1927, Stresemann quietly began to jettison his own and his party's remaining monarchist ballast. Although he had long been a *Vernunftrepublikaner*, he was still by no means convinced that a republican form of government was ideally the best for Germany. At Thoiry, in seeking to explain the popularity of the *Stahlhelm*, the rightist para-military veterans' organization, and other such groups, he had revealed his misgivings to Briand: "The Republic in Germany has shown no consideration for the psychological needs of the masses. It is too stiff in its dull, black frock coat. The people want brightness, joy, and action. . . ."[21] But in spite of his lingering doubts about republicanism, his four years in the cabinet had convinced him that the argument over the form of government was a senseless and wasteful liability that was weakening Germany's position in the world by compounding its internal divisions.[22] As a result, he had by 1927 reached the conclusion that the only solution to the problem was to consolidate the Republic by removing the threat of a restoration altogether.

As a first step in this direction he set out to loosen the links that still bound the DVP to the monarchist cause. On March 20, at a meeting commemorating the sixtieth anniversary of the founding of the National Liberal Party, he publicly pledged the

[20] See *Nachlass*, 3115/7144/150329, letter to Jänecke, 15.8.1927.
[21] *Vermächtnis*, III, 19.
[22] *Nachlass*, 3161/7402/173071, speech of 5.7.1926. Also, *Vermächtnis*, II, 51, article for *Die Zeit*, 19.4.1925.

DVP to continue to cooperate within the Republic and referred to it as "our state, republican Germany."[23] Later in the year he ordered the party to use the republican flag, in addition to the customary imperial banner, at all public meetings.[24] On the anniversary of the death of his mentor, Bassermann, he specifically ordered the DVP national headquarters to send a wreath with a white ribbon, rather than the usual black-white-red one.[25] In August still another tradition was broken when the DVP participated actively for the first time in the Reichstag's annual Constitution Day celebration, with Kardorff, one of the several professed republicans among the party's leaders, delivering the principal address of the day.[26]

In addition to this gradual alteration of the DVP's position, Stresemann began to cut the last of his own remaining ties with monarchism. In 1928 he even went so far as to resign from the *Kaiserlicher Yachtklub* of Kiel on the grounds that a Minister of the Republic could not associate with an organization that continued to carry such a title.[27] But although his own position and that of the DVP had become virtually indistinguishable from that of the republican parties, he never explicitly renounced the party's monarchist past or openly identified himself as republican. He avoided such an open break because most of the DVP's rank and file were still staunchly monarchist. Even the comparatively minor shift in the flag question was immediately noticed and resulted in a number of protests.[28] In order to prevent a wholesale exodus, a development that would have benefited only the DNVP, he had to avoid a direct endorsement of the republican form of government.

In February 1928, while Stresemann was recuperating on the French Riviera from a case of pneumonia, he received the

[23] *Nachlass*, 3162/7404/173470.
[24] *Nachlass*, 3162/7405/173626f., letter to Paul Luther, 21.9.1927.
[25] *Ibid.*, 173585, letter to Trucksaess, 19.7.1927.
[26] *Schulthess' Europäischer Geschichtskalender*, LXVIII, 133ff.
[27] *Nachlass*, 3116/7149/151226f., letter to Metzenthin, 6.10.1928.
[28] *Nachlass*, 3162/7405/173662f. *Ibid.*, 137640. *Nachlass*, 3115/7145/150560f.

news that the Marx government had fallen. The cause of the crisis was a bill calling for sweeping church supervision over instruction in elementary schools which was supported by the Reichstag delegations of the Center, the BVP, and the DNVP. Since the proposal was in direct conflict with the traditional secular tenets of German liberalism, it forced the DVP to align itself with the DDP and the SPD and thus divided the coalition. For this reason the issue had been postponed several times during the life of the cabinet and when Stresemann left for his vacation, he had been under the impression that no action was imminent. He was therefore surprised to learn that the Center had provoked a crisis by suddenly demanding a decision.[29] There was no need to intervene in the crisis, however. In view of the fact that the regular quadrennial elections were due to take place in the spring no attempt was made to form a new government. Instead, the Marx cabinet agreed to remain in office on a caretaker basis until after the balloting, which was set for May 20.

As the Reichstag elections of 1928 approached, Stresemann ignored an opportunity to bolster the DVP by adding a prominent personality to its ranks. In the fall of 1927, after more than a year of virtual retirement, ex-Chancellor Luther had quietly associated himself with the local DVP organization in Essen.[30] At first, he showed no interest in playing an active role in the party, but by the beginning of 1928 there were signs that he was seriously considering a political comeback. In January he launched, with much fanfare, a new supra-party organization, the *Bund zur Erneuerung des Reichs*, aimed at strengthening the national government over against the *Länder* and at abolishing the proportional election law of 1920. Then, in February, Luther finally made known his political intentions within the DVP and began working behind the scenes for a Reichstag candidacy in three districts, Düsseldorf-South, East Hanover, and Coblenz.[31]

[29] *Nachlass*, 3116/7147/150859. *Ibid.*, 150900ff.
[30] *Nachlass*, 3162/7405/173620, telegram to Stresemann, 16.9.1927.
[31] *Nachlass*, 3162/7406/173840ff. *Ibid.*, 173887ff.

235

Stresemann, however, gave him no encouragement and even offered to intervene on behalf of one deputy whose nomination Luther had challenged.[32] As a result, Luther's name was rejected in all three districts. Stresemann did not explain his opposition, but in the light of his earlier reactions to Admiral Scheer's bid for recognition and the chancellorship candidacies of Kardorff and Curtius, it is difficult to avoid Luther's conclusion that Stresemann saw him as a potential rival for the leadership of the party.[33]

In the hope that the electorate had begun to recognize the benefits his diplomatic achievements had brought Germany, Stresemann led the DVP in an election campaign that once again placed heavy emphasis on his foreign policy. For the unsophisticated, the appeal was simple and was summed up by the party's principal poster, which consisted of a large photograph of Stresemann over the slogan:

> *Was gehen dich die andern an,*
> *Du wählst wie Gustav Stresemann.*[34]

For the more discerning, the Republic's economic recovery and Germany's growing prestige in the world were presented as the results of his success in securing adoption of the Dawes Plan and the Locarno agreements and in gaining a permanent seat on the Council of the League of Nations.

As his own personal project during the campaign, Stresemann set out to improve the DVP's position in Bavaria, where it had yet to win a single Reichstag seat. Placing his name at the head of the party's lists of candidates in both of the Bavarian electoral districts, he opened a drive to overcome the southerners' traditional hostility to the "Prussian" DVP. In the midst of his cam-

---

[32] *Nachlass*, 3163/7407/173917, telegram to Beythien, March 1928. Also, *Dingeldey Papers*, Vol. 77.

[33] Luther, *Politiker*, p. 412. Luther presents a garbled version of his relationship with the DVP in his memoirs, claiming that he joined only at the beginning of 1929.

[34] Olden, *Stresemann*, p. 254.

paign, in late April, he had his first personal contact with National Socialism. His earlier negative impressions of that movement and its leader were thoroughly confirmed when a flying squad of Nazi toughs invaded a DVP rally at the Bürgerbräu Beer Hall in Munich and so effectively drowned out his attempts to speak that he was forced to leave the platform with his address uncompleted.[35]

In all, the Bavarian campaign proved far more difficult than he had anticipated. But in spite of the fact that his candidacy there was far from secure, he was obliged, as the DVP's most prominent national figure, to aid its campaign in other parts of the country. Beginning in the last week of April, he launched what was supposed to be an extensive speaking tour of a number of important cities. This effort proved too much for his health, which had not been good for some time. On May 10, his fiftieth birthday, he was stricken with a severe kidney ailment and was forced to cancel his remaining campaign engagements and return to Berlin for treatment and recuperation.[36]

The elections of 1928 left Stresemann dismayed.[37] The results of the balloting failed to produce any evidence that the German public was ready to reward his party for what he had accomplished as Foreign Minister. To the contrary, the DVP failed even to hold its own. It received fewer votes than at any time since 1919 and was again reduced to 45 seats in the Reichstag. The other middle parties, the Center and the DDP, suffered losses, too, dropping to 61 and 28 seats. For the first time the Nationalists also had to pay the price of responsibility and had the new experience of being among the losers, retaining only 78 of the 110 seats they had formerly controlled. On the whole, the elections were marked by a shift to the left, with the chief beneficiaries being the Social Democrats and the Communists, who emerged with 152 and 54 seats. Stresemann's

[35] On his Bavarian candidacy, *Nachlass*, 3163/7407/173954f., letter to Raumer, 23.3.1928. On the Nazi incident, *Vermächtnis*, III, 293.
[36] *Nachlass*, 3163/7408/174121, Bernhard to Burger, 4.6.1928.
[37] *Nachlass*, 3163/7407/174112ff., letter to Havemann, 2.6.1928.

personal campaign in Bavaria was not without effect, especially in upper Bavaria, where the DVP more than doubled its votes. But even this gain was far short of the number of votes necessary for a Reichstag seat and he was forced to accept election on the party's national list, which he had headed as national chairman.

Following the elections, Stresemann favored a revival of the Great Coalition. Since the beginning of the year, he had been laying plans for a renewed effort aimed at achieving an early evacuation of the two remaining occupied zones of the Rhineland. In order to deprive the French of any excuse to postpone the question further, he was anxious to enter the negotiations with the support of a stable, majority government. After his experience with the Nationalists in 1925, he feared this would not be the case if the cabinet were dependent on their votes in the Reichstag. When the elections still further weakened the arguments for a government of the right by dealing the DNVP losses and strengthening the SPD, he indicated his preference for a return to the Great Coalition.[38]

President Hindenburg also recognized the need for a Great Coalition. On June 12 he assigned the task of forming such a government to the chairman of the SPD delegation, Hermann Müller, who had served as Chancellor for a brief time in 1920. As usual, the formation of a Great Coalition was held up by differences between the SPD and the DVP. The chief stumbling block was the refusal of the DVP delegation to enter a Great Coalition at the national level unless a similar combination was also formed in Prussia. Since 1925, when the Prussian Great Coalition cabinet established in 1921 had fallen because of the DVP's insistence that the DNVP be admitted, the largest federal *Land* had been ruled by a Weimar Coalition. As a result, the Prussian DVP had been cut off from all of the patronage and influence of government for more than three years. When the

[38] *Nachlass*, 3162/7406/173782f., letter to Spitzfaden, 2.1.1928. Also, *Nachlass*, 3163/7408/174159ff., letter to the DVP delegation, 27.6.1928.

Landtag elections of May 1928, gave the Weimar Coalition parties an absolute majority, the leaders of the DVP in Prussia abandoned hope of altering the situation by their own efforts and prevailed upon the Reichstag delegation to intervene on their behalf.[39] The intervention, however, was indignantly rejected by the Social Democratic Minister-President of Prussia, Otto Braun, as an attempt to subordinate Prussian politics to those of the Reich. The SPD Reichstag delegation supported Braun and thus a full-scale stalemate developed.

Although he was still suffering from the effects of the illness that had forced him out of the election campaign, Stresemann interceded personally in an attempt to remove the obstacles to a Great Coalition. On June 14 he conferred at length with Braun and sought unsuccessfully to find some means of compromise.[40] During the next few days, he persisted in his efforts to resolve the stalemate between the SPD and the DVP, but he was handicapped by a recurrence of his chronic kidney ailment. His condition finally became so alarming that his physicians ordered him to undertake a lengthy rest-cure. On June 20, with the problem of the new government still unresolved, he left for a sanatorium at Bühlerhöhe, near Baden-Baden.[41] His departure left the DVP's side of the negotiations in the hands of Scholz, who was hardly a partisan of cooperation with the SPD. By the 22nd, Müller had decided that there was no hope for a Great Coalition and offered to withdraw his candidacy. The President, however, asked him to make one more attempt. When Müller suggested a Weimar Coalition, Hindenburg gave his consent, but stipulated that Stresemann must remain as Foreign Minister.[42]

[39] *Deutsche Volkspartei Papers*, Vol. 139, minutes of meeting of the Reichstag and Landtag delegations, 13.6.1928.

[40] Otto Braun, *Von Weimar zu Hitler* (New York, 1940), pp. 249f., excerpts from a letter from Stresemann to Braun's State Secretary, Weismann, 14.6.1928.

[41] *Vermächtnis*, III, 298.

[42] *Nachlass*, 3163/7409/174329f., letter to Scholz, 19.7.1928. Also, Carl Severing, *Mein Lebensweg* (2 vols., Cologne, 1950), II, 147f.

Stresemann first learned of the failure of the Great Coalition not from his own party but from Müller, who reached him by telephone at Bühlerhöhe on the morning of June 23. At that time the Chancellor-designate asked him whether he would remain as an expert minister in a Weimar Coalition cabinet. Stresemann rejected this proposal at once. Later in the day he explained his position to Müller in a telegram—soon known as the "shot from Bühlerhöhe"—which he released to the press the next morning.[43] He maintained that a post in a Weimar Coalition cabinet would place him in an impossible position, for it would force him to serve simultaneously as a member of the government and as chairman of an opposition party. But even aside from this complicating factor, he indicated that he felt a Weimar Coalition was unacceptable from the standpoint of foreign policy, which made it imperative to have a government backed by a majority of the Reichstag.

Since it was apparently impossible to form such a government by the customary procedure of assembling a coalition, Stresemann suggested in his telegram that Müller set up a "cabinet of personalities" which would consist of ministers drawn from the Great Coalition parties but which would be free of all ties to the Reichstag delegations of those parties. The parties would then be left to decide whether to support the government or not. He made clear, however, that he was confident they would support it. Concerning his own position, he indicated his willingness to remain as Foreign Minister, but only if Müller would also include Curtius, pointing out that the "cabinet of personalities" would in effect be nothing more than a Weimar Coalition if he were left as the only DVP minister.[44] Müller immediately accepted his suggestions and by the 28th had succeeded in assembling the sort of cabinet outlined in the telegram. It was made up of four ministers from the SPD, two from the DDP, one each from the Center and the BVP, and two, Stresemann and Curtius, from the DVP.

[43] *Nachlass*, 3174/7377/167893ff.   [44] *Ibid.*

Stresemann later admitted that at the time he hoped the "shot from Bühlerhöhe" would force his own party to accept a Great Coalition.[45] He apparently assumed that with two DVP ministers in the cabinet, the party would conclude that there was no alternative except to support the Müller government, thus converting the "cabinet of personalities" into a *de facto* Great Coalition. In making this assumption, however, he overlooked the fact that the new DVP Reichstag delegation was, as he later put it, "oriented very sharply to the right."[46] Largely as a result of his own neglect of the party's internal affairs, the May elections had weakened the left wing and greatly strengthened the right. Particularly important in this regard was a new influx of spokesmen of heavy industry, which had quietly reasserted its domination over the DVP district organizations of the Ruhr and other industrial regions after the brief hiatus occasioned by the National Liberal Union debacle of 1924. In addition, the spokesmen of light industry in the new delegation also tended to align themselves with the right wing, since the concentration movement that followed the stabilization of the Mark had merged many scattered firms into giant corporations which found their interests more similar to those of heavy industry than to those of small-scale light industry. In all, the right wing made up almost half of the Reichstag delegation elected in 1928. The left wing, on the other hand, comprised somewhat less than a third, with the remaining deputies forming an uncommitted middle group.

As soon as the text of Stresemann's telegram to Müller appeared in the press, the right wing of the delegation reacted angrily, recognizing it at once as an attempt to maneuver the DVP into cooperation with the SPD. The lead was taken by Scholz. Since 1926, the delegation chairman had made no secret of the fact that he considered himself a full-fledged member of the right wing, and after Gildemeister's death earlier in 1928, he had become its unofficial spokesman. Moreover, he had been

---

[45] *Nachlass*, 3101/7155/151939, letter to Kaas, 14.2.1929.
[46] *Ibid.*

personally offended by the "shot from Bühlerhöhe," for in retaliation at being left uninformed about the failure of the Great
Coalition negotiations Stresemann had not consulted with him
before sending the telegram to Müller and releasing it to the
press.

At first, Scholz seemed bent on a full-scale test of strength,
indicating that he would demand that the delegation disavow
Stresemann's action and dissociate the DVP from the new government by forbidding Curtius to enter the cabinet.[47] He reconsidered, however, when a group of the party's veteran deputies,
including spokesmen of both the left and the right wings, protested that such a stand would be certain to set off a bitter intraparty struggle.[48] Finally, to the disappointment of the more militant members of the right wing, Scholz contented himself with
a compromise in the form of three resolutions which were
adopted by the delegation on June 27 and promptly released to
the press.[49] The first of these expressed the delegation's full
confidence in him. The second instructed the party's deputies to
consult with the delegation chairman on all political decisions.
The third announced that the delegation had decided not to obstruct the entry into the new cabinet of Stresemann and Curtius,
but indicated that it considered itself in no way bound to support that cabinet.[50]

Stresemann, who was still confined to the sanatorium at Bühlerhöhe, was surprised and indignant when he learned of Scholz's
attitude and the resolutions of June 27. To his embarrassment,
the second resolution had been interpreted by much of the press
as a reprimand directed specifically at him.[51] He agreed that this
was an unavoidable conclusion and regarded it as a covert attempt to effect a fundamental shift in the power structure of the

[47] *Nachlass*, 3163/7408/174200ff., minutes of delegation executive
committee, 26.6.1928.
[48] *Ibid.*, 174204, minutes of meeting of veteran deputies, 26.6.1928.
[49] *Ibid.*, 174205f., minutes of delegation meeting, 27.6.1928.
[50] *Ibid.*, 174232.
[51] *Ibid.*, 174190, telegram to the delegation, 28.6.1928.

party by elevating the authority of the chairman of the Reichstag delegation above that of the chairman of the Central Committee. The third resolution was also unacceptable in his opinion since it implied that the delegation had the power to prevent its members from accepting ministerial posts as individuals.[52] So strong were his objections that on June 30 he informed Scholz that he was considering resigning from the DVP if the resolutions were not revised.[53]

Although he assured Stresemann in private that the delegation's resolutions had not been intended as an attack on his position, Scholz ignored his demand for an official revision.[54] From his point of view the resolutions were a minimum compensation for what he considered a serious loss of prestige and he was determined to uphold them. But at the same time, he was anxious to keep Stresemann from carrying out his threat to leave the DVP, apparently being unwilling to face the problems that the resignation of the party's leader would bring. Knowing that Stresemann's main concern was the survival of the new Müller government, he sought to smooth over the dispute by throwing the DVP's support behind the cabinet. When the first confidence measure came before the Reichstag on July 5, he led all except the extreme right wing of the delegation in voting with the SPD, the DDP, the Center, and the BVP, for the government, thus giving it a firm majority. But before the vote was taken he emphasized that the DVP delegation considered itself in no way bound to the new cabinet and would not hesitate to withdraw its support if unacceptable policies were adopted.[55]

Scholz's maneuver was successful. Rather than pursuing his grievances and risking a reversal of the DVP's attitude toward the cabinet, Stresemann let the matter drop.[56] He did not aban-

[52] *Ibid.*, 174225ff., draft of a letter to the delegation, 30.6.1928. *Ibid.*, 174265ff., letter to Kempkes, 2.7.1928.
[53] *Ibid.*, 174209ff., letter to Scholz, 30.6.1928.
[54] *Ibid.*, 174261ff., Scholz to Stresemann, 2.7.1928.
[55] *Verhandlungen* (Reichstag), ccccxxxii, 73ff.
[56] *Vermächtnis*, iii, 316f.

don it entirely, however, and began planning almost at once for an eventual test of strength with Scholz and the right wing. In a letter written on July 19 he warned Scholz that as far as he was concerned they were engaged in a "duel." He also served notice that he intended to summon a Party Congress in the autumn in order to obtain a clear decision on the relation of his authority as chairman of the Central Committee to that of Scholz as delegation chairman. In addition, he indicated his awareness that many of the Reichstag deputies were opposed to his belief that the DVP should be a middle party. The fundamental question of whether or not the party was willing to work with the SPD would, he warned Scholz, have to be settled by the Congress.[57]

These plans for bringing the dispute into the open had to be laid aside almost as soon as they were made. In mid-August, while he was continuing his recuperation at Oberhof in Thuringia, Stresemann suffered a mild stroke. It left him with a temporary speech impairment and forced him to return to Berlin for special treatment. Against his physicians' wishes, he insisted on traveling to Paris on August 26 to sign the Kellogg-Briand Peace Pact. This trip so weakened him that he was forced to go at once to Baden-Baden for two months of treatment and rest.

By the time he returned to Berlin in November 1928, Stresemann had abandoned his plans for a test of strength with the right wing of the DVP. The main factor in this change of plans was his success, during his trip to Paris in August, in bringing the French to consider an early evacuation of the Rhineland and to agree to a review of Germany's reparation obligations by another committee of international experts. By November, negotiations on these questions were already well under way and he was reluctant to provoke a dispute within the DVP that might weaken the Müller cabinet. If the government should be weakened and fall, he felt the result could be a paralyzing crisis, for he saw no possibility of putting together another combination

[57] *Nachlass*, 3163/7409/174329ff.

of parties that could command a majority. This was especially true in the wake of the Nationalists' action a month earlier in electing the extreme rightist Alfred Hugenberg as their chairman. When he heard of Hugenberg's election, Stresemann was appalled and voiced concern that the DNVP's turn to the right might eventually lead to civil war.[58] Immediately, though, the effect was to rule out the alternative of a government of the right, thus leaving the existing cabinet as the only possible basis for a majority government.

In view of this situation, and the Reichstag delegation's continued cooperation with the Müller government, he decided against reopening the controversies of the previous June and substituted a meeting of the Central Committee for the projected Party Congress. When the Committee met on November 23 and 24, he carefully avoided the issues he had earlier planned to raise. The right wingers also exercised restraint, for the new Müller cabinet had not proved as objectionable as they had feared. Only a week earlier, for example, the SPD had suffered a severe setback when the DVP, the BVP, the Center, and the DDP joined with the DNVP to defeat a Social Democratic proposal to block the construction of a pocket battleship that had been authorized by the previous Reichstag earlier in the year. In spite of the fact that the SPD held a dominant position in the cabinet, the DVP right wing could therefore hardly complain that it dictated the policies of the government. During the Central Committee session the only indication that not all the DVP was entirely satisfied with the political situation was the resolution adopted at the end of the meetings. It emphasized that the party was still not bound to support the Müller cabinet and revived the troublesome Prussian issue by instructing the Reichstag delegation to demand a place in the Prussian government for the DVP at the earliest opportunity.[59]

[58] *Ibid.*, 174480, letter to Zapf, 23.10.1928.
[59] *Deutsche Volkspartei Papers*, Vol. 105q.

Stresemann was later to regret this resolution, for it was the source of a government crisis in January 1929. At that time Chancellor Müller attempted to convert his cabinet into a formal Great Coalition in order to facilitate the adoption of a new budget. In the opinion of the DVP delegation, Müller's decision brought the resolution of the Central Committee into play. It therefore indicated that it would consent to a Great Coalition in the Reich only if the DVP was admitted to the Prussian cabinet. In contrast to the previous June, the SPD raised no objections to this demand. The Center, however, produced a stalemate by insisting that the DVP accept the pending Prussian concordat with the Papacy. This the DVP Landtag delegation was unwilling to do, since the proposed concordat greatly increased the church's voice in matters of education. As a result, the Great Coalition project collapsed in Prussia. In retaliation, the DVP Reichstag delegation rejected the demand for an additional ministerial post which the Center had put forward as its price for participation in a Great Coalition at the national level. The Center then responded by withdrawing its one minister from the cabinet on February 6, 1929, leaving the Müller government badly shaken.

The withdrawal of the Center was an extremely disturbing development from Stresemann's point of view. It came just as his laborious diplomatic preparations of the fall and winter were about to culminate in the opening of the Paris conference of international experts, which had been assigned the task of drawing up plans for a new reparations settlement. A collapse of the German government at such a moment was almost certain to have an adverse effect on the conference by calling into question the status of the experts who had been sent by the Müller government. Determined not to see his foreign policy obstructed in this manner, Stresemann set out to find a way to bring about the formation of a stable Great Coalition. At first he sought to arrange a compromise between the DVP and the Center. But in spite of his efforts the two parties remained firm in their positions and the stalemate continued.[60] Finally, he concluded that the only solution was to cut the tie between the politics of the Reich and Prussia which had produced the impasse. He therefore called a meeting of the DVP Central Committee for February 26 in order to ask it to repeal its resolution of the previous November.[61]

This decision led to his most violent collision with the DVP opposition since the National Liberal Union revolt of 1924. In summoning the Committee, he obviously assumed that it would obediently comply with his wishes, just as it had always done since the formation of the DVP. He miscalculated badly, however. The right wing of the party, and especially the industrial group, had grown very dissatisfied with the Müller government and was eager to bring about its fall. The source of this dissatisfaction lay with the government's economic policies. Since the final months of 1928, the German economy had been gripped by a recession. By the time the Committee met there were three and a quarter million jobless workers, the highest total since the return of prosperity following the stabilization of the currency. This was a far greater number than had been provided for by the unemployment insurance legislation of 1927. Consequently, the Müller cabinet had decided to meet the extra costs of jobless compensation with funds that had been appropriated for other purposes. By February it was already clear that the budget for the fiscal year 1928 would be greatly unbalanced and it was no secret that the Social Democrats, as well as many Democrats and Centrists, favored a tax increase to cover the deficit. In the opinion of the DVP right wingers, who had never fully accepted the principle of unemployment insurance, this would be a hopelessly unsound move that would only handicap the recovery of the economy. Rather than permit the implementation of such a policy, they preferred to topple the whole cabinet.[62]

---

[60] Braun, *Von Weimar*, p. 273.
[61] *Nachlass*, 3164/7410/174658f., party bulletin of 23.2.1929.
[62] *Nachlass*, 3164/7410/174694ff., memorandum prepared for Strese-

The right wing did not control enough votes in the Central Committee to challenge Stresemann on its own, but by opening the Prussian issue Stresemann provided the opposition group with a powerful ally. This was the large block of Committee members who represented the local DVP organizations in Prussia—well over half of the whole party. They were strenuously opposed to any suggestion that the Reichstag delegation be released from its commitment to the Landtag delegation, feeling that such a move would condemn the DVP to extinction in Prussia. Since its exclusion from the government in 1925, the Landtag delegation's strength had declined sharply; the delegates attributed this to the party's inability to dispense patronage to the large Prussian bureaucracy or exert influence on behalf of the business and commercial interests which had formerly supported it. The only solution, they felt, was to reinstall the DVP in the Prussian cabinet as soon as possible. Because this would probably be impossible without aid from the Reichstag delegation, they were determined to uphold the resolution of November 1928.[63]

The Central Committee session of February 26 was a painful experience for Stresemann. Since he had made his intentions clear in advance, the right wing was well prepared when the meeting opened. Realizing that the Prussian issue offered an ideal means of bringing down the Müller cabinet, they joined with the leaders of the Landtag delegation in protesting vigorously when Stresemann suggested rescinding the resolution of the previous November. In addition, they attacked the government's financial policies and demanded that the DVP withdraw its support unless drastic reductions were made in expenditures, particularly on unemployment insurance.[64]

---

mann by Bernhard, 27.2.1929. Also, *Deutsche Volkspartei Papers*, Vol. 105q. Also, *Nachlass*, 3164/7411/174823ff., Cremer to Stresemann, 23.3.1929.

[63] *Ibid.*

[64] The minutes of the meeting are in *Deutsche Volkspartei Papers*, Vol. 105q.

In contrast to the usual pattern of the Committee's meetings, Stresemann's views found little support. Even his warnings that the DVP's stand on the Prussian issue was endangering the prospects for a revision of the reparations settlement and an early Allied evacuation of the Rhineland had no visible effect. Nor did his assurances that he would use his full influence to press for a revision of the government's unemployment policies once the questions of reparations and the Rhineland had been settled. Virtually his only support came from Scholz. The delegation chairman was still not an advocate of the Great Coalition, but he argued that the most important issue was that of the government's economic policies and that the Prussian question was simply complicating matters. Scholz therefore proposed a resolution releasing the Reichstag delegation from its commitment regarding Prussia and calling upon it to concentrate its efforts on fiscal reform.[65]

Apparently convinced that it was the best that could be hoped for in view of the rebellious mood of the Committee, Stresemann endorsed Scholz's resolution. It found little sympathy among the delegates, however, and was greeted with whistles and shouts of derision, which were highly unusual at a meeting of the normally staid Committee.[66] Otto Hugo of the Ruhr group then came forward with a counterproposal which renewed the party's pledge on Prussia and called for an immediate withdrawal of support from the government if the DVP's economic demands were not accepted by the other parties.[67]

Faced with the possibility of a humiliating defeat at the hands of his own party, Stresemann secured a recess in the middle of the afternoon to provide a cooling-off period. After considering the matter, the leaders of the opposition decided against risking an open break with both the party leader and the chairman of the Reichstag delegation. When the meeting reconvened, Strese-

[65] *Ibid.*, p. 82.
[66] *Nachlass*, 3164/7410/174694ff., Bernhard's memorandum of 27.2. 1929.
[67] *Deutsche Volkspartei Papers*, Vol. 105q, p. 130.

mann was thus able to announce that a compromise resolution had been agreed upon. It upheld the pledge to the Landtag delegation but suspended it until after the end of the Paris conference. It also announced the DVP's determination to oppose any increase in expenditures or taxation, but contained no direct threat of a withdrawal of support from the government if the party's economic demands were not met.[68]

Although he had succeeded in holding the opposition to a draw at the Central Committee meeting, Stresemann had not overcome the right wing's determination to have its way with regard to the government's economic policies, even at the cost of felling the cabinet.[69] When he and Müller undertook during the last days of February to remove the obstacles to a Great Coalition, the right wing succeeded in bringing a majority of the DVP delegation to make the formation of such a government contingent on immediate revisions in fiscal policies. Since the other parties were unwilling to accept this ultimatum another stalemate resulted. In the midst of the interparty negotiations, on March 1, Stresemann was obliged to go to Geneva to prepare for a session of the League of Nations Council. When he arrived in Switzerland, he was dismayed to learn that the DVP Reichstag delegation had brought the attempt at a Great Coalition to a stalemate by rejecting Müller's final compromise plan.[70] With the rump cabinet on the verge of falling, he threatened once again to resign from the party unless the delegation adopted a more reasonable position.[71] This threat shifted enough votes within the delegation to place the right wing in the minority again, at least temporarily. The delegation therefore agreed to reopen the talks with the other parties. By the time he returned to Berlin in April a compromise had been reached which brought the Center back into the cabinet and created a *de facto* Great

[68] *Ibid.*, Appendix, copy of *Nationalliberale Correspondenz*, 27.2.1929.
[69] *Nachlass*, 3164/7411/174823ff., Cremer to Stresemann, 23.3.1929.
[70] *Vermächtnis*, III, 434.
[71] *Nachlass*, 3101/7155/151943ff., letter to Curtius, 11.3.1929. Also, *Nachlass*, 3164/7411/174722ff., letter to Kahl, 13.3.1929.

Coalition. The April agreement bound all the parties to support a compromise budget and only the DVP's refusal to commit itself to the cabinet's future policies blocked the formation of a full coalition.[72]

The rebelliousness of the Central Committee and the subsequent obstinacy of the Reichstag delegation finally forced Stresemann to recognize the extent to which he had lost control of his own party. In a letter written to his old friend and colleague Wilhelm Kahl on March 13, he expressed his disillusionment: "I wanted to be the bridge between the old and the new Germany, and a part of our party has also recognized this historic mission. Others have never changed the old gramophone record and only want to hear the same melody over and over again." It was obvious, he told Kahl, that the DVP was simply no longer willing to bear the responsibilities of government: "Everyone approves the Great Coalition in principle and then most of them strive to block it."[73] In a letter to Curtius on March 11 he gave his views on the opposition's motives: "They want to get out of the government, they want to turn over all responsibility to the SPD . . . and are thinking of a fine 'national' opposition that will make it possible for them to let go with all the catchwords they have learned from the *Stahlhelm* and from Hugenberg." But if their aim was to strengthen the right in German politics, he felt they were hopelessly shortsighted. In his opinion the policy they had in mind could only drive the SPD into the arms of the Communists and so greatly increase the danger of a full-fledged leftist government.[74]

Stresemann realized that his difficulties with the Reichstag delegation were the result of a shift to the right in its composition, but he had no clear understanding of how or why that shift had taken place. In his letter of March 13 to Kahl he gave belated recognition to the fact that the DVP was "no longer a party

[72] *Nachlass*, 3164/7412/174982, Trucksaess to Stresemann, 23.4.1929.
[73] *Nachlass*, 3164/7411/174724.
[74] *Nachlass*, 3101/7155/151943ff.

251

of *Weltanschauung*," but was "becoming more and more a purely industrial party."[75] In other statements he made it clear that he felt the responsibility for this lay with the industrialists and their hirelings. On March 26 he wrote to Scholz: "Busy people are at work in the party, attempting to discredit its leaders and to transfer control of the party to the hands of certain economic special interest groups."[76] This line of argument could legitimately be offered as a partial explanation for the resurgence of the DVP right wing since there was little doubt about the determination of heavy industry to increase its influence in the party. It was hardly a complete or adequate explanation, however, for by falling back on this facile theory of an industrial conspiracy, Stresemann failed to face up to the fact that the opposition's resurgence had been made possible only by his own neglect of the party's internal affairs.

Although the Reichstag delegation's acceptance of the April compromise on the budget was a pleasing development from Stresemann's standpoint, it did not alter his views about the DVP. Since he made no effort to conceal his dissatisfaction with the party, there were frequent rumors in the press throughout the spring of 1929 to the effect that he was about to bolt the DVP and either join one of the old parties or form a new one.[77] His actual intentions, however, lay in a different direction. He had in fact concluded that it would be impossible to continue much longer with the DVP in its existing form. But instead of breaking with the party altogether, he planned to solve the problem of the opposition group by relegating it to the position of a small minority in a greatly expanded organization in which the DVP would serve as the core. Ever since the election of Hugenberg as chairman of the DNVP the previous October, Stresemann had been hopeful that the left-wing Nationalists would break with their party. By the spring of 1929 their in-

---

[75] *Nachlass*, 3164/7411/174724.

[76] *Ibid.*, 174862.

[77] *Nachlass*, 3164/7411/174786f. *Ibid.*, 174799f.; *Nachlass*, 3164/7412/174941ff.

creasing dissatisfaction made such a development only a matter of time in his opinion. He saw no obstacles to their eventual amalgamation with the DVP and regarded it as a way of weakening his party's right wing, for although the dissident Nationalists would be coming from the right, he felt their views coincided more closely with those of the DVP left wing. In addition to this influx from the right, his plans for a new and expanded organization also called for an extension to the left. In this regard he had finally accepted the fact that it was impossible to break the right-wing Democrats away from the rest of the DDP and had reconciled himself to a fusion with the entire party, including its left wing.[78]

Since a far-reaching political realignment of the sort he had in mind would probably affect the status of the Müller cabinet, Stresemann decided against any overt actions until the crucial reparations question had been settled. But a venture of such dimensions could hardly be carried out without some advance preparation and he began to take preliminary steps during the summer of 1929. Having learned that the leaders of the DNVP left wing planned to retain their independence for a time if they broke with Hugenberg, he set a merger between the DVP and the DDP as his first target.[79] As an initial step in that direction he gave confidential encouragement to the efforts of two organizations, the *Front 1929*, a new group committed to a consolidation of the forces of moderation within the Republic, and the *Liberale Vereinigung*, which had been formed in 1924 specifically to work for a restoration of liberal unity. The *Front*, which was headed by Rochus von Rheinbaben, the young author of a popularized biography of Stresemann that had appeared in 1928, consisted largely of intellectuals and had little influence outside Berlin.[80] The *Vereinigung*, on the other hand, had a broader

[78] *Nachlass*, 3163/7408/174305f., letter to R. Schneider, 11.7.1928. Also, *Nachlass*, 3164/7412/174987f., memorandum of 26.4.1929.

[79] *Nachlass*, 3164/7412/174987f., memorandum of 26.4.1929.

[80] *Ibid.* Also, *Nachlass*, 3165/7413/175316, Rheinbaben to Stresemann, 28.9.1929.

base, counting among its members a number of important figures of the DDP and the DVP, including Wilhelm Kahl, one of Stresemann's closest associates in the DVP Reichstag delegation. Previously, Stresemann had held aloof from it because of its insistence that a fusion must encompass all of both parties, including the left wing of the DDP. But after he dropped his opposition to the left-wing group, he saw the *Vereinigung* as a useful vehicle for lessening the distance between the two parties. In July he called upon its chairman, August Weber, to schedule a series of luncheons and dinners during the coming fall so that the leaders of the DDP and the DVP could have an opportunity to communicate informally on a regular basis.[81]

He took still another step toward a merger with the DDP in September 1929. At that time he informed its chairman, Erich Koch-Weser, of his disillusionment with the DVP and his determination to form a broad new political organization. Koch-Weser, who had repeatedly sought to interest him in a fusion of the DDP and the DVP ever since the subject had been broached after the elections of 1924, at once indicated his readiness to cooperate. In the course of a lengthy conversation the two agreed that the best way to remove the obstacles to a merger was to coordinate the policies of their two parties and to bring them into close cooperation on all important issues. Once that had been done they were confident that the actual merger would present no insuperable problems.[82]

Realizing that his plans would encounter stiff resistance from the right wing of the DVP, Stresemann set out to strengthen his position within the party. In the spring of 1929 he abandoned his pose of neutrality within the Reichstag delegation and agreed to take part in regular weekly strategy sessions with the leaders of the left wing.[83] In addition, he made preparations for a sweeping organizational reform that would replace the decentralized

---

[81] *Nachlass*, 3164/7412/175126f., letter of 5.7.1929.

[82] *Koch-Weser Papers*, Vol. 101, diary for 29.11.1929. Also, Koch-Weser, *Hitler and Beyond* (New York, 1945), p. 40.

[83] *Nachlass*, 3164/7412/174974, Dingeldey to Stresemann, 18.4.1929.

structure inherited from the National Liberal Party with a more centralized organization. By September the details of the reform plan had been worked out by a committee headed by his loyal follower Adolf Kempkes and Stresemann planned to submit it to a Party Congress for adoption in late October. Under its terms Stresemann's authority as head of the party was to be increased and he was to receive the more imposing title of *Parteiführer*. The chairmanship of the Reichstag delegation, on the other hand, was to lose much of its importance, since the delegation was for the first time explicitly subordinated to both the *Parteiführer* and the party's central bodies. The plan also penalized the Central Committee for its rebellious performance in February, expanding its membership and increasing, at its expense, the policy-making power of the thirteen-man Party Executive Committee, which had formerly been limited to making short-term tactical decisions. Finally, it struck at the entrenched position of the right wing in the electoral district organizations by giving the central bodies effective authority to veto the Reichstag candidates named by those organizations.[84]

One of the primary aims of Stresemann's reform projects was to break the power of the industrial interests within the DVP. There are indications he felt that in order to accomplish this, more than a party realignment and reorganization would be necessary. For some time he had been concerned with the question of the influence of money in politics and in 1928 he suggested publicly that since it was a problem common to many of the Republic's parties, it might best be solved by national legislation. His own proposal was that the parties' dependence on business interests might be reduced by using the state as a vehicle to ease their financial burdens: "The parties participate . . . in the government with far greater responsibility than ever before and for that reason we have an interest in keeping capitalistic powers from obtaining an excessive influence over the formation

[84] See *Nachlass*, 3165/7413/175228ff. *Ibid.*, 175284. *Ibid.*, 175298f. Also, *Nachlass*, 3163/7409/174479.

of the Reichstag. It is therefore worth discussing whether the parties should not have their campaign expenses reimbursed [by the state] in proportion to the number of votes they receive."[85] It thus seems probable that he hoped to supplement his projected party reforms by proposing legislation of this sort.

Stresemann's plans did not stop with these projects, for his disillusionment with the political situation went deeper. As a result of the long series of government crises and, more immediately, the continual harassment to which the Müller cabinet had been subjected while he was involved in delicate negotiations with the French, Stresemann had come to the conclusion that there was something fundamentally wrong with Germany's political machinery. His own diagnosis was that the Reichstag had, at least for the time being, shown itself incapable of meeting the responsibilities that went with its power. This situation could be remedied without altering the constitution, he told the Englishman Bruce Lockhart in April 1929, by simply asserting more fully the existing authority of the Chancellor and the President. And in February, before the Central Committee, he had revealed the direction his thoughts were taking, indicating that he would not object to government by presidential emergency decree if the parties proved unable or unwilling to provide a workable majority. In making this proposal, however, he emphasized that he saw such an arrangement not as a desirable development, but as a last resort; not as a means of undermining parliamentary government, but as a means of shocking the Reichstag back to its senses.[86]

Although his failing health handicapped him greatly and forced him to spend part of July in the sanatorium at Bühlerhöhe, Stresemann was busy during the summer of 1929 with the arrangements for the new reparations settlement. On June 7, after four months of deliberation in Paris under the chairmanship of

---

[85] Starkulla, "Organisation und Technik," p. 36, quoted from *Hallesche Nachrichten*, 22.3.1928.

[86] R. H. B. Lockhart, *Retreat from Glory* (London, 1934), p. 360. Also, *Deutsche Volkspartei Papers*, Vol. 105q, minutes of Central Committee, 26.2.1929, pp. 7, 14ff.

the American industrialist Owen D. Young, the international committee of experts had published a comprehensive set of proposals which quickly became known as the Young Plan. The Plan, which provided for a substantial reduction in German payments, was in Stresemann's opinion a significant step forward. When the spokesmen of the countries involved met at The Hague in August to consider the experts' proposals, he therefore pressed for adoption of the Plan in its entirety.

The Hague conference was an outstanding success for Stresemann. After some initial disagreement occasioned by a British demand for a larger share of the German payments, the Young Plan was accepted, as he had hoped, with only minor changes. Moreover, he achieved a major victory when French Premier Briand finally gave in to his requests for an early evacuation of the Rhineland and agreed to withdraw the last occupation troops by June 30, 1930. But in spite of the successful outcome of the conference from Stresemann's point of view, it did not lead to a speedy settlement of the issues involved. Since the participating countries had decided that a number of other issues—including the troublesome question of the claims arising from the confiscation of enemy property during the war—must be resolved before the final details of the Young Plan could be determined, action on its ratification had to be postponed for several months. Stresemann was thus faced with the task of holding together the unstable Müller government until the Plan could be ratified.

When he returned to Berlin at the beginning of September, he discovered that the new reparations agreement was by no means universally accepted. Once again, the Nationalists had rejected his foreign policy and were attacking the Young Plan as another example of cowardly fulfillment. In addition, their leader, Hugenberg, had joined with Hitler and other extremists in sponsoring a special plebiscite against the Plan. But in spite of its virulent polemics, this group offered no serious threat, for it was evident that it did not have sufficient support to obtain the

21 million signatures necessary to secure adoption of the plebiscite.

Far more dangerous than the vociferous opposition of the rightists was the prosaic and undramatic issue of unemployment insurance, which threatened to split the government parties and set off a crisis that could greatly complicate the ratification of the Young Plan. Although the economy had recovered from the recession of the previous winter, unemployment had remained above normal during the spring and summer. As a result, the government's deficit continued to increase steadily. Moreover, a number of temporary provisions of the insurance program were scheduled to expire at the end of September, thus requiring action by the Reichstag. This created a dangerous situation for the Müller government, since the DVP demanded that the deficit be eliminated by reducing compensation benefits while the SPD insisted that more money be raised by increasing the compulsory contributions of employers and employed workers which were supposed to finance the program under the 1927 law. In an effort to avert a clash between the two parties the cabinet hastily drew up a compromise plan calling for the elimination of a number of categories of compensation and a slight rise in contributions. Led by its industrial group, however, the DVP delegation objected to even a small increase in contributions as a covert and unsound form of taxation and indicated that it would reject the compromise.[87]

Stresemann was unable to intervene personally in the insurance dispute during most of September, for shortly after his return to Berlin at the beginning of the month he again had to leave for Switzerland. There he attended a session of the League of Nations Council and then, because of another recurrence of his illness, undertook a rest-cure at the resort of Vitznau on Lake Lucerne. When informed of the impending clash on the insurance issue, he urgently advised the cabinet to postpone all

[87] Helga Timm, *Die deutsche Sozialpolitik und der Bruch der grossen Koalition im März 1930* (Düsseldorf, 1952), pp. 132ff.

action on it until the Young Plan had been ratified.[88] But with the temporary provisions of the program due to lapse at the end of the month, the other members of the cabinet decided they had no choice except to bring the matter before the Reichstag when the fall session began on September 30.

After learning of the cabinet's decision, Stresemann broke off his stay at Vitznau in spite of his ill-health and his doctors' warnings and returning to Berlin in the hope of averting a government crisis. When he arrived back in the capital on September 25 the debilitating effects of his illness were quite evident. He had lost much weight and his strength had declined markedly, leaving him subject to sudden spells of weakness and exhaustion. In the words of one observer he was already *vom Tode gezeichnet*, marked by death.[89] Nevertheless, he threw himself into the parliamentary struggle in an attempt to bring about a compromise that would hold the government together.

His efforts were frustrated by his own party's Reichstag delegation. To his disappointment, he found that the right wing, backed by the country's two biggest industrial associations, the *Reichsverband der deutschen Industrie* and the *Vereinigung der deutschen Arbeitgeberverbände*, had won over enough of the middle group of uncommitted deputies to command a majority of the delegation. Even after a committee of the Reichstag had still further diluted the government's compromise bill on September 30 by removing the provision for an increase in contributions entirely, the right wing remained stubbornly opposed to it. Such a truncated measure, they warned, would leave the basic problem of excessive compensation unsolved and continue to saddle the government with a deficit that would have to be paid by business and the general public.[90]

[88] *Schleicher Papers*, Bundesarchiv, Koblenz, Vol. 17/II, pp. 123ff., memorandum by State Secretary Pünder of the Reich Chancellery on Stresemann's call from Vitznau, 18.9.1929.

[89] Grete Neubeiser, correspondent for the New York *Staats Zeitung*, after a press conference given by Stresemann on 27.9.1929: Lochner, *Always the Unexpected*, p. 135.

[90] *Verhandlungen* (Reichstag), ccccxxvi, 3147ff., 3205f., speeches of

With the final vote on the insurance bill scheduled for the morning of October 3, Stresemann's last chance to alter the DVP's stand came on the 2nd. In spite of a serious cold he took part in a stormy three-hour meeting of the delegation that began shortly before noon. He called upon the deputies to support the measure and warned that there might be grave consequences in the realm of foreign policy if they opposed it and toppled the government. In reply, the right wing, led by the industrial spokesmen Adolf Hueck, Friedrich Pfeffer, and Carl Schmid, counterattacked vigorously, arguing that it was impossible to go on countenancing unsound economic policies. In the middle of the afternoon the meeting was recessed for several hours. When the deputies reassembled Stresemann was absent, having returned home because of his illness. After two additional hours of heated discussion the question was finally put to a vote. Of the 38 deputies present, 19 favored acceptance of the government bill and 17 were for rejection, with 2 abstaining.[91]

Since Chancellor Müller had let it be known that he would consider his cabinet dissolved only if the bulk of the DVP voted against the government bill and thus caused its defeat, the outcome of the vote was a victory for Stresemann. However, in view of the sharp division it had revealed in the delegation, many of those present favored abstaining as a bloc in order to preserve at least the appearance of unity. But when he was informed of the situation by telephone, Stresemann asked the delegation to free its members to vote as they chose, apparently hoping to bolster the government by demonstrating that the majority of the DVP was behind it. His request, however, was rejected and it was decided to withhold the party's votes the next day. He was thus deprived of a full victory in what proved to be his last battle with the delegation. That evening he suffered a paralytic stroke

---

the industrial spokesmen Friedrich Pfeffer (30.9.1929), and Adolf Hueck (1.10.1929).

[91] *Deutsche Volkspartei Papers*, Vol. 139, minutes of the meeting.

and early on the morning of the next day, October 3, he died at the age of fifty-one after a second stroke.[92]

❖

Stresemann's sudden death left unfinished the political projects he had been preparing to launch during the last months of his life. Nothing was ever to come of his plan for a sweeping political realignment that would create a broad new party of the middle. Instead, his death delivered the DVP into the hands of its right wing. Under the leadership of Scholz, who was elected to succeed him as Chairman of the Central Committee, the party began to move steadily to the right. It remained in the Müller government until the Young Plan was ratified in March 1930. But immediately thereafter it demanded a revision of the unemployment insurance program, thus producing the crisis that ended parliamentary government in the Republic. After the crisis had brought down the Müller cabinet, the DVP supported the cabinet of Heinrich Brüning, which was able to govern only with the aid of the emergency powers of President Hindenburg. The Reichstag elections of September 1930, reduced the party's strength by one-third, to 30 seats, but added another group of rightists, including General von Seeckt, to the delegation. As a result of the election defeat, Scholz was ousted at the end of 1930 in favor of Eduard Dingeldey, who had been one of Stresemann's followers in the delegation. Dingeldey proved to be a weak and ineffectual leader and capitulated completely to the right wing. At its insistence he broke with the Brüning govern-

[92] *Ibid.* Cf. Curtius, *Sechs Jahre*, p. 88. Curtius was one of the last persons to see Stresemann alive, having called on him on the evening of October 2. But the first-hand evidence does not support his contention that he found Stresemann pleased at the unity of the party. See also Hermann Pünder, *Politik in der Reichskanzlei. Aufzeichnungen aus den Jahren 1929-1932*, ed. Thilo Vogelsang (Stuttgart, 1961), pp. 12f. Pünder also saw Stresemann on the afternoon of the 2nd and although his diary confirms Curtius' account of Stresemann's general good spirits it contains no indication that the latter was pleased with the DVP.

ment in October 1931, and took the party into the opposition. In February 1932, he expelled the leaders of the remaining left-wing group, Curtius and Kardorff, from the Reichstag delegation. Then, after the elections of July 1932 had left the DVP with only 7 seats, he took the lead in reducing it to the level of a satellite, first of the DNVP and then of the onrushing Nazi movement. Finally, in July 1933, the party Stresemann had founded fourteen and a half years earlier was voluntarily dissolved by its leader after having endorsed the new regime of Adolf Hitler.

VIII. STRESEMANN AS POLITICIAN

STRESEMANN's record entitles him to recognition not only as the Weimar Republic's most successful Foreign Minister but also as one of the leading figures of its domestic politics. Without his contributions, in fact, the course of Germany's first experiment in democratic government might have been quite different. In its stormy early years the Republic would clearly have been much less firmly established if he had not committed his party, and hence a strategically important portion of the electorate, to cooperation within the new state and with the Social Democrats, thus significantly widening the base upon which parliamentary majorities could be built. It is also questionable whether the new state could have survived the multiple threats that beset it in 1923 without the firm and courageous leadership he provided during his short term as Chancellor. Even after his attention had focused mainly on foreign affairs, Stresemann continued to exert an often decisive influence on the Republic's politics. As a member of every cabinet from 1923 until his death in 1929 he served as the principal element of stability and continuity in the rapid succession of governments that marked those years. Finally, his achievements as Foreign Minister contributed to the stabilization of the Republic by easing Germany's financial burdens and bringing the foreign occupation to an end.

The most controversial aspect of his career in the politics of the Republic was his transition from opponent to defender of the new regime. In an effort to explain this, numerous theories have been set forth, ranging from sudden conversion to outright opportunism. The simplest and most satisfactory explanation, however, has been overlooked—namely, that he was that rarity among the German politicians of his day, a pragmatic conservative. Throughout his career in the Republic his goals remained the same as those of most Germans who could be termed, in the broadest sense of the word, conservatives: the restoration of the

263

country's power and prosperity and the preservation of as much of the prerevolutionary social and economic order as was possible. But in contrast to most of his conservative compatriots, he was, as a pragmatist, willing to be flexible about the political means of achieving these goals.

In the wake of the revolution of 1918 he went along with most conservatively inclined Germans in rejecting the republican system as the product of an unworthy rebellion and the source of a humiliating peace treaty. Like many others, he was hopeful that it would be of short duration, but had no clear idea as to what should replace it. Apparently, he looked toward some sort of return to the past, perhaps to the constitutional monarchy established in October 1918, which most closely approached his political ideal. The events of the turbulent early years of the Republic, however, gradually convinced him of the folly of relying on any such facile solution to Germany's problems. As a realistic man of common sense, he recognized that the alternative to the existing system was not a restoration of past glories but a development that would imperil his basic goals: a dictatorship, either of the left or of the right. Equally important, he recognized that the parliamentary Republic could be used for conservative as well as for revolutionary purposes. As a result, he made the important decision to pursue his goals within its framework.

This same pragmatic readiness to accept unpleasant realities and to settle for something less than the optimal was evident in Stresemann's approach to most of the major problems he faced during his career in the Republic. This attitude was especially apparent in his handling of the question of monarchism. Personally, he regarded constitutional monarchy as the soundest basis for government in Germany. But when he became convinced that the country was hopelessly divided on the issue and that strife over the form of government could only obstruct recovery, he dissociated himself and his party from the monarchist cause. Similarly, he did not, like most conservatives, flatly reject the idea of cooperation with the Social Democrats because of their commitment to a fundamental alteration of the economic and social order. Instead, he recognized that such a stubborn refusal to cooperate with the country's largest party would either deliver the state completely into the hands of the left or produce a paralysis of the governmental machinery, thus opening the way for extremism of the left or the right. Since neither of these developments would contribute to the achievement of his goals, he preferred to work with the Social Democrats, making concessions where necessary to their point of view and in return bringing them to drop, or at least postpone, the more far-reaching points of their program. There, as on most other issues, his pragmatism made him that indispensable component of democratic government—a man of compromise. He recognized this himself and the political philosophy of his mature years was best expressed in an observation he made in the spring of 1927. "In my life," he remarked at that time, "I have come to the opinion that nothing great which has been created in this world has ever proved lasting without compromise."[1]

Stresemann's record in the Republic's politics is by no means without its negative aspects. The most conspicuous entry on the debit side of the ledger was his response to the Kapp Putsch. It demonstrated that as late as the spring of 1920 he had still not abandoned the vain hope of a short-cut return to past greatness and was capable of being swept into accepting the outcome of an apparently successful overthrow of the Weimar system. In addition, his conduct during the aftermath of the Putsch revealed that he was not above employing some of the less reputable tools of the politician's trade in an effort to extricate himself and his party from a difficult predicament. Still another serious blemish on his record was his failure to act on his convictions at the time of the second presidential campaign of 1925 and to make known his opposition to Hindenburg.

More serious than these lapses of judgment was the fact that

[1] *Vermächtnis*, III, 457.

Stresemann failed to achieve the political mission he had set for himself in the Republic. This was, as he himself expressed it, to serve as "the bridge between the old and the new Germany," bringing the adherents of the two together on the basis of constructive cooperation within the Weimar state. Through his own personal achievements he came closer to this goal than any of the Republic's leaders and became in his latter years the symbol for many, both at home and abroad, of a Germany based on a synthesis of the old and the new. As the events that followed his death were to show, however, he had failed to heal the fundamental breach that was finally to paralyze the parliamentary system and open the way for the Republic's fall.

In part, this was due to factors beyond Stresemann's control, in particular the susceptibility of a large part of the electorate to the reactionary nationalism of the Nationalists and the utopian radicalism of the extremists of the left and right. On the other hand, he must bear the heavy responsibility for the fact that his achievement in bringing his party, and the conservative interests it represented, to cooperate with the SPD proved to be only temporary. Throughout his lifetime he succeeded in holding his party behind him, though often not without difficulty. But he failed to give his accomplishments as party leader a firm institutional basis by forging a political organization fully committed to the course he had set. His influence in domestic politics thus remained basically personal and, when he died, it vanished with him.

There were a number of factors in Stresemann's failure to build a loyal party. Among these was the animosity toward the left-wing Democrats which he carried with him out of the bitter days that followed the revolution. In later years this enmity repeatedly blocked the formation of a united liberal party, a solution which would not only have strengthened the moderate elements in the Republic but which would also have reduced the right wing of the DVP to a helpless minority. Also important was his evident desire, until the last months of his life, to remain as the undisputed leader of his small party, an arrangement which he undoubtedly realized would be difficult to duplicate in a larger organization. The most important factor, though, was his decision, following the elections of 1924, to subordinate domestic politics to foreign policy in the hope that his diplomatic successes would eventually break through the voting patterns established in the Republic's early years. It was this that led him to neglect the internal affairs of his own party. And it was this neglect in turn which made possible the resurgence of those elements which had never been reconciled to his insistence on a readiness to cooperate with the Social Democrats.

Although he never admitted that it might be his own fault, Stresemann recognized in the last months of his life that he was perilously close to losing control of his party. As his plans for a sweeping political realignment indicate, he was hopeful of remedying this situation. But even if he had been given more time it seems probable that it was too late to correct the errors of omission of earlier years. The right wing of the DVP had grown much too strong ever to submit to the merger with the DDP which he had in mind. As a result, the outcome of his efforts would probably have been a division of the party between the DDP and the DNVP. This would have strengthened the middle portion of the Republic's political spectrum somewhat, but the gain would have been largely offset by the increase in the strength of the right.

✧

In the mass of uncritical and adulatory literature dealing with his career, Stresemann's increasing aloofness from the affairs of his party during his latter years is usually presented as a commendable achievement, as a surmounting of the pettiness of partisan politics. In reality, it was his great failing, since it robbed Germany of the full benefits of his acceptance of, and reconciliation to, the Weimar Republic. It marks, in fact, his failure in one of the dual roles with which the republican period confronted

267

him: that of party politician. And in failing in this role he contributed, ironically, to the perversion of his remarkable accomplishments as Foreign Minister. For his own party's sharp shift to the right after his death played a decisive role in triggering the string of developments that eventually delivered the greatly strengthened Germany he left behind him into the hands of an aggressive, irresponsible regime he would have found reprehensible in every respect.

SOURCES AND BIBLIOGRAPHY

(Because of the extent of the literature dealing with Stresemann, much of which is concerned solely with his foreign policy, this listing contains only those items that were of direct use in the preparation of this study.)

DESIGNATIONS USED IN THE FOOTNOTES

Nachlass Germany, Auswärtiges Amt, Politisches Archiv, *Nachlass des Reichsaussenministers Dr. Gustav Stresemann,* microfilm, National Archives of the United States.

Vermächtnis Gustav Stresemann, *Vermächtnis. Der Nachlass in drei Bänden,* ed. Henry Bernhard (3 vols., Berlin, 1932-1933).

AR, *Kabinett* Germany, Alte Reichskanzlei, *Kabinett-Protokolle,* microfilm, National Archives of the United States.

I. PRIMARY SOURCES

A. Unpublished Materials

Deutsche Volkspartei Papers, Bundesarchiv, Koblenz. A large collection of material taken from the party's archive by its last leader, Eduard Dingeldey, before it was seized by the Nazis. The rest of the archive, mostly less important material according to those who have seen it, is in the East German Zentralarchiv in Potsdam and was unavailable for this study.

Dingeldey Papers, Bundesarchiv, Koblenz. Dingeldey's own correspondence and records.

Germany, Alte Reichskanzlei, *Kabinett-Protokolle,* microfilm, National Archives of the United States.

Germany, Auswärtiges Amt, Büro des Staatssekretärs, *Innere Politik,* microfilm, National Archives of the United States.

Germany, Auswärtiges Amt, Politisches Archiv, *Nachlass des Reichsaussenministers Dr. Gustav Stresemann,* microfilm, National Archives of the United States. Photographed in Great

Britain following the war, the microfilmed copy of the *Nachlass* contains the bulk of the Stresemann papers captured by the Allies. It is now clear, however, that part of the *Nachlass* was removed by Stresemann's private secretary, Henry Bernhard, even before the collection was seized by the Nazis (see above, p. 66, note 85). The originals of the captured *Nachlass*, as well as some of the papers removed by Bernhard, are now available for research purposes in the Political Archive of the Foreign Ministry, Bonn. For a convenient guide to the filmed copy, see Hans W. Gatzke, "The Stresemann Papers," *Journal of Modern History*, xxvi (1954), 49ff.

Gothein Papers, Bundesarchiv, Koblenz. The papers of Georg Gothein, Democratic politician.

Koch-Weser Papers, Bundesarchiv, Koblenz. The papers of Erich Koch-Weser, leader of the Democratic Party from 1924 to 1930.

Schiffer Papers, Hauptarchiv, Berlin. The papers of Eugen Schiffer, National Liberal and Democratic politician.

Schleicher Papers, Bundesarchiv, Koblenz. A partial collection of General von Schleicher's papers.

Seeckt Papers, microfilm, Institut für Zeitgeschichte, Munich.

B. Published Materials

1. STRESEMANN'S WRITINGS

Deutsche Stimmen. Stresemann's articles in his magazine were usually signed with the cipher Δ. Bound volumes for the following years are available at the Institut für Zeitgeschichte, Munich: 1919, 1920, 1922, 1923, 1924, 1927. The Bundestag-Bibliothek, Bonn, has bound volumes for the following years: 1920, 1921, 1922, 1924, 1925, 1926, 1927, 1928. The Library of Congress, Washington, D.C., has part of the volume for 1918.

Deutsches Ringen und Deutsches Hoffen (Berlin, 1914).

Englands Wirtschaftskrieg gegen Deutschland (Stuttgart, 1916).

Michel Horch, Der Seewind Pfeift: Kriegsbetrachtungen (Berlin, 1916).

Macht und Freiheit (Halle, 1918).

Von der Revolution bis zum Frieden von Versailles (Berlin, 1919).

Weimar und die Politik (Berlin, 1919).

Die Entstehung der Deutschen Volkspartei (unsigned, published in the name of the DVP) (Berlin, 1920).

Die Märzereignisse und die Deutsche Volkspartei (Berlin, 1920).

"Das Kabinett Stresemann," *Deutsche Stimmen.* A series of four articles written by Stresemann with the collaboration of his private secretary, Henry Bernhard, and published in late 1923 and early 1924 under the latter's name.

Reden und Schriften (2 vols., Dresden, 1926).

Vermächtnis. Der Nachlass in drei Bänden, edited by Henry Bernhard (3 vols., Berlin, 1932-1933). A selection of documents from the *Nachlass,* covering the period 1923-1929. Often heavily edited. (See Gatzke, "The Stresemann Papers," *Journal of Modern History,* XXVI [1954], 49ff.)

2. MEMOIRS AND DIARIES

D'Abernon, Viscount Edgar. *An Ambassador of Peace* (3 vols., London, 1929-1930).

Braun, Otto. *Von Weimar zu Hitler* (New York, 1940).

Curtius, Julius. *Sechs Jahre Minister der Deutschen Republik* (Heidelberg, 1948).

Erzberger, Matthias. *Erlebnisse im Weltkrieg* (Stuttgart, 1920).

Gessler, Otto. *Reichswehrpolitik in der Weimarer Zeit* (Stuttgart, 1958).

Kessler, Graf Harry. *Tagebücher, 1918-1937* (Frankfurt/Main, 1961).

Lochner, Louis P. *Always the Unexpected* (New York, 1956).

Lockhart, R. H. Bruce, *Retreat from Glory* (London 1934).

Lüttwitz, Walther Freiherr von. *Im Kampf gegen die November-Revolution* (Berlin, 1934).

Luther, Hans. "Erinnerungen an Gustav Stresemann," *Schweizer Monatshefte*, xxxiv (1954).

―――. "Luther und Stresemann in Locarno," *Politische Studien*, viii, Heft 84 (1957).

―――. *Politiker Ohne Partei* (Stuttgart, 1960).

Noske, Gustav. *Von Kiel bis Kapp* (Berlin, 1920).

Payer, Friedrich. *Von Bethmann-Hollweg bis Ebert* (Frankfurt/Main, 1923).

Pünder, Hermann. *Politik in der Reichskanzlei. Aufzeichnungen aus den Jahren 1929-1932*, ed. Thilo Vogelsang (Stuttgart, 1961).

Rheinbaben, Werner Freiherr von. *Viermal Deutschland, 1895-1954* (Berlin, 1954).

Rippler, Heinrich. "Wie die DVP entstand," a memoir in *Erneuerung*, 13.5.1933.

Schacht, Hjalmar. *76 Jahre Meines Lebens* (Bad Wörishofen, 1953).

Scheidemann, Philipp. *Memoiren eines Sozialdemokraten* (2 vols., Dresden, 1928).

Schiffer, Eugen. *Ein Leben für den Liberalismus* (Berlin, 1951).

Severing, Carl. *Mein Lebensweg* (2 vols., Cologne, 1950).

Wolff, Theodor. *Der Marsch Durch Zwei Jahrzehnte* (Amsterdam, 1937).

3. YEARBOOKS AND GOVERNMENT PUBLICATIONS

Deutscher Geschichtskalender, ed. Friedrich Purlitz and Siegfrid Sternberg (Leipzig, 1918ff.).

Germany, Büro des Reichstags, *Reichstag Handbuch, I. Wahlperiode, 1920* (Berlin, 1920).

Germany, Büro des Reichstags, *Verhandlungen des Reichstags.*

Germany, Büro des Reichstags, *Verhandlungen der Verfassunggebenden Deutschen Nationalversammlung.*

Schulthess' Europäischer Geschichtskalender, ed. Ulrich Thürauf (Munich, 1918ff.).

4. PARTY PUBLICATIONS

DVP, *Archiv der Deutschen Volkspartei* (title for 1919, *Vertrauliche Mitteilungen*) (Berlin, 1919ff.) An information bulletin for party officials and members.

―――. *Bericht über den Ersten Parteitag* (Berlin, 1919).

―――. *Bericht über den Zweiten Parteitag* (Berlin, 1920).

―――. *Deutscher Aufbau,* ed. Adolf Kempkes (Berlin, 1927).

―――. *Die Entstehung der Deutschen Volkspartei* (written by Stresemann) (Berlin, 1920).

―――. *Grundsätze der Deutschen Volkspartei* (Leipzig, 1919).

―――. *Nationalliberale Correspondenz* (Berlin, 1919ff.).

NLP, *Rundschreiben. Die Einigungsverhandlungen mit der Fortschrittlichen Volkspartei.—Gründung der Deutschen Volkspartei.* (One-page leaflet distributed with the magazine, *Deutsche Stimmen,* 24.11.1918.)

5. NEWSPAPERS AND PERIODICALS

Berliner Tageblatt.

Deutsche Allgemeine Zeitung, Berlin.

Deutsche Stimmen, Berlin (published by Stresemann).

Frankfurter Zeitung.

Le Temps, Paris.

Manchester Guardian.

New York Times.

Tägliche Rundschau, Berlin.

Times, London.

Vossische Zeitung, Berlin.

Die Zeit, Berlin.

II. SECONDARY SOURCES

A. Studies of Stresemann

Bauer, Heinrich. *Stresemann, Ein Deutscher Staatsmann* (Berlin, 1930).

Bernhard, Henry. "Das Kabinett Stresemann," *Deutsche Stimmen*, 1923–1924. (See: Stresemann's writings.)

————. "Seeckt und Stresemann," *Deutsche Rundschau*, LXXIX (1953).

Bretton, Henry L., *Stresemann and the Revision of Versailles* (Stanford, 1953).

Edwards, Marvin L. *Stresemann and the Greater Germany, 1914-1918* (New York, 1963).

Gatzke, Hans W. *Stresemann and the Rearmament of Germany* (Baltimore, 1954).

————. "Stresemann und Litwin." *Vierteljahrshefte für Zeitgeschichte*, V (1957).

Göhring, Martin. *Stresemann, Mensch, Staatsmann, Europäer* (Mainz, 1956).

Görlitz, Walter. *Gustav Stresemann* (Heidelberg, 1947).

Hertzman, Lewis. "Gustav Stresemann: The Problem of Political Leadership in the Weimar Republic," *International Review of Social History*, V (1960), 361ff.

Hirsch, Felix. "Stresemann, Ballin und die Vereinigten Staaten," *Vierteljahrshefte für Zeitgeschichte*, III (1955), 30f.

Hirth, Friedrich. *Stresemann* (Paris, 1930).

Olden, Rudolf. *Stresemann* (Berlin, 1929).

Rheinbaben, Freiherr Rochus von. *Stresemann* (Dresden, 1928).

Schlottner, Erich Heinz. *Stresemann, der Kapp-Putsch und die Ereignisse in Mitteldeutschland und in Bayern im Herbst 1923* (printed dissertation, Frankfurt/Main 1948).

Starkulla, Heinz. "Organisation und Technik der Pressepolitik des Staatsmannes Gustav Stresemann 1923 bis 1929" (Munich dissertation, 1951).

Stern-Rubarth, Edgar. *Stresemann, der Europäer* (Berlin, 1929).

Thimme, Annelise. "Gustav Stresemann, Legende und Wirklichkeit," *Historische Zeitschrift*, CLXXXI (1956).

———. *Gustav Stresemann* (Hanover & Frankfurt/Main, 1957).

———. "Stresemann als Reichskanzler," *Die Welt als Geschichte*, XVII (1957).

Thimme, Roland. *Stresemann und die deutsche Volkspartei 1923–1925* (Lübeck & Hamburg, 1961).

Vallentin, Antonina. *Stresemann, Vom Werden Einer Staatsidee* (Leipzig, 1930).

Warren, Donald Jr. "Gustav Stresemann as Organizer of German Business Interests, 1901–1914" (Columbia dissertation, 1959).

Zimmermann, Ludwig. *Das Stresemannbild in der Wandlung* (Erlanger Forschungen, Reihe A, Band 6, 1956).

B. Others

Brammer, Karl. (ed.) *Verfassungsgrundlagen und Hochverrat* (Berlin, 1922).

Eyck, Erich. *Geschichte der Weimarer Republik* (2 vols., Zürich & Stuttgart, 1954-1955).

Gatzke, Hans W. *Germany's Drive to the West* (Baltimore, 1950).

Görlitz, Walter. *Hindenburg* (Bonn, 1953).

Gordon, Harold J. *The Reichswehr and the German Republic, 1919-1926* (Princeton, 1957).

Hallgarten, G. W. F. *Hitler, Reichswehr und Industrie* (Frankfurt/Main, 1955).

Hartenstein, Wolfgang. *Die Anfänge der Deutschen Volkspartei 1918–1920* (Düsseldorf, 1962).

Herre, Paul. *Kronprinz Wilhelm* (Munich, 1954).

Hertzman, Lewis. "The German National People's Party (DNVP), 1918-1924" (Harvard dissertation, 1955).

Horkenbach, Cuno. *Das Deutsche Reich von 1918 bis Heute* (Berlin, 1930).

Koch-Weser, Erich. *Hitler and Beyond* (New York, 1945).

Liebe, Werner. *Die Deutschnationale Volkspartei, 1918-1924* (Düsseldorf, 1956).

Lochner, Louis P. "Die aussenpolitische Wirkung der Nachricht," *Zeitungswissenschaft*, 1.7.1934.

Michels, Rudolf K. *Cartels, Combines and Trusts in Post-War Germany* (New York, 1928).

Nipperdey, Thomas. *Die Organisation der deutschen Parteien vor 1918* (Düsseldorf, 1961).

Nuschke, Otto. "Wie die Demokratische Partei Wurde," in *Zehn Jahre Deutsche Republik*, ed. Anton Erkelenz (Berlin, 1928).

Rabenau, General Friedrich von. *Seeckt. Aus seinem Leben, 1918-1936* (Leipzig, 1940).

Salomon, Felix. *Die Deutschen Parteiprogramme*, Heft 3 (Berlin, 1920).

Schinkel, Harald. *Entstehung und Zerfall der Regierung Luther* (printed dissertation, Berlin, 1959).

Stern, Fritz. "Adenauer and a Crisis in Weimar Democracy," *Political Science Quarterly*, LXXIII (1958).

Timm, Helga. *Die deutsche Sozialpolitik und der Bruch der grossen Koalition im März 1930* (Düsseldorf, 1952).

Vereinigung der deutschen Arbeitgeberverbände, *Geschäftsbericht 1923 und 1924* (Berlin, 1925).

Weymar, Paul. *Konrad Adenauer* (Munich, 1955).

Wheeler-Bennett, John W. *The Nemesis of Power* (London, 1953).

and separatism, 147; entanglement with politics of Reich, 238f, 245ff, 248; concordat, 246
Pünder, Hermann, 261n

Quaatz, Reinhold, 71, 79f, 94, 115, 137, 139, 158, 161

railroads, 132, 169
Rapallo Treaty, 97, 221
Rathenau, Walther, 90n; appointed Foreign Minister, 96; assassination, 97ff, 111
Raumer, Hans von, 70f, 74, 78, 85, 116; on Stresemann's fear of rivals, 230f
Realpolitik, Stresemann and, 99, 179
rearmament, 203, 227f
Reichsblock, 195ff
Reichsbürgerrat, 192
Reichsverband der deutschen Industrie, Stresemann excluded, 70; and DVP, 71; approves Dawes Plan, 163; and unemployment insurance crisis, 259
Reichsverband des deutschen Handwerks, 71
Reichswehr, see German Army
Reichswirtschaftsrat, 75
Rentenmark, 146
reparations, 83f, 86, 105, 109, 119f, 154f, 168, 244, 246, 249
republican constitution, *see* constitution (republican)
restoration, *see* monarchism
revolution, of 1918, 3f, 11ff, 82, 264
Rheinbaben, Baron Rochus von, 253
Rheinbaben, Baron Werner von, 72, 122
Rhineland, evacuation of, 171, 189f, 208f, 212, 214f, 232, 238, 244, 249, 257
Richter, Ernst von, 36, 160
Richthofen, Baron Hartmann von, 19
Riesser, Jacob, 14, 28, 62

Rippler, Heinrich, 23, 95
Roggenmark, 132
Ruhr, occupation, 105, 116f, 163, 168, 170n, 171, 178
Ruhrort, occupation (1921), 83
Russia, 150, 203, 227; revolution, 9n, 12; Rapallo Treaty, 97, 221; Treaty of Berlin (1926), 220f

Saar, 232
Saxony, 4; Communists in government, 124ff; cabinet deposed, 127f; new cabinet formed, 132; state of emergency, 148; Stresemann's policy, 151
Schacht, Hjalmar, 146
Scheer, Admiral Reinhard, rivals Stresemann in DVP, 230, 236
Scheidemann, Philipp, 4, 35; attacks secret rearmament, 227f
Schiele, Martin, 58f, 188, 209, 211, 213f
Schiffer, Eugen, 27; and Kapp Putsch, 57ff
Schleicher, Colonel Kurt von, 122
Schmid, Carl, 260
Schneyder, Erich, 185
Schoch, General Karl von, 72
Scholz, Ernst, 78, 131, 137ff, 222f, 239, 252; chairman of DVP delegation, 131; favors coalition with DNVP, 134f; defends Stresemann, 141; proposes rightward orientation for DVP, 226f; leads opposition against Stresemann, 241ff; brings DVP behind Müller cabinet, 243; supports Stresemann, 249; succeeds Stresemann, 261; ousted, 261
Schubert, Carl von, 206
Seeckt, General Hans von, 122, 130, 148f, 196; seeks removal of Stresemann, 136ff; Stresemann's views on, 136, 193; given emergency powers, 142; presidential candidacy, 193f; and Locarno, 203, 215; and rearmament, 203; enters DVP, 261
separatism, 123, 146f

government, 143, 151; permits return of Crown Prince, 143ff; and currency stabilization, 145ff; opposition to separatism, 146f; fall of second cabinet, 150; break with the right completed, 153; appointed Foreign Minister, 154; in Marx cabinet (1923-24), 154ff, 183; and Dawes Plan, 154f, 163f, 168, 170f, 175; rebellion of DVP (1924), 155ff; and first campaign of 1924, 162ff; rejection of DVP and DDP merger, 166f; subordination of domestic to foreign policy, 174, 181; brings down Marx cabinet, 178; and second campaign of 1924, 178ff; nomination for chancellorship (1925), 182; unique position in republican politics, 183ff; in Luther cabinet, 183ff; and the press, 184f; and Locarno Pact, 186ff, 202ff, 211ff, 220, 229f; and presidential election (1925), 193ff, 197ff; negotiation of German entry into League of Nations, 220; Treaty of Berlin (1926), 220f; and Adenauer candidacy for chancellorship, 222f; campaign in Bavaria (1928), 236ff; stricken (1928), 237; role in formation of Müller government (1928), 239f; suffers stroke (1928), 244; Kellogg-Briand Peace Pact, 244; seeks reparations revision, 244; and revolt of Central Committee of DVP (1929), 247ff; plans for new party, 252ff; favors merger with DDP, 253f; plan for financing of election campaigns, 255f; favors stronger executive powers, 256; and Young Plan, 257ff; and Hague Conference (1929), 257; secures evacuation of Rhineland, 257; and unemployment insurance crisis, 258ff; suffers paralytic strokes, dies, 260f; assessment, 267f

business career: 4, 29, 29n, 70; in *Bund der Industriellen*, 5, 70; in *Verband Sächsischer Industrieller*, 29; excluded from *Reichsverband der deutschen Industrie*, 70

journalistic activities: 6, 95, 184f, 210; *Deutsche Stimmen*, 6; *Die Zeit*, 95

and liberalism: 8, 14f, 72ff; and failure of liberal unity (1918), 14ff, 21ff, 25f

and the military: 12, 53, 56, 82, 125f, 136, 151, 228; and secret rearmament, 227f

and the parties:

DDP: attitude at formation, 17; accepts merger (1918), 21; excluded from governing bodies, 21; offered candidacy, 21; rejects merger (1918), 22; animosity toward left wing, 34, 166f, 266; blocks merger (1924), 166f; agrees to merger, 253f

DVP: formation, 19ff; elected to head, 25; finances, 29f, 68ff, 159, 161; chairman of Central and Managing committees, 31; opposition, 45f, 53f, 79f, 92, 94, 100, 115, 131ff, 137ff, 155ff, 194f, 225ff, 229, 241ff, 245, 247ff, 258ff; delegation chairman, 78; resigns as Chairman of Managing Committee, 79; dissociates from right, 91; designates as middle party, 157; neglects, 181, 225, 252, 266f; fear of rivals, 230f, 253f, 267; threatens to resign, 243, 250; plans merger with DDP, 253f; plans organizational reform, 254f

DNVP: refuses to join, 24; rejects merger with DVP, 33f; agrees to seek coalition, 160; on Dawes Plan, 170ff; favors entry into government, 174ff; on Locarno Pact, 187ff, 203f, 208ff, 213, 223; pleased by modera-